A Good-Looking Corpse

Also by Mike Nicol

The Powers That Be

A
Good-Looking
Corpse

MIKE NICOL

Secker & Warburg
LONDON

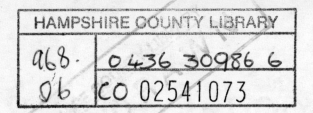
First published in Great Britain in 1991
by Martin Secker & Warburg Limited
Michelin House, 81 Fulham Road, London sw3 6rb

Copyright © 1991 Tortuga Publishing Limited

A CIP catalogue record for this book
is available from the British Library
isbn 0 436 30986 6

Grateful acknowledgement is
made to Longman Publishers for
permission to reprint material from
Home and Exile by Lewis Nkosi

The author has asserted his moral rights

Printed in Great Britain
by Clays Ltd, St. Ives plc

Contents

Illustrations

Photographs by Jurgen Schadeberg (4, 12, 13, 14, 16, 17, 22, 24, 25, 30, 33), Bob Gosani (8, 11, 19, 20, 27, 32) and Peter Magubane (5, 26)

Preface

It is always disconcerting when history shifts beneath your feet; when the past is suddenly no longer what you believed. Overnight, the country you knew becomes a different place. In South Africa nowadays it happens all the time, as historians uncover what colonial chroniclers and – more recently – official scribes deliberately ignored or never thought important as they laid out chapter and verse of white history. But it is even more unsettling discovering a period – and one during my lifetime at that – which had been banned and silenced by government decree. Of course, from time to time odd messages from this 'vanquished' land would permeate the silence: a book here, an article there, an academic study, even a piece of music. But that wasn't enough to people the place; and I tried to find out what had been said and written that was so feared by the state.

And then in the '80s, suddenly, arbitrarily, the 'lost' country was gradually revealed, the voices could be heard again. 'It is now not undesirable,' said the censor in his peculiar officialese, 'to possess or distribute the following works . . .' as book after book was unbanned.

The country released was township South Africa of the '50s. A place of jazz and beauty queens, of gangsters, folk heroes and witch-doctors, a vibrant, laughing, deadly world. Yes, deadly. There was misery, suffering, violence and poverty there. But there was also optimism, a strange unreal sense of hope possibly occasioned by the Defiance Campaign – a milestone in black resistance to white hegemony – and by a measure of political freedom that gave rise to meetings, marches, boycotts, stayaways and strikes.

And the hope continued even as the Nationalist government wrote racial law after racial law into the statutes, even as the security police harassed and detained political leaders; even as a massive dawn raid led to the arrest of 156 people and started the long and futile Treason Trial. If township life in the '50s was hectic and dangerous, then in parliament the activity to suppress it and disinherit it was just as frenzied. By the end of the decade apartheid was fully entrenched. Equally disconcerting, it was enforced by efficient and ruthless policemen.

The first time I saw this 'country' was in 1986 when a photographer named Jurgen Schadeberg showed me the mock-ups of two photographic books he had edited. The photographs were from a magazine called *Drum*, which had started in the '50s and flourished during that decade, but although still published had never regained the vitality of those brief, almost delirious ten years. I was immediately enthralled. Here was a romantic, madcap world that was about as far removed from my '50s of Beezer comics and the Famous Five as it was possible to get. Yet, and this is the awesome paradox of the many 'countries' that make up South Africa, it had all happened on the same land mass at the same time. But what had happened? What had it been like? As I leafed through the 'dummies', I came across photographs of famous politicians, of historic events, of boxing stars, of ballroom dancers, of thugs and freaks. Here, too, were the pictures of those banished writers: the journalists who had recorded their age and been silenced for their efforts. Men like Es'kia Mphahlele, Can Themba, Bloke Modisane and Todd Matshikiza, who in 1962 were banned under the Suppression of Communism Act, and whose work had effectively ceased to exist for more than twenty years.

After this exposure to the '50s, *Drum* became an obsession, not only with me but with many others. Quite why is difficult to say. Maybe the magic that so captivated readers in the '50s was still as potent as ever. Maybe it was this

rediscovered country that lured us. Maybe, maybe . . .
Certainly, no other magazine in the world has generated as
much publicity so long after its heyday as has *Drum*. In
recent years its stories, both fact and fiction, have been
anthologised in at least six books; and, following the publication of Schadeberg's photographic selections, its pictures
continue to be used again and again throughout the world.
And still more books are planned, as are a television series
and a Hollywood movie. But then *Drum* has already given
rise to a play, *Sophiatown!*, which attracted good houses in
South Africa and Britain; a photographic exhibition which
toured Europe, Britain and the United States; and two
popular documentaries. All this without counting the journalists' or the editors' own books inspired by working on
Drum, or the newspaper articles, academic studies, even a
university course at one of South Africa's oldest institutions,
which have followed in its wake.

Like so many, I was caught up in the romance of the
township '50s. Maybe I was merely a latter-day voyeur, a
charge which, I soon discovered, blacks had often levelled
privately at liberal whites jiving in the shebeens of Sophiatown. Maybe, but did it really matter, and wasn't it time
that this attitude changed anyhow? At first the '50s seemed
a 'golden age', an endless dance in the rain, as one veteran
from those years put it. Surely here was a time when South
Africa stood a chance of being decent, when, I was told,
'there was a hunger from whites for blacks and vice versa'.
For a while the glitter was so dazzling it kept hidden the
violence and poverty underneath. But as I interviewed those
who had been there and lived through those years, the
sparkle dimmed. Culturally the township '50s may have
been rich, but in almost every other respect they were
desperately poor. And towards the end of my research, I
was left with that peculiarly South African feeling of loving
and fearing the country and its people. For who cannot be
moved by such strength in adversity; and who cannot weep
at what we have done to one another?

These emotions are reflected time and again in this book. As I rummaged through *Drum*'s thin columns of type, jammed between adverts for Karroo nerve-pain tablets, Puritone blood-purifying mixture, Ipana toothpaste, Boxer tobacco, Bongo shoes, Battersby hats, Waverly blankets – or the boxing hero of the time, Jake Tuli, advertising Post Toasties, Blue Seal petroleum jelly, Coca-Cola or Commando Round cigarettes – I was always aware of them, both in the stories before me and the voices I had listened to, spilling out their anger, hurt, frustrations and good times.

Apart from *Drum*'s importance as a record of those years, it was also a vehicle, at least initially, for an imaginative writing which marked the beginning of the modern short story by blacks in South Africa. Among *Drum*'s contributors were Peter Abrahams, Alex la Guma, Es'kia Mphahlele and Richard Rive, who all later reached international audiences. But perhaps more importantly, *Drum* attracted a coterie of young writing talent into its newsroom. They were highly literate, sophisticated men with an understanding and love of the English language. But theirs was an irreverent love, because their models were American – more specifically Langston Hughes, Damon Runyon and the movies of Humphrey Bogart – and they were attracted to the fast, slangy, mixed-language talk of the streets. So Casey Motsisi would write: 'By the way, pardner, let me introduction you' when he meant 'introduce'. Or their highly inventive imaginations would call plain-clothes policemen the 'ghost squad' or prostitutes 'night specials'. While their flamboyant style has been retained here, it was occasionally necessary to correct poor sentence construction and bad grammar, but this was kept to a minimum. In a few cases articles are not credited, mostly because no one can remember who wrote them. By-lines were scarce in the early issues, when the staff was small and every effort was made to counteract the impression that *Drum* was produced by a few dedicated amateurs who knew very little about what they were doing.

Nevertheless, they met their deadlines and told a South

African story full of the bathos and paradoxes which rule our lives as much now as then. Indeed, theirs is a record of naïvety and optimism, frustration and defiance, courage, exile and death.

Acknowledgements

In so many ways this book is a collective effort, a compilation of the opinions and comments of a number of people who gave freely of their time to see me. They are: Jim Bailey, Barney de Vries, Dinah Lefakane, Nadine Gordimer, Jean Hart, Bishop Trevor Huddleston, Arthur Maimane, Esme Matshikiza, Don Mattera, Juby Mayet, George Mbalweni, Es'kia Mphahlele, Obed Musi, Peter Rezant, Anthony Sampson, Jurgen Schadeberg, Sylvester Stein, Walter Sisulu, and the late Sir Tom Hopkinson who answered my queries by letter.

It is also the result of the enthusiasm and encouragement of Dan Franklin and Christopher Hope.

Then for their suggestions and criticisms, which were invariably followed, my thanks to: Clarissa Rushdie (especially, and for much else), Linda and Piet Human, Stephen Watson, Jane Phillips, and Tim Couzins, who also supplied me with unpublished material. However, responsibility for the final shape of the text and for its shortcomings must rest with me.

Acknowledgements are also due to the staff at the Bailey African Photo Archives, especially Marié Human, and the South African Library.

The material from *Drum* and the photographs are published by kind permission of Jim Bailey and the Bailey African Photo Archives.

A special word of appreciation is owed to Vicki Harris, to Hugh Corder, to Pauline Melville for fulfilling the laws of synchronicity, and to Wena van Bergen for taking my side. And likewise to two forebearing and sympathetic friends, Derek and Shelley Conroy, who gave me a second home and car in Johannesburg whenever I needed them and took me out to the mountains to escape the dreariness of Johannesburg weekends.

This book is dedicated to Jill, with thanks for everything.

'Our Little Woodstock'

1

Can Themba would quote Dickens: 'It was the best of times, it was the worst of times . . .' adding, 'and anything can happen.'

Jean Hart: I remember a time when we were all at a party. It was one of John Goldblatt's. He used to give these wild parties of booze and dancing – great fun and a whole lot of noise. This was at his flat in Yeoville. He'd asked over a group of friends from Sophiatown. Arthur was there and Bloke and Can and maybe Henry. At least I think this was before Henry was killed. Any rate, we were drinking and laughing and I suppose one of the neighbours complained to the police, although at that stage the only law we were breaking was supplying blacks with liquor. So the cops broke in. There was pandemonium. People tried to get rid of glasses, emptying liquor out of the window and into pot plants. Two African women jumped into a wardrobe and stayed there for three days. However, the cops weren't going to let us get away with it. Malcolm and I and John Goldblatt and two other whites were arrested and taken away in a van. Some of the *Drum* guys were also taken off. We were all put in the cells at Hillbrow police station. Now this was Friday night, which meant we had to stay there until the case was heard on Monday. On the three mornings, Saturday, Sunday, Monday mornings, black prisoners came in and cleaned our cells. They polished them on their knees. I vaguely knew the woman who had to clean my cell. Once, when she was shuffling around my cell on her hands and knees, she looked up at me and said: 'Who says stone walls do not a prison make or iron bars a cage?'

When the case was finally brought to court we had a regular advocate. The blacks had the SACP [South African Communist Party] advocate, who was much smarter than the one we had paid for. Their case was heard first and the magistrate found them not guilty of receiving liquor. Then our case was heard by the same magistrate, but we were found guilty of supplying it. We were hysterical with laughter at that sentence. I don't think we were fined very much, which in itself was an indication of how marginal the offence was considered in the latter part of the '50s.

Anthony Sampson: There was an innocence, that's what I think it was. Take those famous pictures of people jiving and ballroom dancing: I find that very moving. Also many of the people were intellectually lively. Those years were paradoxical: on the one hand there was prohibition and the Immorality Act and all the other apartheid legislation; on the other it wasn't a problem for whites to visit friends in the townships. I was certainly never stopped going to Sophiatown or Orlando. For all that it was a decade that shattered people's beliefs.

Walter Sisulu: The '50s was a most important decade. It was a landmark in the history of the African National Congress, and in the history of the movement as such. That is the time we came to strength and we really became an organisation. It is ironical that we came to strength when apartheid was being laid down in rigorous laws, but we had been preparing for a situation where all our activities would be suppressed.

Es'kia Mphahlele: The '50s was a highly optimistic period. It was a decade of real idealism in all ways. *Drum* magazine reflects that a lot. It was a coming into being of a big forum where people could say what they wanted to say and there were more political rallies than there had ever been before. People felt freedom was round the corner and the ANC felt that way. When we talked to them about Bantu Education, the ANC said they were not interested in education now, they were interested in liberation. Nelson Mandela himself said that to us. It was that kind of idealism. Also the idealism that you could have a mass democratic movement – black, white together, no matter if it was South African Communist Party or ANC or the Indian Congress. There was that kind of euphoria. Especially when the Defiance Campaigners were given a suspended sentence. Towards the end of the '50s when the Pan Africanist Congress broke away you could see that there was now disillusionment and then it was crowned by Sharpeville: the whole thing was shattered.

Lewis Nkosi: The '50s were important to us as a decade because finally they spelled out the end of one kind of South Africa and foreshadowed the beginning of another.

Jim Bailey: It was an innocent, optimistic and romantic period.

Trevor Huddleston: There was a lot of hope, although I don't think it was a tremendously optimistic era. There had been the Defiance Campaign, of course, which gave people some cause for hope. The maddening thing really is that [Jan] Smuts could have turned the corner when he came back after the war, but he just took it for granted that he would continue in power. Even so, he did nothing to involve the United Nations human rights charter in his own country – despite being an architect of it. But then he has a terrible record of human rights in this country.

Jean Hart: There was a chance of an exciting, nourishing South Africa in the '50s. There was tremendous cross-fertilisation, particularly in music, especially as South African jazz went on to influence British jazz. That was a result of people meeting and playing together. And the theatre that came out of the country was very much the result of European theatre forms which created a way for that passion to express itself. If those are things that happened before

3

the slab came down to crush everything, what could have happened otherwise?

There was a hunger from whites for blacks and vice versa. I don't think that would have solved the political situation, but dear God, culturally it would have been, and still is, potentially one of the most amazing countries. After the murderous twenty or thirty years that have passed since then I don't think you can have that innocent, delighted coming-together again. Ever. In a way it was South Africa's hippie period, everyone sharing peace pipes and throwing flowers and saying Let's all be brothers. You sit at my table, I'll sit at yours. It was really hippie.

I remember going to Lourenço Marques with Can and Bloke and Esme and Todd and Fiki – Bloke's wife – before they got married. We had to put them in the boots of the cars because it was the only way to get them out of the country. We camped on the beach and had picnics and it was a week at the seaside. It was just like Woodstock. We had guitars, we had dope, we had booze: it was our little Woodstock. That was indicative of what things could be like . . . if only . . . There was a lot of that feeling that this is what the world could be like if only they left us alone.

2

Legal apartheid didn't begin in South Africa when the Nationalists came to power in 1948. Discriminatory regulations had been a feature of the various colonial regimes, be they Dutch or British, throughout the history of white settlement on the sub-continent. But it wasn't until the proclamation of Union in 1910 that parliament began passing such legislation as the 1911 Mines and Works Act, which reserved jobs for whites, or the hated Natives Land Act of 1913, which allocated seven per cent of the country to blacks, who then made up sixty-nine per cent of the population. Overnight this Act displaced hundreds of thousands of people; homeless, they wandered the land, squatting briefly wherever they could, eking out a living as sharecroppers, or succumbing to disease and starvation. Throughout the '20s and '30s racial prejudice continued to become ingrained in statute, so that by the time the Nationalists took over there was a solid foundation on which to build their ideology. With a will, they did.

Act No. 55 of 1949: Prohibition of Mixed Marriages Act
Act No. 21 of 1950: Immorality Amendment Act
Act No. 30 of 1950: Population Registration Act
Act No. 41 of 1950: Group Areas Act
Act No. 46 of 1951: Separate Representation of Voters Act
Act No. 52 of 1951: Prevention of Illegal Squatting Act
Act No. 68 of 1951: Bantu Authorities Act
Act No. 67 of 1952: Natives Act
Act No. 3 of 1953: Public Safety Act
Act No. 8 of 1953: Criminal Law Amendment Act

Act No. 47 of 1953: Bantu Education Act
Act No. 49 of 1953: Preservation of Separate Amenities Act
Act No. 19 of 1954: Natives Resettlement Act
Act No. 69 of 1955: Group Areas Development Act
Act No. 64 of 1956: Natives (Prohibition of Interdicts) Act
Act No. 46 of 1959: Bantu Self-Government Act

Such was the progress of apartheid through the '50s: marriages between different race groups were outlawed; 'immoral' acts between whites and blacks were prohibited; everyone was classified according to race; residential separation was enforced; allowance was made to establish homelands; pass laws were instituted compelling blacks to carry identification at all times; provision was made for the proclamation of a state of emergency; special powers were granted to suppress public unrest; education became a racial issue; beaches, parks, benches, resorts, even state institutions became for 'Europeans Only' or for 'Non-Europeans Only'; forced removal of people was entrenched; the homelands were given the opportunity of self-government.

There were other laws, too – many others, which prohibited drinking, imposed curfews, or turned people into criminals if they stayed in town for longer than seventy-two hours without consent.

3

The cast of characters I have chosen from that period is not large nor is it complete. It focuses on a disparate bunch who have become known as the 'Drum writers' because they achieved journalistic fame or literary success both while working for the magazine and afterwards. They cannot be seen as a literary movement, except perhaps in their fascination with urban living, but their efforts, both in fact and fiction, were often extraordinary and brave. In many ways they were a phenomenon, a quick moment when lives, talents and interests coalesced, documented their age and then parted. Had it not been for *Drum*, for the perception of the first editor Anthony Sampson and the proprietor Jim Bailey, that quick moment would probably never have been realised.

In order of joining the magazine they were:

Henry Nxumalo (from 1951 until his death in 1956)
Todd Matshikiza (from 1952 until he went into exile in 1960)
Arthur Maimane (from 1952 until he went into exile in 1958)
Can Themba (from 1953 until he was fired in 1962)
Casey Motsisi (from 1954 until his death in 1977)
Es'kia Mphahlele (from 1955 until he went into exile in 1957)
Bloke Modisane (from 1955 until he went into exile in 1959)
Lewis Nkosi (from 1957 until he went into exile in 1961)
Nat Nakasa (from 1957 until he went into exile in 1964).

About them circled three editors – Anthony Sampson (from 1951 to 1955), Sylvester Stein (1956–1957), Tom Hopkinson (1958–1961) – and the proprietor Jim Bailey. And there is one other to be mentioned here, Jurgen Schadeberg (1951–1960), who, newly arrived in South Africa from a war-ravaged Berlin, became *Drum*'s photographer, back-stop editor, and instructor to some of the first and best black photographers, such as Bob Gosani and Peter Magubane. Of course there were other reporters, other photographers, but none of them gained the reputations of the group whose efforts made the magazine what it was.

Unfortunately, of those nine reporters only three are still alive. Arthur Maimane returned to South Africa in 1990 to take up a position as features editor on *The Weekly Mail*; Es'kia Mphahlele, who returned in 1978, now an internationally renowned author and academic, is a professor of Comparative and African Literature at the University of the Witwatersrand; Lewis Nkosi is still in exile.

In the Dead, Silent, Dark Night

4

Stories end when people die; and the best of the stories to be told about those years ended badly. It's a story of murder and courage. Perhaps not the most delicate of beginnings, but in one way it's a tribute; in another it sets the tone for the times.

This murder takes place at night, in a badly lit street in Newclare township, Johannesburg, late in December 1956. The victim is Henry Nxumalo.

What happens is this.

All Saturday afternoon Nxumalo has been wandering around Sophiatown looking for Can Themba, a colleague and friend. Three times he knocks at the door of the House of Truth, as Themba called his home, three times he's told Themba is out. Eventually, he goes to see another reporter friend, Bloke Modisane, who lives nearby and chats with him about nothing of consequence into the early evening.

In the Transvaal, night falls suddenly, there's no lingering light: the sun goes down and it gets dark within minutes. And in Sophiatown the dark is not a good place to be alone.

Modisane thinks Nxumalo should be getting home because the boys – the *tsotsis* (young hoodlums) – are always knife-happy in the Christmas season.

Not yet, replies Nxumalo, he has a job in Newclare and will probably sleep at his cousin's in Western.

That's all Modisane knows of Nxumalo's movements.

So at about seven o'clock, Nxumalo leaves Sunset Boulevard – Modisane's home – and goes to Western Township, across the railway line.

It's dark by the time he gets to Percy Hlubi's house. He

9

explains that he wants to stay the night but first he has a job to do. He'll come back afterwards to sleep.

'OK,' says Hlubi, and the men sit talking while Mrs Hlubi prepares a bed.

'We'll be asleep when you get back,' she tells Nxumalo when she's finished. 'Don't knock, just open the door and go to bed.'

'Thanks,' says Nxumalo, and he and Percy Hlubi talk on until close to eleven.

'Why don't you leave your job till tomorrow?' suggests Hlubi.

'No,' says Nxumalo. 'Never put off for tomorrow . . .' and he grins.

Then he goes out into the night and never comes back to the bed Mrs Hlubi made for him. He walks through the dark streets of Western towards Newclare, past shacks and crumbling old houses, past dark alleys where cats scavenge, across vacant lots where a thin horse and some goats nibble at the grass. Lightning flickers in the sky all around, but it doesn't rain that night.

Not a hundred yards from Coronation Hospital, in the dark between street-lights, the knifeman gets him. Maybe Nxumalo sees a woman waiting for him, maybe he sees her gesture. Maybe he senses someone coming at him, maybe he senses nothing. Maybe a man passes him, maybe they look into each other's eyes; then the man turns and slashes with a long blade, once, twice, again, again, twenty-two times stabbing and cutting, at the body, at the head. It doesn't matter. This is no clean assassination, this is a butchering. But Nxumalo won't go down, he stumbles and loses a shoe but he won't go down. And because he won't go down the man stabs madly. Then with Nxumalo still staggering, blood in his eyes, blood filling up his lungs, the man runs back into the night where no dogs bark.

Still Nxumalo lurches about the street, blood in his shoe, blood on the dust. He turns back towards Western, totters

10

in circles, goes down on some grass with his head pressed hard against the ground.

That's where Mrs Hlubi finds him. She's a nurse and is due on duty at six. At quarter-past five she's on her way to the hospital. At the corner of Malotane Street and Ballenden Avenue she notices a body on the grass, one shoe off, an arm twisted behind, the head pressed hard against the ground. There are bloody wounds all over the head and body.

It's Henry Nxumalo.

Crying, sobbing, screaming, she rushes home, drags her husband out of bed, gets him to the body. But there's nothing to be done. Except curse, except ask Why, why, why? The sun comes up and it soon gets hot. A crowd gathers. Someone puts two thin rags over the corpse.

That's how it is when Can Themba gets there. That's how he remembers it: 'There he lay, the great gallant Henry Nxumalo, who had fought bravely to bare cruelty, injustice and narrow-mindedness; there he lay in the broiling sun, covered by two flimsy rags.'

Themba stood there looking on, weeping, but Modisane wouldn't go anywhere near his slain friend. When Gwigwi Mrwebi's wife told him, as she told all the *Drum* boys, 'Henry's dead, Bloke, with twenty-two stab wounds. He's passed away. His body is waiting for the Black Maria . . .', Modisane wouldn't go and pay his last respects. He wanted to vomit, for he was caught in the aftermath of stale sex and brandy and gin. He couldn't think, he couldn't stand on his legs, he wanted to be alone with his pain. He kept thinking of the gored, mutilated body of his father and he didn't want that to be the last image of someone he knew and loved.

Mrs Mrwebi went away, but she never understood why Modisane wouldn't go to the place of his friend's death, never forgave.

Even with all those people standing round the body, the

police still wanted a white to identify it. They phoned Sylvester Stein, then *Drum*'s editor.

'I remember I was woken up early that Sunday morning by somebody from Western Native police station who said he had one of my "boys" there. I thought, "Oh God not again." There was a curfew for blacks at the time and it happened regularly that Can would be out late or one of the others and they'd be picked up and the cops would ring me. I said to the policeman, "Who is it?" He replied, "Henry Nxumalo." Would I come and identify the body. You can imagine the shock. There he was, still lying in the gutter when I identified him.'

But why? As everyone was asking, Why, why, why had he been killed?

'In those days we all had this paranoia about the government,' says Stein, 'we thought it was them. And it might have been. Or it might have been a passing *tsotsi*, or his girlfriend's husband. Not much work was done on his murder at the time and we didn't give it the publicity or make of it the kind of issue that it would be today.'

Was it a *tsotsi*? A jealous husband? The government? Or Mr Big, the white abortionist?

'It is unlikely that Henry's death was a *tsotsi* killing, because of the manner of the stabbing of a man like that,' thinks Es'kia Mphahlele. 'I mean *tsotsis* do things differently. Henry was well known to them, which should have given him some protection.'

'The way I remember it,' says Esme Matshikiza, wife of Todd Matshikiza, 'was that he was investigating a story to do with abortion. There were all sorts of rumours going round as to who it was. Lots of people said it was Mr Big who put somebody on to him to kill him, but I don't know and nobody ever seriously investigated it. What I heard was that Mr Big was a white man, but again there were such vague rumours. The sort of thing you don't really talk about because you don't really know. It was a terribly shocking thing that happened. It was a trauma for all of us. Henry

12

was an extraordinary man. He was certainly the best journalist that *Drum* had. He had no fear whatsoever. He was a very very intelligent man. I called him Boet [Brother] Henry.'

So Boet Henry's death went uninvestigated and people still wonder about who did it. What they know is that he was squeezing a nurse for details of women who had died at the hands of a white surgeon giving illegal abortions. At the time Nxumalo was freelancing while he wrote his autobiography for an American publisher. But he couldn't ignore this smell of death and money. So he arranged for photographer Bob Gosani to take pictures through a skylight during an abortion. Then he went out into the Newclare streets on that Saturday night to meet the nurse for a last time to find out the date of the next operation. The story has it that she was used as a decoy by the murderers.

'Some months later,' recalls Jim Bailey, 'in a shebeen in what used to be Salisbury, Rhodesia, I came across one of Henry's friends who had been driving him around at the time. He told me that a few days before Henry was murdered they had been shot at in his car in an attempt to kill Henry. Henry had paid to have the bullet holes repaired and the car resprayed so it would not be easily identifiable.

'I took all this information to the police, but they told me they were underpaid and understaffed and certainly nothing was ever achieved by whatever enquiries they made.

'Many years later a black prisoner, apparently haunted by Henry's ghost, confessed that Henry's murder was on his conscience. He said that a man named Lefty had arranged it with him. He was paid £120 for the murder. This somewhat supported the other evidence that the real murderer was a white man, because the going rate for a murder in the townships at that time, so my enquiries had assured me, was £25. Only a white man, it seemed to me, would so grossly overpay.'

There is another story, one told in her last years by Nxumalo's wife, Florence. She thought Nxumalo was on his way back to the Hlubis' house on that fateful night, having witnessed the abortionist at work. He probably even had a photograph. But it was a set-up. Someone had leaked that Nxumalo was on to the doctor, so that night Mr Big laid a trap. 'Kill Nxumalo and make it look like robbery,' he instructed. The murderers – three men, not one – did, but they forgot to take Henry Nxumalo's watch. That oversight convinced Florence neither *tsotsis* nor a jealous husband was to blame for the death, but the abortionist. And the price he paid wasn't £120, but £246. 'Ja,' she used to say, 'Dr G— was going to be at stake with his profession and the best thing was to get rid of Henry.'

Three months later *Drum* carried a poem by Vil-Nkomo, the man who had phoned the police when Henry Nxumalo's body was discovered:

> Flowers are beautiful
> Cut worms are made for blight
> Hank Nxumalo was useful
> But someone committed sin
> On the grass that was green
> In the dead, silent dark night,
> Hero! you have done your best,
> Facing condemnation,
> And now you have gone to rest;
> Reward to your nation.
> Black storms on the horizon
> Martyr of a great nation
> To eternal peace and rest
> To the Good Lord, you are blest!

5

Those *Drum* boys, as they've become known – Henry Nxumalo, Can Themba, Bloke Modisane, Todd Matshikiza, Casey Motsisi – lived hard, lived by a maxim out of Willard Motley's book *Knock on any Door*: 'Live fast, die young, and have a good-looking corpse.' Only it didn't work out that way for any of them. Certainly not for Nxumalo. But then neither for Themba nor Matshikiza nor Motsisi, because it was the booze, the European liquor as it was known in those prohibition days, that got them. And Modisane, well, it was probably the drink and a lot more that he took to his grave a few years ago. Things like bitterness and hatred and exile.

But they all died later; Nxumalo was the only one of the *Drum* staffers to die in the '50s. Because of that his death is an anomaly, and considering the violence of the time – didn't another of them, Arthur Maimane, pack a gun in case he met up with the gangsters he wrote about? – it's lucky he was the only one to go that way. For some of the rest of them the '50s had a more insidious fate in store.

Henry Nxumalo's death also marks a turning point, the end of the years of innocence, because from then on things got worse for them all – personally as the drink really started ravaging their lives, professionally with the magazine never again measuring up to the high-kicking vibrancy of the mid-'50s, and politically as the concrete of apartheid solidified about their ankles. Not only had they lost their best journalist, they were losing history.

That Nxumalo was *Drum*'s best journalist has never been disputed; in fact he's still regarded by some as the greatest investigative journalist South Africa has ever produced. You'll hear that from people like Arthur Maimane, Es'kia Mphahlele or Obed Musi, and they all worked with him and survived those years.

Mphahlele is not entirely uncritical however. He says Nxumalo wrote a sort of 'English English which doesn't say very much about what you're thinking. He distanced himself from his material. This may have been his way of handling the situation, I don't know. He was a loner much of the time, he didn't keep company despite common beliefs or the same occupation. He was not really one of the *Drum* boys; he went out on his own. He was older than the rest of us, for one thing. He'd come from news broadcasting on Radio Bantu and political life didn't seep into him at all. Certainly Henry never showed any political sensitivity. Whereas I just had to go into a shanty town and try to do a story and the situation would hit me like that, but it would not hit Henry in the same way. He would look at it as a professional reporter *par excellence* and he would not be shaken by the other things he saw, which would shake me up to the degree where it would mess up my story from the editor's point of view. He was a man of outstanding courage, but the actual reporting itself is so deadpan. I don't think he read much. The other journalists read a lot of American writing and used that way of capturing a dramatic scene and putting it across in a vivid style. This came from their reading of Langston Hughes and Richard Wright and even Damon Runyon. But not Henry; he just reported things almost unemotionally.'

'I only knew Henry for a year,' says Obed Musi. 'I can't say I remember much except he stressed to us the power of being able to adapt and mix easily. He was against us drinking, but he drank a lot himself. I remember thinking that he knew everybody who mattered. I know many of us tried to copy his bravery in getting stories.'

It was that bravery which made Nxumalo's name and gave *Drum* an international reputation. Henry Nxumalo today is really just a name the old-timers know, a fond memory banging around in history. Some young journalists have heard of him but mostly not, let alone his exploits.

He was young when he died, only thirty-nine, and left a wife, two daughters and a son. All his life he'd had to fend for himself, as his parents had died when he was still at school. After matriculation he'd been a kitchen-boy in Durban, then worked in a boiler maker's shop in Johannesburg, all the time writing poetry for *Bantu World*. Later he got a job on that newspaper as a messenger and hung on for three years until he became sports editor.

Then came the war and he went north.

'The world beyond showed him how other people thought and lived and when he came back he was a frustrated man,' wrote Can Themba in an obituary.

After the war and until he joined *Drum* in 1951, Nxumalo worked variously for *Bantu World*, as a stringer for the *Pittsburgh Courier*, in a gold mine, and even did clerical work for the British Empire Service League.

Then came *Drum*, and by the end of its first year he was known as 'Mr Drum'. If found in a township street with a rolled-up copy of the magazine under his arm, he would dish out £5 to anyone who recognised him.

GET READY FOR MR DRUM trumpeted the headline in the January 1952 edition. Below that was a photograph of Henry Nxumalo and an exhortation to readers to 'look at it carefully and remember what he looks like'. Because 'Mr Drum will be touring round the towns of South Africa in the next few months. The first *Drum* reader to recognise him in each place he visits will get £5. All you have to do is: walk up to Mr Drum holding a copy of *The African Drum* magazine and say: "You are Mr Drum. I claim the *African Drum* prize." He will then present the winner with a £5 note.'

Right up to his death people were trying to earn a fiver off Henry Nxumalo.

There are memories of the man still to be gleaned in parts of Johannesburg and London, some explanations for why he did what he did, for the hard-edged way he ran his life, but that's all that's left. That and what he wrote.

'It was fascinating watching Henry with newcomers,' remembers Anthony Sampson, 'particularly with white secretaries. He would turn on the charm and there were few who could resist him. It was most interesting watching him charm white girls who'd never had these sort of conversations with a black man. They'd be completely overwhelmed. It was nothing for Henry to have these women talking to him for two hours at a time. He was very disarming, a very unusual man. He had an absolute natural authority and could bring out the best in everyone.

'Drink though was his terrible problem and I suspect that in one way it was how he coped with that society and apartheid.'

'There was a time when the author Peter Abrahams stayed with Henry,' says Jim Bailey. 'When I asked him about Henry's drinking he replied that it could be said that he – Henry – was pioneering his profession for all the black journalists of the future and so the strains on him were much greater than they would be on them.'

Jurgen Schadeberg, the photographer, has an addition to this story: 'Henry had first met Peter Abrahams in London and when Peter came out here he wanted to meet some of the politicians. We arranged for him to meet Nelson Mandela and Walter Sisulu and some teachers and other intellectuals.

'As I remember it, Henry and I arrived at the house where we were all due to meet. As we organised drinks the hostess came up to me and said, "This Mr Nxumalo, he's a very nice man, charming." And then as the evening went on Henry got a little pissed and we started running out of liquor and the next thing he began reaching over everybody and pouring their glasses into his. He was also pushing everybody and falling about. Eventually I carried him out, put him in the car and dropped him round the corner in the office and put him on the floor there. I went back and this lady said to me, "My word, but he's actually a terrible man." So he had these two sides to him. The heavy drinking might have been a reaction to society.'

Nxumalo's daughter, Suzette, was only eight when he died but she has one cherished memory.

'My mother disapproved of his wild, reckless way of life filled with heavy drinking and his weakness for the skirt. But at the same time she loved him and was very protective towards him. I also loved him, but because of the minimal amount of time he spent at home – sometimes disappearing for days on end – I never really got close to him.

'I guess, though, I have some sort of romantic fixation about him. I have reached into the back of my mind for memories of him in an effort to reconstruct my image of him. I also spent a lot of time talking about him to my mother.

'One of the times I most cherish was when he took me to a shebeen. I was about five years old. We stayed there till late and my mother locked us out. He used me to get her to open up. That's one of the things that made me believe my father was crazy. I mean, what sane man would take a child that young to a shebeen?

'At the same time I am fascinated by his madness. I think he couldn't have been the kind of journalist he was if he didn't have that streak of insanity.

'At one stage I became intrigued by this good-looking man who had been my father. I wished he had lived long enough for me to get to know him. In a desperate effort to establish some sort of contact with him, I read all his works, hoping to find some mention of me in them. I was deeply disappointed when I didn't find any.

'I suppose my choice of career, public relations, is a subconscious effort at identifying with him – to keep alive the memory of Henry Nxumalo, the man who lived and died for the typewriter.'

'Why the bloody hell did they have to choose him to murder?' Can Themba asked angrily at the time of his death. 'I cannot hide my bitterness at all. But, dear Henry, Mr Drum is not dead. Indeed, even while you lived others were practising the game of Mr Drum. Now, we shall take over where you left off. We want you, as you look down on us from among the angels, to mutter, "The boys sure make a good job of that game, and looks like they might get the world a little cleaner from what I left it."'

6

In the hills north of Johannesburg there is a farm where Jim Bailey has lived since those *Drum* years. It is a place Nxumalo would have known, as he partied there whenever Bailey threw his all-night affairs. In the jumble of photo files and the myriad of negatives at the Bailey archives is a photograph of Nxumalo's funeral. It shows a hot day with the crowd sheltering under umbrellas. Carrying the coffin from the church are four young men, three of whom are to figure prominently in the stories still to be told.

In the front on the right is Bloke Modisane, his brows furrowed, his eyes in shadow staring with what could be anger out of the picture. His mouth is set firmly. Behind him, with hooded eyes, his mouth full of grief, is Can Themba; and opposite him on the other side of the coffin, Arthur Maimane: short, his fist clenched at his side, tense, drawn.

A Bunch of Rather Wild People

7

Drum was many things, and probably in a sane society it wouldn't have stood a chance of surviving. But South Africa in the '50s was a mad place. If you were white you could launch a magazine for blacks and still be deaf to howling ironies and paradoxes. What's more you could keep it going, you could reach a six-figure circulation, you could have credibility, you could even try, and for a while succeed, in putting together a publishing empire across Africa. But to do it you had to be a little weird, a little out of the ordinary. On the other hand, if you were black you could work on the magazine, you could risk your neck, write great stuff and great rubbish, but you knew it would get you in the end. Either way you also had to be an eccentric.

Jim Bailey was a strange character. And as you'll see so were the others: Can Themba, Todd Matshikiza, Bloke Modisane, Casey Motsisi, Lewis Nkosi, Nat Nakasa, Jurgen Schadeberg; and in other ways so were Anthony Sampson, Sylvester Stein, Tom Hopkinson – the troika of editors.

But Bailey first.

As the son of the diamond and gold Randlord Sir Abe Bailey, he was rich. Many would say stinking rich. The family millions gave him what he called a 'thumping income'.

In his late teens he was flying RAF Spitfires against the Luftwaffe. Or going out on night bombing-raids in machines where sometimes the instrumentation measured little more than speed and altitude, where if the enemy didn't get you there was a good chance the cold would, or that turbulence would shake the plane to pieces. At that age, after meeting death each day, not much is left for an encore. Which is maybe why risking your money to build a publishing empire in Africa is not so out of the ordinary.

Today around Bailey swirl legends of hard drinking, of seemingly endless parties, of meanness, generosity, wilfulness and a pig-headed attitude that ended in bad words with practically everybody who worked for him. And of an extraordinary concern and kindness as well. Ask anyone who's known Bailey and they'll respond: 'I love him dearly but . . .' Or mention his name in some quarters and you'll be stone-walled so quickly you'll feel like a tourist in a deserted city centre late at night.

Anthony Sampson: He was very generous to me. He had a streak of genius and a tremendous amount of flare and drive in him, but he wasn't a businessman.

Sylvester Stein: Bailey was a difficult man, everybody had problems with him. But by the same token he achieved some amazing results.

Es'kia Mphahlele: Bailey was very hard and tight-fisted, he didn't want to lose a penny. He was a manipulator with money. He had a way of treating his staff as a kind of clan that he could invite to his farm as often as he wanted to. They would bring their girlfriends and he would serve them all drinks. This was paternalism, as well as a kind of wicked streak in him that wanted some amusement. This gave him power. He felt he had their fate in his hands.

Obed Musi: The parties at Bailey's were swinging occasions. Bailey's done a lot to put black journalism on the map and to break down racial barriers. To this day if you walk into *Drum* publications you walk into a different world entirely.

The photograph of Bailey that's become the icon of those years shows him with his feet against the desk, tilting his chair back, a laughing young man with his top button undone, tie pulled loose, sleeves rolled up. Behind him is a stippled-glass window with papers and magazines on the ledge. Today he has a mane of white hair, pulls his sleeves up on to his forearms, and laughs with a rasp at his funny memories.

8

Although *Drum* became Bailey's, it wasn't started by him. The founder was a local hero of sorts – a Springbok fast bowler, a tank commander with a DSO and bar, a journalist and broadcaster who had fond dreams of selling his African magazine right across the continent. His name was Robert Crisp: he had the vision but he needed finance. And finance wasn't all that easy to raise for such philanthropic ventures in early 1951.

Crisp approached a respected Cape Town QC, Robin Stratford, who agreed to help raise £5,000 as capital. One of the people Stratford touched for a thousand was Bailey, who was then farming sheep near Colesberg in the north-eastern Cape. Thanks to a wool boom he was being paid a pound for a pound of wool and thought the idea sounded, if not profitable, at least interesting. He went in, although he knew nothing about publishing. In March 1951, *The African Drum* appeared.

Four issues later the balance sheet showed a total outflow of funds, circulation had dropped from twenty-four thousand to sixteen thousand, and Stratford had gone to live in England because he wanted to talk to dukes and earls.

Bailey took charge and set about trying to change the magazine's content. He moved the office from Cape Town to Johannesburg, and cabled Anthony Sampson, a former Oxford friend, to come and join him on a 'Negro periodical' at a salary of £50 a month. Sampson wrote back to say he'd come but didn't want to get mixed up in politics, then booked a ticket on the *Llangibby Castle* to Cape Town. He was twenty-five years old, with an uninspiring career record that included two and a half years in the Navy, three years at Oxford and a knowledge of 243 Elizabethan plays, which was to stand him in good stead when it came to understanding South African township life.

He took to that life with a zest that astounded local whites who, no matter how liberal their outlook, still viewed the black world as alien, even hostile. But not Sampson. He was soon being shown through the shebeens, invited to eat at friends' and colleagues' houses in Soweto or Sophiatown, and not many months had gone by before the man with the black cap and the scooter felt himself welcome, if not entirely at home, in this other reality.

'I think I must have looked a very cold fish in all that frenzied activity which seemed to me to be every bit a Shakespearean play with terror and murder waiting in the wings. On many occasions I felt a blundering Englishman who had stumbled into something he didn't understand: a history that was being played out between Africans and Afrikaners.'

It was just as well that Sampson was driven by what others have seen as 'recklessness' or 'sowing his wild oats', because the urban life he quickly came to relish was not appreciated by *The African Drum*'s first editor, Bob Crisp. For all Crisp's bright ideas, he was too imbued with the concept of the noble savage. He thought great copy was a series called *Know Yourselves*, a history of the various tribes, or articles on tribal music, or features on religion, farming and famous men, to say nothing of strip cartoons about Gulliver and St Paul. He serialised Alan Paton's novel *Cry, the Beloved Country* and ran epic religious poems by obscure poets.

> I the King of kings, am not
> Opponent, bluffer, competitor,
> A mirage leading sojourners astray:
> A dream like unto a sham death,
> Through the midst of which a man may stray.

I, your father, am not a snare and a lure
I, the immortal, am not a maker of mischief.
In my realm
Where there are no ills
Where no fake trails exist
Evil is the hurt of hares by hounds.

His efforts might have attracted praise from liberal whites, the Nationalist government might have sent copies to their information centres abroad as an example of black achievement, but the magazine wasn't going down a storm in the townships. What was wanted there were hot dames, jazz, pin-ups, sport. Kraals, chiefs and tribes were out. So was the white hand. And in those early editions of *Drum*, or *The African Drum* as it was rather staidly called, the white hand was everywhere. *The African Drum* was what white men wanted blacks to be.

But how to get rid of the white hand? Firstly, hire black reporters, although black reporters in those days weren't exactly thick on the ground. And deliver what township dwellers wanted. Superficially that was an answer; in practice it was more complex.

When Sampson arrived as circulation manager, Bob Crisp was editing; Jurgen Schadeberg, that German refugee from a bombed-out Berlin, taking photographs; and the dapper, jaunty Henry Nxumalo valiantly kept up the black side. For a black magazine there was an odd preponderance of whites.

At the time relations between Crisp and Bailey were tense, as the founder fought to retain his ideal and the proprietor started to push for a diet of crime, sex and sport. Something had to go; not surprisingly it was Crisp. Sampson became editor and Bailey started looking for advisers.

'It is the intention of the directors,' he proclaimed, 'to secure, as soon as possible, the assistance of an African advisory board, composed of eminent African men of letters and leaders of thought. Their role will be to keep *The African*

Drum in close touch with Africa and the Africans. The names of the advisory board will be announced at a later date.'

Two issues later the advisory board was announced. It comprised: Joe Rathebe, Johannesburg businessman, social worker and chairman of the Transvaal Boxing Board; Dan Twala, sports commentator and founder member of the Soccer Federation; Dr Alfred Xuma, a former ANC president; and Andy Anderson, a printer with a taste for cover girls. Over sandwiches and milk they showed Bailey and Sampson the way to go. It was the path Bailey had already chosen.

Sampson has always felt it was to his advantage that he knew nothing about journalism and even less about South Africa when he accepted the editorship. At least he had no preconceived ideas and prejudices. At least he would let the writers have it their way. And in the main they did.

'I was always aware of this anomaly of having a white editor. But I think we were preparing the way for black successors, which eventually happened. In the mean time I could at least make sure that blacks did the writing and not whites. Which was important because it broke a long tradition of white liberals interpreting black life. At last the blacks could have their own say.'

Nevertheless there has also been criticism, charges that *Drum* acted as a means of social and political control by reinforcing (if only implicitly), and very seldom challenging the social, political and economic order of the day. Partly that's true, but then *Drum* never pretended to be anything other than a popular magazine, with all that this implies. It skidded across the surface of the '50s, out of control, dizzy, spinning, going nowhere in particular because there was nowhere in particular to go, because there was only this slippery surface with nothing underneath.

As Sampson, with more seriousness than flippancy, puts it: 'We were just a bunch of rather wild people having an exciting time.'

28

However, others look on it all rather differently. One of the magazine's sternest critics at the time, Es'kia Mphahlele, feels the publication should have aimed at loftier ideals instead of succumbing to a racy mediocrity, a level he ascribes to the ubiquitous white hand.

'I think to a large extent the dominant white hand was all but sublimated because we had pretty strong writers who wrote the way they wanted to write. So I would say the white-hand influence was a much more generalised factor, an overall influence rather than noticeable in particular stories. But in shaping the magazine the white hand was very strong, in particular from Bailey behind the scenes. He had a strong desire to avoid confrontational material. For instance, the mines were a subject *Drum* stayed away from. There is no doubt about it, he would not touch the mines. It was a grave omission. There was one picture story I recall, not a full-fledged story, that showed conditions in the hostels. That was the one and only story that appeared in the years I was there. And I tend to think the story was a side issue, that it didn't have anything to do with the mines themselves.'

'We were discouraged from writing about the mines,' agrees Arthur Maimane. 'It was Bailey's children's inheritance.'

Certainly at a time when the mines were hiring vast numbers of workers, when conditions in the mine hostels were abysmal, it is surprising that only some half a dozen photographs depicting concrete bunks and rudimentary shower rooms were ever used, with a brief story that avoided all mention of the miners' conditions, even glossing over them in the picture captions.

This charge Bailey counters somewhat disingenuously. 'It's not true that I disallowed mining stories. We never ran them on the basis that miners themselves were illiterate. Besides, trying to get mine managers to allow us to sell the magazine on the mines was impossible because mine managers are so conservative anyway. So that was why mining never came into it.'

Sampson has a more straightforward answer. 'Now that *Drum* has become the subject of doctoral theses and solemn analyses I'm always amused at the way these people want to see a white capitalist conspiracy to portray blacks in a certain way. Of course it was never like that at all. We were all feeling our way. Jim Bailey, myself and probably quite a lot of the black staff were undergoing our political education day by day. We were just trying to find out what the hell was going on. Probably we should have given more attention to the mine compounds, but because the staff didn't have any link with the migrant mine workers none of those stories came our way. It's quite as simple as that. It had nothing to do with Jim's connections with the mining industry; it was just that the miners lived in a totally separate world from our writers and readers and we just never got to hear about their stories. It's important to understand that the *Drum* journalists were writers first and political analysts afterwards. They were also young, most of them under thirty, and engrossed with their extraordinary world.'

But there are other ways, too, in which Mphahlele would have preferred to see a more progressive publication. 'For instance, up to the mid-'50s there hadn't been much political reporting in *Drum*. When Henry went out for the Bethal farm labour story, that's when political reporting began. But you must remember there was never much text in *Drum* because it was always regarded as a picture magazine: it went for the dramatic scenes and the dramatic personalities, the Mandelas and Tambos. Admittedly there was that kind of political reporting around established profiles, but there was no commentary. Much more analytical writing could have been done, but nobody seemed to want it. The editors were not interested in that kind of thing. They wanted investigative reporting such as Henry's prison story. I think they could have done much more at the time.

'It's now common to see *Drum* as an island in an abnormal world. And yes, *Drum* was an island, an island where things were being created, but it was overseen by an authoritarian attitude which said This is what people want. The editor and publisher had already formulated the criteria on which people read magazines. So it was a kind of dictator's taste. Of course it so happened that there was an urban readership ready to lap up a good deal of this material, and it cashed in on that. It also created a standard which would have to be accepted by the reading public while at the same time they created a vicious cycle: the people want *this* and they want us to do *that* so this is what we give them.

'It was an island in another sense too. The very way in which the reporters comported themselves made you feel that they had a kind of power to dictate taste to the people.

'I would say that *Drum* succeeded in stimulating an interest among a number of people, which satisfied management. For instance, when *Drum* went in for pin-ups it believed that there was a segment of the population that loved this kind of thing, that people loved to see pictures but didn't want much text. However, investigative reporting was one thing that they could swallow. I was unhappy about this approach; the editorial approach could have gone further and elevated the reader, there was no upward movement. They – management – used a word, "uplift", as in "we don't want too much uplift stuff here".

'Yet there was a vibrancy. *Drum* lived a life which seemed to say Life is normal, things are going the way we would like them to go. The magazine wasn't interested in long-term discussions about society, about what it would be like. *Drum* wasn't interested in projecting that kind of view, even through the politicians they were interviewing. For them it was Live fast, die young, have a good-looking corpse. I think this attitude clouded what was really happening.'

However, at a time when the press wasn't interested in black politics, the ANC found an interested ear.

'The press was absolutely hostile to us,' recalls Walter Sisulu. 'You would be surprised at how hostile the entire press was. There would be no follow-up of party conferences, and a lot of inaccuracies. Even *Bantu World* was completely hostile, and that was a paper which had been started by the ANC, but the editor wasn't sympathetic to us. He favoured the Africanists in Congress. So there was only the Communist Party's paper. When *Drum* came up, and later *Golden City Post*, it more or less took a different attitude. I think they had men who were able to read the situation. Men like Anthony Sampson and Bailey, that combination, they were able men who could see things better than the rest of the press. So they were not hostile, they were shaping things.'

'At the time,' says Sampson, 'at the start of the '50s, amazingly little was known about the ANC. I remember going to a Congress meeting and there were only two other white people in the hall. One of them was Ruth First. We tried to take photographs but the black delegates weren't very co-operative because they saw it as an invasion of privacy. You see, they just weren't used to being covered seriously at all. It was then I got to know people like Mandela and Tambo, and because no other whites were really interested in them we had a sort of political opportunity. I don't think we ever sat down and thought through a political line; we certainly never had editorial conferences to discuss our political stance. Perhaps things were influenced by Henry Nxumalo because he was a friend of many Congress people. I would say that in some ways he was the most politically mature among us.'

In other areas, though, Bailey had fixed ideas about what *Drum* was going to do and how it was going to do it. Sure there were editorial meetings of all the staff where issues were discussed and debated, and sure the bulk of the stories originated in the township shebeens – they had to, it was after all a black magazine. But it's Bailey's hand that paints the broad brush-strokes.

'When I took over I asked Henry to gather a number of burglars together so that we could assess what they wanted in a magazine. We went out to a place in Orlando to meet them. I distinctly remember there was no electricity, so the room was lit by a flickering candle which cast shadows of an extraordinary size on the walls.

'The group of men started arguing among themselves about what should be in a magazine, and it was very difficult to make head or tail of their decisions because they had drunk so much. One of them took it on himself to be chairman, and in parliamentary-style language tried to make sense of the drunken horde but couldn't. I had brought a lot of brandy with me, which kept the party going until they started flaking out one after the other. Eventually in the early hours of the morning there were only three left on their feet so I played an old Air Force game called Cardinal Puff – a drinking game where you go through a ritual which looks simple but if you make a mistake you have to drink up and start again – and that finished them off. I walked out over the body of my host who was unconscious at the door and drove back to the city.

'The next morning when I woke up I wondered what it was they had agreed they wanted to read, but couldn't remember. There was, however, one thing they had agreed on and that was that no crime should be reported. So I thought that was a good topic to start with.' And he laughs that dry laugh with his mouth wide open.

Crime, sex – mostly sex across the colour line which was now forbidden by the Immorality Act – and sport became the basis for the revamped *Drum*.

'Obviously,' he continues, 'I had a lot of input from beginning to end. It was too tricky not to. The world we were in was too bloody dangerous, you had to have more or less everything at your fingertips.

'That initial recipe gave us the foundation. Even so, Sampson and I had hard discussions on this topic of an evening. With popular publishing you can produce something that is widely read and isn't worth reading or something that is immensely worth reading and isn't read. The problem was to produce something rather like a pill that

33

had a sugar coating on the outside and the worthwhile message inside.'

So did *Drum* succeed?

Sampson says yes. 'I think *Drum* caught all aspects of its age, simply because we had the best writers. It became a natural mirror of society. I never had any doubts about the authenticity of it. The basis of *Drum*'s expansion rested on the vigour and strength with which those first *Drum* writers recreated their world, its dangers, its miseries, its joys. Their lives were caught up in it. Perhaps in retrospect you could say that the early *Drum* was too optimistic, too light-hearted, that we weren't giving enough attention to the younger generation growing up in the townships. Maybe. But Henry and Todd and Can recorded their lives and times with a courage and energy that couldn't be ignored.'

Similar thoughts come from Bishop Trevor Huddleston, who spent many years living in Sophiatown: 'I saw *Drum* founded in a very unattractive form, which would never have made anything. It was Sampson who really brought the sparkle into *Drum*, him and the photographers. It did serve a purpose at that time, but I think it was too much dominated by the Bailey hand.'

And Nadine Gordimer: 'Many whites read *Drum*, and now there are some blacks who argue that *Drum* was aimed at whites and was not nearly close enough to the people and to their lives. But I don't think this criticism is true of the period when Sampson was editor. This was urban life and the *Drum* people were writing what they saw and knew.'

And *Drum* reporter Obed Musi: 'I think *Drum* gave its readers what they wanted. I'll say *Drum* was the mirror of township life. Many of the writers were palsy-walsy with the gangsters, the guys who mattered – we were on first-name terms with many of them. Many of us were of the people, that's why there was an open policy on *Drum* towards these people. Almost all the magazines before *Drum* were about "Jim goes to Jo'burg". *Drum* came out with the

"Jim is *in* Jo'burg" reality. As for the political coverage, I feel there was ample. *Drum* was the ANC magazine. Towards the end of the '50s it may have been reflecting the Pan Africanist movement more than the ANC but that was because it seemed a good story and it was the start of the black consciousness movement.'

Lewis Nkosi agrees: 'In those days when I went to join the paper, *Drum* was a curious institution. It wasn't so much a magazine as a symbol of the new African cut adrift from the tribal reserve – urbanised, eager, fast-talking and brash . . . By the end of the '50s *Drum* and *Golden City Post* had become so widely accepted as the most authoritative newspapers on the life of black South Africans that visiting writers and journalists would almost inevitably call at the *Drum* offices on their way across the country.'

But perhaps the question, Did *Drum* succeed?, is nonsensical. All that can really be said is that here was a magazine which created an impression of a highly romantic age decked out in American clothing, American drawls, American gangsterism, American-style prohibition. Somehow even Henry Nxumalo's exploits are surrounded by a romanticism, the spirit of the crusader; and although the gangsters that terrorised township streets are never glorified in print the photographs treat them as movie stars. And yes, there were horror features on alcoholism and benzine kids and *muti* (medicine) killings by witch-doctors and political marches, but they were all stories and the first task of stories is to enthral.

9

There must have been quiet days in the *Drum* newsroom, days when nothing out of the ordinary happened, when Henry Nxumalo or Can Themba or Arthur Maimane quietly typed out their stories or answered the occasional telephone. Office days, punctuated with cups of coffee and not much to do, especially when an edition was on the presses.

'No,' says Jurgen Schadeberg, 'I can't ever remember a time like that. It always seemed to be a madhouse. There was always something going on.'

In fact 'Madhouse' was the popular name for *Drum*'s editorial office, a name cheerfully conferred by a reporter in a caption to a double-page photograph of the staff taken to celebrate the magazine's fourth anniversary in March 1955. It shows Nxumalo, in a bow-tie, sucking his pipe, straddling a chair, his arms encircling its back as he 'bashes out his latest hair-raising Mr Drum exposure', as the caption has it. Behind him Es'kia Mphahlele scratches his head in bafflement at a short story; then there's Casey Motsisi and Can Themba and a photographer, Jerry Ntsipe, crouched on a desk. Next, Arthur Maimane looking like his detective creation, the 'Chief', hat tilted back, cigarette dangling from his lips. And others, Victor Xashimba, Dan Chocho, Benson Dyantyi, Ken Mtetwa and chief photographer Bob Gosani posed in the corner. It's a madhouse photograph of a chaotic office packed with desks and littered with paper. The caption ends: 'Doesn't it surprise you that you get your *Drum* every month with no pages missing?'

Yes, I can hear the three editors, Anthony Sampson, Sylvester Stein and Tom Hopkinson, answering with a

36

smile. Because to look at the pictures both in the magazine and in the archives is to get an impression of a constant surge of frantic activity.

There is a photograph of them all on the roof of a Johannesburg building kicking a football. It appeared with Casey Motsisi's article SPORT IS DARNED CRAZY, SIR, and so is the picture. Unfortunately it is too indistinct to make out the faces, but Gosani's got his camera round his neck, Maimane's in dark glasses and hat, someone's pretending he's a waiter in a long white coat with a silver tray balanced on his fingers. This one's got a guitar, that one's reading an issue of *Drum* and the rest look like they're dancing rather than chasing a ball.

There is another picture that must have involved the photographer lying on the floor. Even then he has the model posing on a box in the newsroom so that her long legs go on for ever. Surely Can Themba was riveted with delight. Or this one of a cover girl in a bathing costume seated on the sub-editor's desk, while he, surrounded by jars of glue, cups, pencils and paper, carries on earnestly with his work. 'Francina Monarens, 22, of Sophiatown' reads the caption. '[She] has been discovered by Africa's trick-up-the-sleeve talent scout [probably Henry Nxumalo]. Francina says that her secret for a lovely appearance is a combination of the right clothes for the right girl in the right mood on the right day. Quite a formula huh! But when she came in everybody in the office thought everything was absolutely right!'

Then of course there's this wonderful photograph of Anthony Sampson, eyes closed, mouth slightly open, an image of satisfaction because in his outstretched hand rests the heel of a smiling beauty posing on a chair before him. No doubt about it, this is a Jurgen Schadeberg photograph, where long shapely legs are given top priority. Or here, Bloke Modisane has a tape measure around a woman's waist and a look of barely contained enthusiasm on his face. Putting a stethoscope to her thigh for some absurd reason is Es'kia Mphahlele.

But it wasn't only cover girls and any passing 'lovely' that got talked into the newsroom for a photographic session. When it came to taking photographs for Maimane's detective series a certain madcap flair was called for. Here's the Chief (an actor hired for the occasion) in two-tone shoes and Woodrow hat, jumping through the window into the (out-of-picture) newsroom. To capture the action, the text is as zany as the image: 'First a dame phones me she's in trouble. Then I lose her. Then an old gizzard asks me to find his kid. Then Detective-Sergeant Fourie and I go to see a girl drowned in the Wemmer Pan. And it's the baby the old gizzard wanted me to find. So I go to see Lui Hong, and oh, boy! The whole bezuzus pops! I pose on the window-sill, give a cough, and as he swings round I dive for him.'

Anthony Sampson recalls an occasion when he asked Henry Nxumalo to find someone to pose as a *tsotsi*. Nxumalo went off and came back with a young man called Spike whom he introduced as a sax player by night and a clerk in town during the day. He was dressed in wide 'sixteen-bottom' trousers, a long floppy coat, bright scarf and a hat – *tsotsi* gear. After the photographic session Sampson remarked that Spike had certainly acted the part. 'Oh he wasn't acting,' replied Nxumalo nonchalantly. 'He is a *tsotsi*.'

'We never needed to go out and search for news,' says Anthony Sampson; 'it was something that just seemed to come into the office. If it wasn't a *tsotsi* who wanted to tell us how he'd been converted to the straight and narrow, then it was some of Todd's jazz friends giving an impromptu session, or Henry's contacts recounting extraordinary run-ins with the police. Once, after we'd published a piece on ritual murders, seven witch-doctors in headdresses, beads, skins, studded belts, bangles – the full regalia – came in to complain about our allegations. One man introduced himself as the president of the African National Herbalist Association and the others as the members of his board. So you see it was happening all around us. The problem was to fit it into forty-eight pages a month.'

In the early days that wasn't the only problem. They also had to contend with the magical process of turning typed stories and photographic prints into exciting magazine pages. To Sampson, who didn't even know what a by-line was, it must have seemed a daunting prospect. Schadeberg was little better equipped, although he had spent three years with a press agency before coming to South Africa. Nxumalo was probably the most skilled, but he was needed to write the copy. All these disadvantages notwithstanding, *Drum* met its monthly deadlines.

As soon as possible a white sub-editor was hired: the first was Joe Bloomberg; later came Humphrey Tyler. Schadeberg did rough layouts, sized up the photographs and sent them away for processing. When the typeset galleys returned the sub-editor took over and saw the various proof stages through production until the sections were on the press – an old four-colour machine which had been bought from a printing company in India. Although it worked efficiently enough, the quality of the newsprint was poor, so *Drum* never looked a flashy magazine. Towards the end of the decade *Drum* was being printed on presses owned by the Afrikaans newspaper *Die Vaderland*. And because the *Vaderland* management were on good terms with the paper manufacturers, the quality of *Drum*'s stock improved slightly.

'I think part of the reason we had white subs, at least in the opening years,' says Schadeberg, 'was because there were so few black journalists and certainly none with editing skills, and also because it would have been difficult for Henry to go into the works – which were all run by conservative whites – and ask them to change something in his story. They would have thought he was the tea-boy being cheeky. So having a white sub was a way of overcoming that problem.'

Sampson also makes the point that in those days seeing

blacks typing, proof-reading or answering the telephone was enough to make many whites stop in their tracks. He recounts an occasion when a young reporter from an Afrikaans paper arrived to borrow a photograph. He was so astonished to see 'kaffirs' working in his profession that he went away and wrote about his meeting with these intelligent 'natives'.

Sylvester Stein has a similar story, except the terms are cruder. He says some members of the Afrikaans press came round one day to view this anomaly and a man stood aghast, repeating over and over again; 'Truly, truly, those baboons are typing, to think of those baboons sitting there and typing.'

Working on a black paper in a white world wasn't easy, especially when the advertising department – all white – wouldn't have anything to do with the reporters and were rather ashamed at having to sell space in a black publication. But they did, and filled forty to fifty per cent of the magazine, which left between thirty and forty pages to be turned into racy crime, sex and sport reports.

'That meant,' says Schadeberg, 'that once you'd allowed for the contents page, the letters and a few columns, there were about twenty pages left. In a month that wasn't a dramatic demand. We did things well in advance anyway so I can't remember that there was a scramble to meet deadlines although I'm sure there must have been occasionally. Obviously, being a monthly, we couldn't do any hot news stories although some of the things – the Defiance Campaign, the Evaton bus boycott – we brought out within a month or six weeks of the event. Of course six weeks is a long time, but when no other newspaper is covering the events it doesn't matter.'

The first *Drum* office in Johannesburg was in a small backyard room just off Eloff Street. It was totally unsuitable: so small there was just enough room for Schadeberg, Nxumalo, Crisp and a secretary to squeeze their way between the desks. It was a dim, sunless place surrounded by office blocks. From there *Drum* moved in 1952 to the old *Rand Daily Mail* building in Main Street where Anthony Sampson had an office of glass partitions which looked on to the smoky, noisy newsroom. When those premises were rebuilt *Drum* was given space on the first floor. And there the magazine stayed until just before Tom Hopkinson joined in 1958. By then it had moved to Samkay House in Eloff Street.

Samkay House is still there, although today many of the upper-floor windows are smashed, the concrete is chipped from the stairs and the lift is not something you use if you value your life. Most of the rooms are locked or their doors broken in to reveal the filth of passing itinerants. It was there I talked with Obed Musi, a journalist who started on *Drum* in the late '50s. We found two chairs in a room where a woman with a baby was sewing. Somewhere below us a group called the Jazz Pioneers – relics from those times – were practising. 'It's hard to imagine that it all used to happen here,' sighed Musi. 'Oh ja, those were good times.' As we were about to leave a drunk staggered in. He wanted to know what we were doing. Musi told him.

'I knew Henry Nxumalo,' he slurred. 'He was my cousin. Fabuloos man. Fabuloos.'

'He's lying,' said Musi as he steered me out into the street.

Tsotsis *and Gangsters*

10

March 1951: Volume 1 No. 1. In the centre of the cover was a stylised map of Africa; on the left a man with an assegai; on the right a city skyline and a man in a suit.

This picture stayed the same for the first three issues, and only the colours changed.

Then came issue No. 4 which marked the move to Johannesburg. On the cover was a young child looking at a globe of the world. Next month a smiling young man against a hut. Then a girl leaping a tennis net. And then October 1951. Nothing had prepared its readers for this.

The cover shows a gangster in a Woodrow hat, his eyes manic, his lower face masked by a handkerchief, one hand raised, the other bunched, the dance of stab-kick-kill in his body. His legs disappear into the lights and buildings of a city at night. The caption reads: 'Shadow over Johannesburg'.

Here for the first time, *Drum* takes on what is to become almost an obsession: crime, gangsters, thugs, *tsotsis*.

The story is headed: INSIDE JOHANNESBURG'S UNDER-WORLD. The sub-head says: *While you are reading this . . . an African is being murdered or an African is being robbed or an African is committing a robbery or an African is being raped.*

There's a photograph next to this of a darkened Victoria Road in Sophiatown. A group of young men crouch in the foreground throwing dice; behind them the long street is empty. It is like a stage set with faint street-lights, dimly lit houses, a lone figure on the left looking on. The caption calls it murder street, 'where no decent African dares walk alone at night'.

The story goes:

Every African on the Reef knows the miseries and terrors of the crime city; they know what it is to be imprisoned in their own homes and not to dare to cross the road alone. They know how even in broad daylight they may be assaulted, robbed and stripped, and yet have no means to retaliate; they know how even in their daily journey to and from work they run the risk of encountering thieves, thugs and murderers. Everyone on the Reef has close friends who have been stabbed and murdered; and almost everyone has a story to tell himself. The fear and misery which hang over Johannesburg have already made the Golden City notorious for its black record of crime.

Yet how many people outside the Reef know the real facts of this new Chicago? Crimes against Europeans are widely known, and bad enough; but the crimes by Africans against Africans are worse by far, and a staggering indictment of the conditions and circumstances that have brought them about. Official police figures reveal that at the present rate one in twenty-four of all Africans on the Reef will be murdered in the course of their lifetime. In the first seven months of this year 447 Africans were murdered, an average of two a day, and by stabbing alone an African is killed every day. The non-European population of the Reef is 965,000 by the 1951 census, so that nearly one in a thousand is killed each year, as many raped, and one in a hundred assaulted; and the numbers are rising each year. If this rate continues as it is, every other African will have been assaulted once in his life. To the African on the Reef, crime is not something set aside for bioscope [cinema] shows; it is a terrible everyday reality, a shadow over his daily life, and a constant anxiety and fear.

From time to time journalists and others attempt to whitewash these black facts; they say that Johannesburg is no worse than other cities, but only more famous.

43

They quote America and yet, in proportion to population, there are twenty times as many murders on the Reef than in the USA. And in Britain, with forty times the population of the Reef, there is only one murder every three days. Egoli [Johannesburg] has a worse record than anywhere else in the civilised world.

The major crimes are common enough; but the lesser crimes, which breed the greater, are so familiar to the man on the Reef that they have stopped frightening him altogether. The *tsotsi* and his fellow thugs are more familiar to the Johannesburger than the policeman, they parade themselves openly and arrogantly in the streets, dressed in their conspicuous 'uniforms', and with little fear of the law. The sordid underworld of petty crime is something which many Africans encounter daily. Every year one man in ten appears on a charge involving illicit liquor, and for every man caught, how many are not? The shebeens, the dagga dens and liquor houses are not the secret resorts of a few; they are open doors of vice for all who wish to enter, known and frequented by thousands. And it is in such places that killers are reared and recruited.

The breeding grounds of crime are the shebeens. They produce both the criminals and the victims. Many of them are the haunts and meeting places of murderers and robbers, who very often are in league with the 'queens' who run them, and at the same time the drunkards that shebeens produce are easy and welcome prey for thugs.

Johannesburg is thick with shebeens, both in and outside the city, behind the most innocent façades, and in the most unexpected places. Well-known public buildings, office blocks and flats take on a different life after working hours. Often while men are working in offices, others are drinking, carousing in the very same building. Boys who clean and look after buildings run

44

shebeens in their rooms to make more money, sometimes with the knowledge and connivance of European caretakers, who take a rake-off in return.

And apart from these there are any number of full-time drinking dens, devoted to selling liquor all day and night. They are most thick in Jeppe, Fordsburg, Doornfontein or Malay Camp [Ferreirastown]; but others are isolated in the heart of the city, like the notorious Cabin in the Sky, not far from police headquarters!

Some are even out in the open, for all to see, like the much frequented Sip and Fly off Von Wielligh Street. Tired of drinking kaffir beer at the Municipal Beer Hall, many Africans move along to where they can have doctored beer with a kick in it. Liquor queens dig holes in the ground to hide their wares, and football players sometimes trip on cans of liquor.

But most illicit liquor is brewed in private homes, and hidden under the floors. Sometimes shebeen queens are the wives of sober working men, and bring misery to their homes.

The shebeens thrive on vice and most of all on drunkenness, and usually the liquor they sell is not clean, but doped or polluted with other liquids, chemicals and spirits. Bad and dangerous liquor is the cause of hundreds of stabbings, murders and assaults.

Shebeens are run sometimes by queens, sometimes by men. The queens in Malay Camp and Fordsburg are mostly Europeans who employ Africans as their assistants to sell the liquor. Many of the queens are women who have seen better days, and have succumbed to temptation and frustration. Often they trade as well in stolen goods, brought to them by the gangs who frequent their houses. A lot of queens lead double lives, like one religious woman who lives in a large house in the suburbs, with most respectable friends. She has one or two murders to her credit.

Although the shebeen queens have some influence
and do much to foster and encourage crime, the people
who organise and control the underworld are the various criminal gangs, whose ultimate aim is to dominate
the whole city. They stop at nothing to achieve their
end. They are reckless, brutal and without scruples,
and their strength is growing every day.

Most notorious and common are the *tsotsis* or 'Zoot
Suits', with their tight-fitting zoot trousers, wide-
brimmed hats, loud shirts and ties. Originally a single
gang, they are now found in every location on the Reef.
They live by stealing, stabbing and killing anyone who
stops them. They are usually young lads of between
sixteen and twenty-five, sometimes their parents cannot
control them, but very often parents have been found
encouraging their children in crime, and taking some of
their earnings.

Many *tsotsis* are illegitimate children, who have fallen
in with gangsters. Often they begin their career as a
kitchen-boy or servant, in league with a gang of thieves.
They get to know the house and then the gang burgles
it, and the young *tsotsi* leaves the house soon after.

Now they are so numerous that they divide locations
into slices, with a gang in each like Orlando's 'Otto-
town', 'Salamas', and 'Kid Rauchers', or Kliptown's
'Slagpaal' and 'Vaalkamers', or the Russians' district of
Racecourse Township.

Tsotsis roam the streets in gangs at night, and drink
and gamble during the day. They gamble recklessly and
violently. Sometimes the winning gambler is murdered
by the losers, and often *tsotsis* fight among themselves,
and kill each other quarrelling over crimes.

Tsotsis, being young and familiar with the places
where they live, can study their victims carefully, and
take care to catch them off their guard. Their thefts are
often carefully planned for weeks ahead. They work
mostly at weekends, when their prey may be both rich

and drunk; or at the end of the month, when all their richer victims are paid.

Then there are the Russians, the Americans and the Berliners. The Russians are the most dangerous gang on the Rand, and they specialise in murder. They are older and more experienced men than the *tsotsis* and hardened criminals. They are easily recognisable by their dress – big black and white Basuto blankets which conceal their knives, daggers or revolvers, gaberdine trousers, shirts and black felt hats. They operate in Johannesburg's worst crime spots, Newclare, Sophia-town, Moroka and Pimville, where they can often be seen by day, usually at night or at weekends. They take their name from the country which, they say, won the war.

A favourite device of the Russians is to use a woman to attract their victim: a man hears a woman shout for help, runs to her assistance, and is set upon by the hiding gang. Russians are paid handsomely by many businessmen and shopkeepers in return for protection from attack by *tsotsis* or other Russians. And these 'cost of living' boys fleece the poorest families by demanding protection money every week, which they are forced to give as the only alternative to assault and possibly a crippling injury.

not just streets/

The Russians are a new gang, who have grown quickly in numbers and strength, and grow more dangerous every day. Newer still are their rivals, the Americans, with their bush shirts and peaked caps, and the Berliners, who employ similar tactics to the Russians.

public space

analyse

Then there are other lesser gangs like the Amalaita, who consist mostly of Vendas from the northern Trans-vaal. Many of them work during the week as domestic servants in the suburbs, but at weekends they roam the middle of the city in big gangs chanting their songs and blowing whistles, and beating up anyone who gets in their way. They wear white shorts and shirts and tennis shoes, with bangles on their arms and knuckledusters round their fingers concealed by handkerchiefs.

At the back of African gangs, or working with them, there are often gangs of Europeans, planning, financing and abetting their crimes, and taking a big slice of the booty. They realise that there is big money in crime. There is, for instance, the white 'Professor' of Ferreirastown, who is used as a fence by African gangs; or 'Van' of Kliptown, who supplies liquor to the shebeens.

'White *tsotsis*' are becoming more and more common: they strengthen and reinforce the position of the African gangsters, and use them to their own ends.

The position of gangsters on the Rand today is so strong that they need not keep themselves secret. There are many well-known murderers and thugs at large who no one dares betray for fear of reprisals. The safety of crime is shown by the low prices of illegal goods. Revolvers can be had for only £10 and black-market prices of liquor are low enough to show how little danger is involved. And there are some wealthy men with cars and businesses whose record is known to all.

All the gangs have their own habits and favourite settings for their crimes, which Africans have come to know of all too well. The daily activities of the ordinary African are hemmed in by this background of crime. Every location has its Murder Street, its passages where men are stripped and robbed, its dark corners where no one dares to go. These danger spots can be mapped out by any African. Even in his daily life the ordinary working African faces risks and dangers. Crime locations like Sophiatown or Newclare are well known, but take even Johannesburg's model location, Orlando.

No one who is not foolhardy will travel by the late 11.18 train at night alone; he knows what has happened in the past, how there are compartments full of thugs, waiting for some man like him; he knows that there are

sensationalist

black authors?

48

times when the European ticket collectors will not take tickets from some compartments. And then he may have to change at Canada, and wait on the platform where assaults are notorious. When he reaches Orlando he must come out of the subway into the dark patch where men are stripped nearly every night; and finally he must walk across the dimly lit location which is a thugs' paradise. Little wonder that the late train is the 'gangster special'. Even in his own house he can never feel quite safe or visit a neighbour without risk. Thugs know that they can assault and rob a man alone in the house with little danger of being caught, that many people have been attacked within a stone's throw of their own house.

Few people who know the facts can have serious doubts at the real causes of crime on the Rand. Bad housing, low wages and high cost of living, not enough facilities for education and recreation, few opportunities for advancement lawfully, and often no work. It is inevitable that frustration and apathy should turn weak-willed young men to the easy life of crime. With little discipline, and family respect often down, it is all too easy to understand how *tsotsis* are made. And every year more Africans flow into the towns, often straight from the kraal and not knowing the ways of city life; and so every year crime becomes more uncontrollable, and gathers force. The unpoliced streets, the lack of regular patrols, makes criminals far more feared than the police, and gives gangsters free rein in the locations. People are more glad to keep on friendly terms with crooks than with the law. The vicious circle grows worse each year.

Apart from the dreadful misery and suffering it causes, crime is a ghastly waste for the whole country, in money and manpower. Each year there are more watchmen, more guards, more windows barred, more doors double-locked, the jails are full, the courts

49

crowded, the whole legal system strained to the limits of inefficiency. For every gangster at large several men are needed to safeguard and protect the citizen. And yet crime grows. The huge crime rate is an incalculable open drain on the resources of the country which no country could afford. The solutions usually offered – more police, stiffer sentences, more corporal punishment, flying squads – these are palliatives, and not cures. Crime must be stopped at the source. The conditions and frustrations that breed *tsotsis* must be done away with. The incentives and attractions of crime must be destroyed. Family discipline and respect must be built up again, and homes made fit to live in. The law must become a stronger force than crime, strong not only by force but by attraction.

Part at least of the solution lies with Africans themselves. Africans alone can build up discipline in the locations from inside, and outlaw *tsotsis* from the homes. A start has come already: vigilantes have been formed by citizens themselves to patrol the streets and protect the householders. Children are being stopped from wandering after dark. African detectives are being used, who understand the criminals they hunt. But every African on the Reef knows how much more must be done before this dreadful wave of crime is stopped.

(October 1951)

11

From THE BIRTH OF A TSOTSI:

EK praat my nooit verby nie [I never shout my mouth off].
I am a *tsotsi*, it is true. I don't care to work. Working at
a regular job does not pay. I can make more money by
stealing – at least most of my friends do. That is why
they don't work.

But that is nothing. On the whole it is quite easy to
get fixed up with a pass. In fact the real criminal has
nothing to fear on that score. It is easy to get either a
Chinaman or an Indian to take out a pass for you so
long as you are able to find the pass fees. Some African
businessmen also help sometimes.

There are no organised coloured gangs as such in
Kliptown. Although the boys may meet and plan their
operations, they are mostly lone wolves. Their oper-
ational base is by a church on the main road: from there
they move all along the bus stops, particularly on
weekends. They rob, drink and smoke dagga.

Around Suikerbossie – on the East Rand – is one of
the most notorious spots in Kliptown. Assaults, drink,
stabbings and loose women – these can be had there.
This is the coloured *tsotsi* boys' happy hunting ground.

At Dukathole, also in Kliptown, you will find mostly
Africans, representative of all tribes you can think of.
There they drink, play dice, smoke dagga and enjoy the
company of bad women. Nearly every hut there is a
shebeen – specialising in 'Barberton' and 'Korean'
booze.

'Tamatievlei', just on the ridge behind Sansouci bio-scope, is another bad spot. There are to be found the Bashoeshoe, notorious for fighting among themselves for the favours of their womenfolk.

The Chinese are the greatest sinners in so far as supplying illicit liquor is concerned in Kliptown. Customers come from all the neighbouring townships and locations. They sell liquor from distilleries operated by their countrymen. Innocent-looking shops are known to have a big turnover in liquor. A contributory factor to the success of these hooch merchants are the *stockfel* [money-lending] parties, parties when the guests pay for the liquor – the Devil take the hindmost. Nearly every location and township has these clubs where weekend debauchery has a lot to do with the large numbers of murders and assaults.

. . .

I was born in Randfontein and my parents moved to Alexandra when I was still very young. I went to school when I was ten but already I had heard about picking pockets and snatching handbags.

Our heroes were the boys who could steal and stab. The more stabbings they did, the bigger they were. The 'biggest shot' of all was the one who had killed somebody – either with a knife or a gun.

These boys used to have a lot of money and they were able to have a good time with the girls and buy them many presents. It was not long before I wanted to be a *tsotsi*.

I was about thirteen when I committed my first crime. My friend and I were drinking pineapple brew in Alexandra. It is made with *mtombo* [corn], pineapple, sugar, oats, carbide and so on.

The quick-service brew is made at six-thirty in the evening and can be swallowed just after. A glass jar for carrying fruit full of pineapple brew costs a shilling. I used to get drunk after about half a gallon.

The first time I got drunk my friend and I decided to go and steal something. We went over to the Inanda Club. It was a Sunday afternoon and all the white people were watching the game they play with horses. We each had a six-inch knife.

I saw some Africans working near the club house and said, 'Hey, folks, I'm looking for a job.'

They told me to come back the next morning and see the boss.

As I talked to them I looked in the door of the secretary's office and saw a lady's handbag and a grey sports jacket lying on a chair. I went in and took them.

I was walking away when one of the stable-boys shouted at me to put the things back in the office. I told him to come and get them himself and threw the bag and the coat on the ground. As he bent down to pick them up I stabbed him with my knife three times in the back – one up near his neck, the other in his ribs and the other in his buttocks. My friend and I picked up the things and ran away.

We crossed the road near the club and saw a servant-girl in the backyard of the house belonging to Mrs —. My friend asked the girl for a drink of water and when she went to the tap to get it I walked into the kitchen.

I was looking for money, but could find none. But in one of the bedrooms, under a pillow, I found a Baby Browning gun. This was better than money.

I took it out to my friend. 'Listen,' I said, 'I've got something very important. I'm going to make money out of this.' And I showed him the gun. There were five bullets in it.

We went to work at Bramley. Always we had something to drink or smoked some dagga to give us a big heart.

Every Friday and Saturday we held up somebody at Bramley. Mostly they were Europeans and nearly always in daylight.

Why did I do it? Because I wanted to be a big shot among my friends and my girlfriends. I wanted a lot of money to have a good time and give my girls a good time. Sometimes I made £50 in one day with the gun. I would spend it all in three or four days and then go and get some more.

When I leave Diepkloof [Prison] I am going straight. I hope to get a good job. I have stabbed fifteen or sixteen people – sometimes when I robbed them and sometimes when one of my friends didn't have any money to buy me drink. But all that is finished now.

I think the best way not to start stealing and stabbing is not to make friends with a boy who has got a bad spirit. He says to you, What a fool you are. You only can make a few pounds a month while I can get £50 a day and all the girls I want.

It's not our parents' fault. They don't even know we are doing it. Sometimes they think we are working or still at school. We always sleep at our homes.

(November 1951)

12

Anthony Sampson: I was once threatened by a man who phoned to say his name was Solly and he heard that we were going to run a piece on him in the next issue. I told him I'd never heard of him. He said I had, that he was the 'Sheik's' brother. The previous issue we'd run an exposure on the Sheik, a man called Gonny Govender who wasn't too happy about what we'd done and even had his thugs follow one of our reporters. But that was all. And now I was being warned that if I put Solly in *Drum* I'd end up looking like I'd had six train accidents. As it turned out Solly – a petty housebreaker – did appear in the next issue, but he never followed up his threat.

Sylvester Stein: Once we did have gangsters after us, which was rather frightening. They came to my office and threatened me but I don't think they pulled guns. They might have mentioned them, but that was all. They were far more threatening to the black staff than to me.

Arthur Maimane: I had enough friends who were *tsotsis* for one gang to protect me against another. We used to have our arms twisted by our editors and publisher saying, You've got to do this exposé on the gangs. We'd say, Yes we'll do it but we could get killed. You had to do it or you got fired. Comes the time we run the story then all hell breaks loose and then we get threats from the gangsters saying they'll kill us. At least the editor can call the police or get a permit for a gun, but what about us? Fortunately we were never really given a rough time by the gangs – we

55

knew enough of them to play one against another. But if we'd written about a gang we had to be careful not to go to their area for a few weeks.

13

I first met Don Mattera at a poetry reading at the University of the Witwatersrand. It was 1972 and Mongane Wally Serote was to read from his recently published collection, *Yakhal'inkomo*. There were perhaps a dozen other people. I was the only white. Serote, with the support of his audience, refused to read until I left the lecture room. Mattera said, 'Leave him. Let him stay.'

Four years later I met Mattera again: he was working as a sub-editor on *The Star*; I was a reporter. He had recently been served a severe banning order which prevented him from writing, restricted him to his house at night and weekends and made it illegal for him to be in a group of more than three people. These conditions were to last for nine years. We would spend odd moments during the day talking about poetry, but it was years before he spoke of his other life. Yet once he had been the leader of a vicious gang of teenage thugs known as the 'Vultures'.

Don Mattera: On May Day 1952 there was heavy fighting in Sophiatown. The cops came on horses, the *skietkommando* they were called. They had long lances and .303 rifles. We were told by our school principal that the school was closing early and that we shouldn't be on the streets because there was going to be a big war. I was already a Young Vulture; I think we had started the gang in '51.

So we took our weapons, our knives, our things, because if this war was going to happen then we wanted to be part of it.

There were these mounties riding around attacking and

whipping people, so we pelted them with stones. At dusk we went to the Putco bus depot and took the waste oil that is drained from the buses. This we poured all over Victoria Street and Good Street and Gold Street and Tucker Street and at the bus stop in Gibson Street. When we lured the mounties they just slid on the oil and fell and we attacked them. We stabbed. One guy, Vivian from the Berliners gang, actually dived from the roofs the way he'd seen it done in the movies . . . he dived, he stabbed, he took. The police lost so many .303s, that dangerous rifle. I remember how you pull the bolt. I remember it was so heavy. Our gang had one too. So many of those .303 rifles landed among the gangs.

That day we attacked the *skietkommando* from the roof-tops. Some of the guys even mixed the crude oil with petrol and lit it on the streets. It was a heavy day. The police brought in reinforcements, and it was a helluva war. May of 1952 was a helluva war in Sophiatown and we were part of it.

I don't think *Drum* reported this. But it was a helluva battle. It happened because of the oppression at the time, because we felt we were fighting an enemy, we felt we were fighting the government. Let me tell you, when the Second World War broke out many people named their sons Hitler because Hitler was fighting against white South Africans. In a gang called the 'Whibsey Kids' there were about six or seven Hitlers. And that's also why there was a 'Berlin' gang, because the Germans were the heroes. Their slogan was 'No retreat in Germany'.

It was a twisted, absurd, paradoxical terminology. The Germans were finally the enemy of the black people, but because they were fighting the white enemy government in South Africa many people saw them as saviours. That's why when we fought the cops we were actually fighting an enemy, it was a life-and-death battle against an enemy, just as we saw portrayed in the movies. So when we forced the cops to flee, leaving guns and rifles in the streets, we took these weapons just like the movies showed us. Especially I remember a film where the Germans are caught in the desert and when they attack they shout: 'Guns for water, water for guns.' This became our slogan. When we went for the cops we screamed, 'Guns for water, water for guns' – this cliché, which had nothing to do with what was happening, which was just a war-cry which we emulated.

The gangs were a great paradox. People couldn't understand why they would rob them, stab them, and then also fight the police. So there was this love–hate relationship. Sophiatown was full of that. Full of this paradoxical lifestyle. This guy Vivian was a brutal man, he was the boss of the Berliners gang. I tell you, this guy would kick women, men, children, but the fact that he hated police, that he stood his ground with them, won him so many admirers, and yet he was a cruel and vicious man who had committed two or three murders and had served long gaol sentences. But the fact that he fought the enemy made him a model we tried to emulate. Again this twisted emulation. We had no other role-models. Our fathers were so preoccupied with survival, with self-preservation, and also with pleasure. My own father must have had fifty to sixty women that I know of. And it was the same with my uncles. I emulated them, I did the same.

Our gang was started because of the bullies. Older guys used to pick on us. They would send us to town to fetch cigarette butts with lipstick on, white women's lipstick. They would spit in the sand and tell us to complete the errand before the spit was dry.

The first 'recitation' Mattera wrote – he was hesitant then about calling his literary efforts poems – was in 1950 while at a Catholic school in Durban. This is what he showed to the nuns:

> To the veld I would like to wander
> there where sun sets a golden splendour
> honey bees hum sweet melodies

and the white veld flowers scent the morning breeze.
Oh how my heart there longs to roam
the wide open world that is my home
to hear birds sing of dew drops that shine
and to know that life can be sweet and divine.

14

In the Bailey Archives is a photograph taken by Bob Gosani that says a great deal about Sophiatown and the gangsters. In the foreground is a flashy left-hand-drive Cadillac coupé occupied by five men. Behind them, on the opposite side of the street next to the tailor's shop, a group of people stand around, chatting, leaning against walls: but only one has his back to the camera. The others are too curious about what's going on. It makes you wonder what they thought of it, this portrait of some hoodlums. Were they resentful? Were they proud? Or were they just drawn to the distraction of something different happening in the empty hours of Sunday afternoon? This would seem to be the most likely explanation because about their postures – the child tangled around a lamp-post; the man in that classic position for street-corner talking, his right leg crossed over his left at the ankle, his body supported by a raised right arm leaning against a pillar – is an ennui, a listlessness. When the photograph's taken they will drift off, alone or in couples, back into their lives, this single moment of their existence caught in a photograph of five gangsters. The gangsters are all wearing Woodrow hats and white shirts. The coupé is one of the few cars they ever bought. It is new, shiny, the chrome trim and the white-walled tyres gleaming. It idles in the rutted Sophiatown street, a stark contrast to the shacks of corrugated iron, the boarded-up windows and the litter that are its props. The three men in the back seat all smile, amused by their notoriety. The driver's face is obscured, but it is the man in the passenger seat who is the focus of the picture. He lounges in the luxury of the car, his hat tilted back, his eyes focused down the road, a half-smoked cigarette in his mouth. His name is Kort Boy. His gang is known as the 'Americans'.

In September and October 1954 *Drum* devoted two long articles to this gang; the second one gave the story of George 'Kort Boy' Mbalweni. Today it is difficult to see in George Mbalweni the hard face of the Kort Boy who stared so humourlessly out of the Cadillac almost thirty years ago, or to believe his exploits. Today those features have softened and he frequently wipes his hand over his face: a gesture of fatigue, sometimes of embarrassment. Yet this man, with his friend Chanam, became known as the 'homicide squad', this man got the reputation that he couldn't be hanged.

When *Drum* wrote his story, Kort (Afrikaans for short) Boy was already in gaol with an eighteen-year sentence to serve. Nevertheless he read the story and was not amused. Yet he wasn't sufficiently troubled to seek revenge. Instead, irritated, he asked for royalties. None were ever paid.

The sub-head read: *Crime-life of the short killer*.

> The name 'Kort Boy' has become a legend on the Reef. It spelled terror and ruthlessness, arrogance and cunning. For George 'Kort Boy' Mbalweni, five-foot-nothing, was one of the two strongmen of Sophiatown's notorious Americans. And people thought that he was beyond the law, that no charge could be made to stick on him – until last year he was sentenced to eighteen years' hard labour for murder, commuted from the death sentence. Now he is in Pretoria Central Gaol.
>
> Kort Boy's story is the old, old story of the man who turns to crime and thinks he can get away with it. And the end of that story is always the same . . .
>
> . . .
>
> Kort Boy was the so-called knife 'artist' of the Americans in the [gang] battles. The knife had long been his bloody companion and he used it brutally and recklessly on any who dared interfere with him or any other

member of the gang. A young, smiling man with the curious name of Chanam had also been attracted to the Americans. He became the gunman of the gang. He carried two guns – a .38 Colt revolver and a .25 automatic – that he shot often and indiscriminately, scaring off any enemies though hardly ever hitting one with his abundant bullets. He also carried a long-bladed knife for emergencies.

These two, between them, were the backbone of the Americans as far as physical fighting was concerned. They were the Americans' 'Homicide Squad'.

With the fading of the Berliners and Gestapo, the Americans remained the only organised gang in Sophiatown. They had no more 'wars' to fight, so Kort Boy, with his knife, would start his own for his private entertainment.

One day he and some other Americans were walking up Good Street. The bus terminus was in that street then, and there was a long queue of people patiently waiting for a bus to take them to town. And there were the usual knobkerried and strict queue-marshallers patrolling the line to see that no 'bright boy' tried to join it in the middle.

Out of boredom and a craving for excitement, Kort Boy brazenly and openly stepped into the queue near its head. Two of the marshallers rushed up to him to eject him from the line. He told them to 'go jump in the lake' and when they prepared to remove him forcefully, he pulled out his knife and seriously stabbed one of them, Sponono.

For the bus company this was serious. None of their employees had been defied in this manner before. So, to prevent any further incidents and safeguard their employees, the local managers of the bus service called a meeting with all Sophiatown gang leaders, including the Americans, and came to some kind of 'truce'. Kort Boy was not charged for the criminal assault.

63

This is only one of many incidents he was involved in. There were many others which spread his name over the location as someone to be feared and hated for his quickness with the knife.

Knifemen have always been feared – even more than gunmen, who can easily miss and often lose their nerve to pull a trigger at point-blank range – and this five-foot-nothing man was feared above them all.

And it seemed the police were powerless against him, for nobody was brave enough to give evidence in court against him – or any of the Americans at that – for his many misdeeds. The young and foolish admired him; the older and wiser who lived in his world flattered and humoured him to keep away from the business end of his knife.

And so he thought he was a big shot; everybody was scared of him, so he could afford to be as short-tempered as he was short in height – and any weakling who was his 'laitie' [boy] and wanted protection from bullies or anyone else could come to him and get it. He thought he was so big that he could have any girl he wanted – and that nobody would dare stand in his way.

He was wrong. Sophiatown still had people who were not cowed by his reputation. Honest, upstanding citizens who would not tolerate his type of bravado . . .

Mr P. Mokhoetsi was at the time principal of St Cyprian's Primary School in Sophiatown. As principal, he lived on the school grounds; and at the house was staying a young girl who attended the school. One evening in 1947, he sent the girl to the corner shop. Kort Boy had long had his eye on the girl, and had asked one other American, Big Joe, to talk to the girl for him. At the corner the girl met Big Joe, who started propositioning her for Boy. She wouldn't hear anything about it, so he started manhandling her and refusing to let her go about her errand.

Mokhoetsi waited impatiently for her return. At last

he decided to go out and look for her. To protect himself on the dangerous street, he took a sjambok. At the corner he found the girl detained by Big Joe. He was angry, and after a few hot words, he thrashed Big Joe with the sjambok, and Joe ran away. As far as Mokhoetsi was concerned, that was the end of the incident.

But not for the Americans and Boy. When Joe told him about the thrashing he got, Kort Boy told him that he would give him a knife to go and kill the teacher, it is rumoured. Boy said Joe wouldn't be hanged for the murder as he was still a juvenile; he would only be sent to the reformatory for a few years. But Joe would have no part of it.

A few days later, the Americans had a brawl with the Berliners. There were some casualties, including Big Joe, who was admitted to Coronation Hospital a mile out of Sophiatown. That evening in hospital, an assault victim was brought in on a stretcher, suffering from serious knife-wounds. Joe recognised him to be Mokhoetsi, and guessed what had happened. Silently and quickly, he walked out of the hospital and back to Sophiatown. He was frightened.

What had happened? On the evening of the brawl with the Berliners, Kort Boy was probably still hot-blooded. And he met Mokhoetsi, the man who had dared stand in his way. He started an argument, it is said. He was short-tempered. So he drew his knife and stabbed the principal teacher. Mr Mokhoetsi died in hospital from the wounds.

It was his first killing. He went into hiding. But that could not be for long. A first killing is unnerving even for the most callous hoodlum. After a few days he went to the St Cyprian's Mission and gave himself up to the priests there.

He confessed to the killing and explained that he had done it in a rash moment of lost temper. The priest escorted him to Newlands Police Station where he was charged with the killing and locked up to await trial.

At the trial the Americans engaged a lawyer to defend him. The lawyer was good, and the judge, considering the 'extenuating circumstances', sentenced him to a year's imprisonment with hard labour. Everybody – especially those he had terrorised – had been sure he would hang. He didn't. And the legend started that he could never be hanged or given the sentence he deserved.

Some time later, Kort Boy joined a gambling school he found in progress in one of the location's many spots [gambling places]. He squatted between the men throwing the dice and the one who would be throwing after him, telling the latter that if he would give him, Kort Boy, his chance of throwing after the present thrower, he would 'jockey' him – place a bet for him. The man agreed. But Lolly, the 'knocks man' – runner of the school – objected. An argument started between him and Kort Boy.

Before the argument could develop into a fight, the police broke up the school and all the players scattered to avoid arrest. Lolly was last seen by a witness walking towards his home. Within an hour he was dead: stabbed to death on the streets. Nobody came forward as an eyewitness when the police arrived. Kort Boy was arrested as a suspect. People say he was the right man to be suspected – but the Crown had no evidence. So, after nineteen days in the cells, he was released. But he was warned. The police had heard a lot about him and his doings. He was warned that the next time he killed a person, he would hang.

And it seems that he really did take the warning seriously. He was not prepared to be involved in anything like this after his release. And he made it plain at a drinking session the gang had after his release.

He told Nicky, a brother of the Americans' leader

Slim, that he, Nicky, should stop going out with them over weekends if he could not behave after a few drinks. He said he was not prepared to end all the fights Nicky started.

A few weeks later on a Sunday evening, Kort Boy, Isaac and a few other members of the gang were walking down Victoria Road – 'the toughest street in South Africa over weekends' – with Nicky. Isaac, it is said, tried to pull a girl away from the man she was standing with. She resisted, and her boyfriend hit Isaac with a fist.

Exactly what happened after that has been argued over and over again; but a few minutes later the boyfriend was stabbed to death.

The police were informed that Kort Boy and Isaac were responsible for the murder. And the word went out that they were wanted by the police.

At the preparatory examination Kort Boy realised that his position was very dangerous. For Nicky had turned Crown Witness. So Kort Boy now 'squealed'. But it was too late. All the evidence that police could dig up was against him. He was found guilty of the murder and sentenced to death, as he had been warned.

He appealed against the sentence while he was in Pretoria's condemned cells. The appeal was sustained, and the death sentence was commuted to eighteen years' hard labour.

Kort Boy realised, too late, that the legend that had grown up around him was a hollow mockery, and that for him, as for all other criminals, the law sooner or later has its revenge.

(October 1954)

I spoke to Kort Boy under less than ideal circumstances. I cannot say where the interview occurred or give any information about George Mbalweni's current situation. And while we talked there was a third, daunting presence in the room. So the interview is stunted. Throughout it, this short man whose feet swung clear of the floor kept his arms tightly folded across his chest and spoke reluctantly in monosyllables: ja, yeah, or naw.

Did your family rent a room in Sophiatown?
  'Ja.'
Did you go to school there?
  'Not so far.'
Why not?
  'I didn't have a chance.'
But you did know Father Trevor Huddleston [head of St Peter's Priory]?
  'Very well.'
You went to him after you stabbed somebody didn't you?
  'A principal.'
How old were you then?
  'I was eighteen or nineteen.'
Why did you stab him?
  'There was a quarrel.'
Was it about a girl?
  'No. They say so, but the girl was a schoolmate of my friend. Some parts of what they wrote in *Drum* are wrong. Some parts right. Some parts wrong.'
So that incident when you stabbed the principal had nothing to do with the girl?
  'No. But actually it was mixed with the girl. My friend was talking to the girl, as they were schoolmates, but the girl was at high school. Then they greet each other but the principal didn't like it. I was also there. He slapped the friend of mine and my friend stabbed him. After he had stabbed him I also stabbed him. Then he died.'
Did you feel guilty about this?
  'No. I didn't feel guilty.'
Did you feel anything at all?
  'Naw.'

Yet you went to Father Huddleston. [According to Huddleston the principal died in his arms.] How long afterwards was that?

'The next day. I just went to tell the father that I was also there. And maybe I had stabbed him [the principal] dead. I don't know.'

It didn't concern you that you had stabbed a man?

'Naw. I don't know.'

Had you stabbed anybody before?

'I think so, but not dead.'

How old were you when you first stabbed somebody?

'Very young.'

Ten? Eleven?

'Thirteen.'

Why did you stab this person?

'We were fighting.'

Fighting about what?

'Just fighting.'

Were you in the Americans then?

'I started the Americans when I came back from the Army [at the end of World War Two].'

How old were you when you started the Americans?

'I was young.'

In your twenties?

'Nearly twenty.'

Did you go to gaol for stabbing the principal?

'Ja.'

For how long?

'Twelve months.'

That was the first time you'd been to prison?

'First time.'

Why did you choose a knife as your weapon?

'Well, that time I used to box also. I always choose a knife. I can't reason it.'

Did you prefer a knife to a gun?

'Ja, but we had a lot of guns at that time.'

Where did you get the guns?

'From the chinas [the Chinese shopkeepers].'
Where did they get them from?
'They bought them from whites.'
You didn't attack policemen to get their guns?
'No. Where did you hear that?'
I was told that.
'Who? Don Mattera?'
Yes. So you didn't attack policemen?
'Sometimes. Then we took .45s.'
What sort of knife did you use?
'A flick-knife.'
How long?
'Seven to nine inches.'
Did somebody teach you to use the knife?
'Naw. I saw it in bioscope then I use it also. MGM films. That time it was black and white. Humphrey Bogart, James Cagney, *Angels with Dirty Faces*. At the Odin.'
Why did you choose the name 'Americans'?
'Because of the clothes we used to wear. We used to dress like Americans.'
Weren't the clothes very expensive?
'Naw.'
How much money were you making as a crook?
(He laughs) 'Ja. About £1,000 a week.'
Who did you rob to get a thousand pounds?
'Railways.'
How did you do that?
'Used to bluff them [the guards] away from the trucks and then steal the stuff [consignments of clothing].'
Did you have cars?
'We hijacked cars.'
What kind of cars?
'Cadillacs. Big cars. American cars. Our cars were open coupés.'
A thousand pounds a week is a lot of money?
'But we were a lot. We had Americans in Alex [Alexandra

township], Orlando, maybe nineteen or twenty. We shared the money.'

During the gang fights, were you ever shot?

'Yes. Here in my leg [he reaches down and rolls up his trouser leg to show me the scar]. Here [he points at his thigh], and here [he indicates his torso].'

Were you stabbed as well?

'Yeah. A lot.'

Did you have the wounds treated at a hospital?

'Yeah.'

Did you take revenge?

'Everybody who stabbed me died. I killed them.'

How many did you kill?

'Eleven.'

All with a knife?

'Ja.'

A long time after they'd stabbed you?

'Within weeks.'

You had a reputation for causing terror?

'Naw. The people liked me because I didn't fight with the people. I only fight with people when I get too cross. But most of the time I don't fight with people.'

Were these people gangsters?

'Yes.'

You killed all these people yet you were only sentenced for one murder excluding that of the principal?

'I was framed up.'

Why do you say that?

'That's part of my life story.'

Can you tell me?

A long silence, then: 'Ja. I'll tell you. I didn't kill that person. But I was walking through the street when this young boy called Chanam saw these boys fighting and he stabbed the one guy. Then two SAPs [South African police-men] wanted to arrest him. So I stepped in and took out a revolver and set him free. It was a Sunday. On Monday they came to me with the police and said I killed that person. So he [Chanam] was the Crown Witness against me. They sentenced me to death. I spent four months, two weeks in Central on death row. There was a reprieve to eighteen years.'

Where did you serve the eighteen years?

'A lot of gaols. I was a "flying squad". My last station was Barberton, 1965. That was the last time I went to gaol. [The next two sentences have been censored to meet the conditions under which this interview was conducted.] After that everybody was afraid of me but I just went straight. I was a plumber.'

Are you married?

'Ja.'

And children?

'Seven. Two died.'

Grandchildren?

'Ten. In Soweto.'

Do you miss your wife?

'Too much.' He wipes his face with his hand.

What did you think about the stories in *Drum*?

'I don't like it. It wasn't fair. They didn't have my full story.'

They were critical of you. They didn't like you.

'But now they do like me.'

Do you like yourself?

'Ja. All the time.'

You weren't bothered about killing people?

'Naw.'

Did you ever think about what you were doing? That you were taking someone's life?

'They made me cross.'

Did life mean anything?

'I'm sure life means something to everybody.'

But you didn't mind killing someone?

'No.'

Why not?

'Because he would have killed me. It was rough on the streets. We had to fight hard.'

Did you go drinking in the shebeens?

'Naw. Not really. I drink but not too much.'

What was it like in the shebeens?

'Rough. Rough.'

But were there good times?

'Yeah. Music. It was OK.'

What was your favourite shebeen in Sophiatown?

'Thirty-Nine Steps. We used to call the woman [who ran it] Fatty.'

Did you go there to find 'nice-time' girls?

'Some.'

Did Can Themba write love letters for you and the other Americans?

'Ja.'

Did you have a lot of girls?

'Naw. Excuse me. [He rubs his hand over his face.] I don't like women.'

Did the other gangsters have a lot of women?

'Ja.'

All the time?

'Ja.'

Could you just pick and choose?

'Ja.'

And if the girl had a boyfriend?

'Well, in Sophiatown you can't walk just with a girlfriend if you're not a tough guy. You must be tough or they take her away from you. Day or night.'

Was anybody safe in Sophiatown?

'We used to protect people in Sophiatown. We didn't like people must be robbed at night.'

Did they pay you protection money?

'Naw.'

So you didn't rob people in Sophiatown?

'No.'

In town?

'A lot.'

Did you know any of the politicians at the time?

'The most.'

Mandela? Sisulu? Xuma? Luthuli?

'The most.'

Did you know Mandela?

'We are one nation. He was in the fourth street from my home. And we are one nation. Both Sisulu and Tambo. And we used to eat with them. Dr Dado. J. B. Marks. The most.'

Did you know the musicians?

'The most. I can say the lot of them – Jazz Maniacs, Harlem Swingsters, Merry Blackbirds. The most. When I came out of gaol they were all gone [mostly into self-imposed exile]. It was just too bad.'

Matshikese

15

Drum's staff seemed to arrive on the magazine more by chance than by an active recruitment policy. Perhaps the metaphor of the island is right: perhaps they were all castaways washing up on its shores. During Anthony Sampson's time Henry Nxumalo brought along his cousin Bob Gosani, who went from being a useless switchboard operator to a fine photographer, and then introduced a short, neat, little man called Todd Matshikiza who was to give *Drum* its upbeat tempo. He was a jazzman, and when the jazzman got behind the typewriter it turned into a musical instrument. His style became known as 'Matshikese', an infectious rhythm, difficult to put down:

> Some called it 'Marabi', others 'Mabokwe'; they called it 'I-Tswari' and 'Fahmoo'. But whatever it was called it was vital . . . and so were the dames that liked it. They made the men, and also broke them. But one thing about the old days, the men didn't kill each other for dames. There was a gentleman's code about double-crossing women. I recall an episode at Newclare, E-Sidikidikini, the place of hell. Jensen Mdaka and Willie Zim were famous singers for whom the girls vied with each other.
>
> Then the two men discovered they were in love with the same girl! She came to the show and at the interval they called her outside. Jansen had a whip. He said to the dame, 'You dirty double-dealing damsel, we'll teach you not to do it again.' Then he whipped her long and bitter, and when he was through, he handed the whip

to Zim who repeated the painful process on the girl who was now almost faint. Then the two men shook hands and went inside to sing again.

In the posher places there was the great singer and pianist Bob Kwaza. The girls showered him with presents every night. One night a woman gave him a scarf. Put it round his neck and Bob forgot to take it off when he went home. He was so tired he fell asleep with the scarf around his neck. He had a very jealous mistress. She looked at him with venom in her heart, then she poured paraffin over his body, and set him on fire. Bob died a painful death, but forgave her in his kind heart. She was never punished for the act.

Bob Kwaza was one of a long line of pianists. They were great, tireless men who played from eight to four, non-stop. Sullivan Mphahlele and his black overcoat in which he lived from day to day. He played all day at the Bantu Men's Social Centre, tickling his long fingers over 'Kitten on the Keys'. He never played requests unless you gave him a cup of tea. We bought albums of popular pieces and rushed to Sullivan, who rattled the pieces off at first sight. There was Douglas Qoqo and his pounding piano. His favourite stunt was to play with his elbow. He'd sing:

Who's that coming down the street,
My heart, my arms are open wide;
Knock knock, who's that
It's Douglas Qoqo

And Samuel Tutu, who always practised the accordion on the train. He told me: 'Boy, I was the lion of the keyboard until one helluva boy came and grabbed the crown right out of my hands. He was Meekley "Fingertips" Matshikiza [Todd Matshikiza's brother]. I was playing at a dance when Meekley walked in. He played after me, and the next morning I took the first train and quit East London for Johannesburg.'

Nbadula Hall memories. I remember scampering

through the back door in 1938. I was a member of a concert party with R. T. Caluza touring the Union. A shot was fired and I remember seeing a dagger in the air. And the little boy that was me made straight for the door. Or the night at the Bantu Sports Club when Snowy Radebe was singing. I had heard great singers: Rhoda Bhengu, Faith Caluza, Marie Dube, Linda Nkosi and numerous polished, trained voices. I loved these women. I loved singers. I loved Rhoda Bhengu, and she became my adopted mother at school.

But when I heard Snowy at the Bantu Sports Club I had never heard a voice of such great power, range, beauty and sheer magnificence. Something hit me, and I knew it was love. I loved Snowy. The kind of love when a little boy loves a big girl and is shy but wants to tell her. I didn't know what it was. But they told me it was calf-love. Love of something magnificent and out of reach. Really, we all loved her music.

I loved the dingy lights of the club house. The smell of roast meat from the kitchen behind the stage. The people muttering through tobacco smoke and the rhythm pounding through my head. I loved the powerful piano tones of Samuel Tutu, and I stood leaning against the piano. His technique dazzled me and I was in a haze. Snowy's soprano. Tutu's piano. Roast meat and jazz overpowered me and I fainted over the piano. Singer Ezekiel Mogale carried me out of the hall and poured cold water over my face. Voices were saying, 'The little boy is overpowered by the music.'

They were fashionable days! The artists were taking show business seriously. And the shows were getting sophisticated.

Promoters were advertising sophisticatedly: 'New faces in de Bantu Follies', 'The show is on', 'Geepers Kreepers, isn't he the man called Ou Boeta Vick?', '*De Juba wat de Maraks moet de chandis speel* (Now what is all this big noise about?)' and 'The Gold City's Most

Spectacular Concert is a Unique Extravaganza . . . Universal, Hilarious, a scream from beginning to end'.

But the days of Marabi were dwindling. Artists were being described as 'Wizards of Mirth'. The printing shops invented phrases like 'The Orlando Geneva Club has pleasure in presenting to you the incomparable stage maestro . . .'

It wasn't so bad ducking the curfew laws then; it was worthwhile going to hear the 'Durban C to C', the 'Brakpan Home Tigers', or the 'Durban Letter Stars'. Or you were inspired by the words, 'Today the whole world looks forward to another Africa for fresh and original music works. Africa is ready. It has been a long time.'

Well, Africa was a long way past original music works. She was drunk with American and English music works and quite inevitably, too. The missionaries had taught that the music of Africa was barbarian. Barbaric. Barbarous. Africa had to abandon African music as such. Africa had to learn Western music. Tonic sol-fa. The hallelujah chorus. 'In this hour of softened splendour'.

1941.

We had a band at college (Lovedale), called the Students' Own Band, the first jazz band in the district of Victoria East. We'd been inspired by the great Merry Blackbirds under Peter Rezant. We'd been reading the first black music magazine, the *African Sunrise*, edited by Wilfred Sentso. We heard about the Synco Fans Downbeat Troupe and the wonderful progress they were making in show business. The paper painted glorious pictures of the jazz world and we weren't gonna be left out. There was Mr Bishop Ntuli, bandmaster of Lovedale. He could play every brass instrument and he taught us the lot.

The Students' Own Band was Willie 'Taai' Shomang (drums), Bennet Lekoma and Macdonald Nyati (trumpets), Bishop Ntuli (trombone) and the host of banjos, ukeleles, mandolins, guitars that the coloured boys from Uitenhage, East London and Port Elizabeth drowned us with. I was playing piano.

We graduated from the SOB and joined the bigger bands in the big cities. We were crazy about the Merry Blackbirds. They were the greatest ballroom-dancing and swing band. They were the best band in Johannesburg amongst black and white. They graced the country's biggest occasions . . . the Empire Exhibition of 1936, where they swung it on a specially constructed boat in a lake; the Jazz Cavalcades at Cape Town, Durban and Port Elizabeth in 1942. They took swing to Lourenço Marques, the Rhodesias, let alone the Union towns. Don't I remember their show in Queenstown in 1940, when the capacity crowd just stood, staring, dazed, thrilled to the big band playing 'In the Mood'. Nobody danced. Everybody stood marvelling. Swing had arrived.

Wilfred Sentso began composing. Swing fever had touched him but he wouldn't touch imported music. He wrote his own numbers which went over well with his Downbeat Band and Synco Fans concert party. Us kids sang his 'Syncopation' like this: 'Syncopation, modulation, obligation, jubilation,' and any other words that rhymed with 'syncopation'. Sentso's music was published in England. But the local bands preferred 'the real berries from America'. The Merry Blackbirds imported orchestrations. They played nothing else, and there was nobody to touch them there.

Then there was a man, a transport driver in Johannesburg, whose ear for sound and mind for creativeness was driving him crazy. His name was 'Zulu Boy' Cele. He said that this big, bold sound was ideal for transporting the musical ideas that he had in mind. He had been for many years a house pianist in the Marabi joints, and he had always wanted to paint Marabi tones on broader canvases and bigger scales. He bought a saxophone and learned to play it. In his band were Wilson Silgee, who studied at the Adams School of Music; Jacob Moeketsi, who had studied classical music; guitarist Victor Hamilton; Palmer Mochumi; and Isaac Nkosi. He said, Let's go and see the movies. 'Pennies from Heaven' they heard there, and Z-Boy said to them, 'Listen carefully to that piece, we've got to play it tonight.' And they played it that night.

Came Vy Nkosi. He liked the trombone and learned its registers trial-and-error-style till he got it. He played a piece by ear; then he went to buy the music. He compared what he was playing with what he saw on the printed sheet. The spaces in between the lines seemed to agree with the notes that he was playing, and that is how Vy Nkosi taught himself to read music.

He got himself one of those five-in-one mutes with which you can produce five different sounds on the trombone, but it wasn't good enough for the sounds that Vy wanted.

He pierced holes in his mute with a knife, and captured the sound he wanted . . . something between a laughing human baritone and a honking, tonking trombone sound that put Vy on the musical map.

Then Z-Boy Cele came across a youngster, Makwenkwe Davashe. Makwenkwe's admirers have since shortened his name to MaKay, MacCay, MacKay. But all his names mean the 'boy that learned to play sax the penny-whistle way'. Makwenkwe was playing the penny whistle, or the flute, if you like, as a schoolboy. But he was intrigued with the sound of the sax. He got hold of one and started fidgeting with it. One day he tackled a number during the interval. He got it right and it got him a job with Sentso's Downbeats. Then he went with Dale Quaker's Merry Mischiefs of 1943.

This was the time which was swing-mad. It was also the time when pianists were syncopation crazy. There was a big demand for piano syncopation methods.

But Z-Boy Cele was the kind of musician who wanted to bring music to those who danced to it, and if the people danced to the new swing sound – loud, forceful and big – the same element was present in Marabi.

So much in demand were the Jazz Maniacs that in 1944 they were accepting double engagements because they did not wish to disappoint their patrons.

They were hired to go to Pretoria. Said yes. Then they took a train on the same night to go on a tour of the Cape. They were heading for Port Elizabeth and Cape Town, but the engagements they had left behind caught up with them. A legal suit followed them to the Cape and they became broke. Dead broke. The great Jazz Maniacs of Johannesburg lived on the charity and goodness of the people of Port Elizabeth. Their instruments were evaluated by a sworn appraiser at 25s. and 30s. each. The instruments were to be impounded, but the players were given the instruments back because, to raise the money required, the players required small jobs, and what's a workman without his tools!

The Maniacs returned to Johannesburg one by one, and by the time they had all returned, they were no longer the strong forceful band that Z-Boy had built up. They were weaker, trading mostly on the name that had achieved the fabulous reputation of the Jazz Maniacs of Zulu Boy Cele.

By this time, the legendary Zulu Boy had died a violent and mysterious death. His body was found on a railway line in Johannesburg. Some say he was murdered at a party and his body carried to the railway line.

Others say he was forcibly thrown in front of a fast-moving train. Wherever you go, musicians say, 'Don't talk too loud about the murder of Z-Boy. His murderer may be around.' But whatever happened to Zulu Boy, his great Maniacs band is dead now.

(July 1957)

16

Esme Matshikiza: I think Todd went to Johannesburg in 1947. He had been working as a teacher down in Queenstown but wanted to move up to the Reef. He applied at the Transvaal Education Department and got a job at Ermelo. He took the job just to get in. We actually met while he was on his way to Ermelo. I'd invited some friends to lunch and they brought Todd along.

Well, he went off for three months, applied for a transfer and was then lucky enough to get a teaching post outside Johannesburg. That didn't last very long before he got the job at Vanguard's [bookshop]. He was working there when we married in December 1950.

Of course by now he was playing music at various places in and around Johannesburg, and you must remember he was already quite well known in the eastern Cape both as a musician and as a composer.

He got roped into *Drum* in February 1952. It was Henry Nxumalo who approached him, because the two of them knew each other very well. He was excited about getting the job, although he'd never written prose before. By this time he'd left Vanguard's and was working as a clerk on a construction site at Springs. To get there on time he had to leave home at four in the morning. That lasted a matter of a few months and then came the *Drum* job.

I can't remember what his pay was like, but I shouldn't think he was well paid. I do recall that his salary was always a matter of grievance to him.

Todd handled society, the apartheid laws, with a mixture of amusement and very strong criticism. A lot of it he found amusing, but amusing in a satirical way. Just as his writing is very satirical. That was his approach to South Africa. It did hurt, but he had so much inborn faith in himself and who he was and where he came from that he was extremely self-confident about being a South African. I don't like to use the words a 'black South African', because for him that was totally irrelevant. There was no question about it, he was a South African and had a right to be there, he was a part of the soil, it was his ancestral home. He was religious from that point of view, not from the point of view of a formal religion. He totally believed in his ancestors.

He did drink, but I never actually saw Todd drunk. He died of liver failure, but nobody can ever tell you he got drunk. He was such a small person and a difficult eater, possibly because he drank too much. The drink was a defence against everything that happened to you if you were black in South Africa and especially if you were in the front line like his generation of journalists was.

He was by emotion and sentiment a supporter of the African National Congress but he was not uncritical of the party or of individuals. Todd never became a member of any organisation and when the Pan Africanist Congress broke away from the ANC, he understood their reasons. He did agree with certain things that the PAC stood for but was critical of them too. He was an observer of the situation more than anything else but at the same time identified with it. Wisely, I think, he decided not to join a political party. Because he was a South African, a nationalist, he felt he stood for the rights of black South Africans, in a way in which all of us do.

Matshikiza's musical career probably took off in 1956 when he was commissioned to compose a cantata for Johannesburg's seventieth anniversary the next year. It was called 'Uxolo' (Peace), and, in seven fragments played out by a seventy-piece brass orchestra and two hundred voices, told the story of a city founded on gold and riddled with racial strife. It ended with a prayer for peace. The concerts were sold out: people stood in the aisles and on the steps outside. They couldn't get enough.

Two years later he wrote the jazz opera *King Kong*, based on the life of a heavyweight boxing champion, Ezekiel Dhlamini, known as 'King Kong' and one of the folk heroes of the '50s, which took Matshikiza to the West End and Broadway. In Johannesburg, too, it played to rapturous applause.

'We were all astonished at the success of his musical,' says Esme Matshikiza. 'We didn't expect it to create such a sensation, especially as the production was such a very modest effort that nobody thought would last more than a few weeks. But it did, and then got much the same sort of response in London that he had in Johannesburg.'

Once there was a prospect of putting *King Kong* on in London, the Matshikizas seriously started thinking about living abroad for a few years. Their children were approaching school age and neither parent wanted them subjected to Bantu Education – the government's none-too-subtle way of making sure blacks received an inferior education to their white counterparts. In 1960, a year before the London staging of *King Kong*, the Matshikizas left.

'We did it for the sake of the children, but at that point we still felt we would go home after three years or whatever. But then South Africa broke away from the Commonwealth and we had to make a choice between going back and losing job opportunities in England. There really was no choice; we decided it was best to take out British citizenship, but it was still an extremely difficult decision to make.

'Once we'd changed our citizenship we realised there was no going back, and in fact Todd never went back. By the end of his life he was a very sad man. He really wanted to go home again.'

But he couldn't. By now he had been banned under the Suppression of Communism Act.

In the latter half of the '60s, Matshikiza tried to get as

close to his home country as he could by working on radio stations in Malawi and Zambia. But that was the nearest he got: he died in Lusaka in 1968. Fourteen years later his autobiography, *Chocolates for my Wife*, was finally unbanned in South Africa.

'I knew Todd best out of them all,' says Anthony Sampson. 'He was in some ways the most talented person on the staff, and a brilliant talker. He transformed *Drum*. He used to go at the typewriter the way he played a piano. There was rhythm in his every sentence, a briskness that mirrored the way he spoke.'

'Todd was a charlatan, I'm sorry to say,' says Obed Musi, one of the junior reporters on *Drum* at the time. 'As you know, he was not a Reef boy and he could hardly speak a line of the ghetto slang which is mostly Afrikaans-orientated. He either spoke English or Xhosa.

'He was a great musician, though. Like the others he drank a lot but he was able to hold it better than them, even though he was so small.'

'The drink didn't affect Todd's work,' says Sylvester Stein. 'It did with some of the other journalists, but never with him. I think his style might have had something of James Joyce about it – it was a flinging-off, a naturally uninhibited style. He was an artist; the others weren't really.'

'It was through Anthony that I became very friendly with the Matshikizas,' recalls Nadine Gordimer. 'They were married then and living in Orlando. I soon became very fond of Todd and that friendship continued even after they left here. In fact I sent him a piano when they were in Zambia and it gave me great pleasure to think of him using it. He was a wonderful little man. He was very affectionate – you have to use the word adorable – he just was an adorable man, very temperamental very easily hurt, immensely talented. He was such a natural person. Todd was my size, you know. People used to laugh when we danced together because we looked like two little dolls. I know Todd drank a lot but it wasn't noticeable. He was certainly not an alcoholic.'

'Matshikiza was just bristling with life. He had that kind of deep-seated irony which was very sophisticated,' says Es'kia Mphahlele.

The last word comes from Jean Hart, a Londoner who was lucky enough to be in the right place at the right time:

'Todd was a fiery, proud, hard, tough man. Lovely, a wonderful man, but so . . . how should I describe him? He was like a sea urchin; you couldn't touch him he was so proud. Todd was such a grand man he could be affable and you could have a wonderful conversation with him about music, he would be open and honest and interested in you, but you couldn't ever get close to him. Not really. There'd be a point at which he'd say, We may have no more intimacy than this.

'I remember when his mother died he was living a few houses down from me. This was in London. I went up to say how sorry I was and I went to hold him and I could feel him pull away. That was how he kept himself. Even in grief he couldn't let go because that was when he'd be most vulnerable.

'Todd was also an angry man, so conscious of daily humiliation. I once asked him why he'd called his son John in a society where every black man was called John by whites. He answered that if a white ever called his son John it would hurt him a little less.'

17

'The greatest ballroom-dancing and swing band. The best band in Johannesburg.' That's what Matshikiza called the Merry Blackbirds. They're all gone now, of TB, cancer, unknown deaths, drink or just the passing years, except for their leader, Peter Rezant. He's not playing music any more. Nowadays, in his seventies but still dapper, still fit, he helps out in the family's small Riverlea supermarket working long hours from early morning until nine in the evening. But long hours have been a feature of Peter Rezant's life. In the '30s, '40s, '50s he used to work as a transport driver all day and then do gigs with the Merry Blackbirds till late at night. They played to whites on the immaculate lawns of Johannesburg's northern suburbs, they played to miners in the hostels, they played in Pretoria, Sophiatown, in hospitals, at circuses, in hangars. They played themselves into a legend.

This is how Matshikiza described the jazzman:

> The hall was chock-full of people. The hall was chock-full of music. It was good music from Peter Rezant and his famous Merry Blackbirds. I said to the fellow next to me, 'What do you think of this fellow, Peter Rezant?' The fellow next to me said, 'Man, firs' class.'
>
> I crossed the floor and asked a lady, 'What do you think of P –?'
>
> She didn't let me finish. 'Firs' class, firs' class. Couldn't be nothing better nowhere.'
>
> The following day I went to Baragwanath Hospital. I went to see his very pretty daughter Violet, who is nursing there.

'Could I please see Nurse Violet?'

The attendant said, 'Which one, Peter-Rezant-of-the-famous-Merry-Blackbirds' daughter?'

I said, 'That's right. That's the one!'

The words were going cling-clong in my mind. 'Firs' class, firs' class Peterezan. Firs' class Peterezan.'

I remember him in 1936. The Great Empire Exhibition in Johannesburg. Huge wonderful exhibition. Gold pieces from Jo'burg. Uncut diamonds from Kimberley.

Washing machines and whales' teeth from Durban. Pygmies from the Sahara. Swings. Ruby rings. They took the finest things on earth and put them there for us to see. Ugh! I saw nothing there. I was too small. But I saw the huge, large, 'Show Boat' on a big lake. 'Peter Rezant and his famous Merry Blackbirds Orchestra appearing here daily and nightly.' I went to the Show Boat every day. Judges, lawyers, policemen and pimps. Ladies and gentlemen and thieves. They didn't come in ones. They didn't come in twos. They came in tens to hear Peter Rezant and his Merry Blackbirds.

'Sfunny. I'm just thinking now, I saw people there . . . people that treat us like I treat my hag-tailed location hound. I saw them gape at this strange blackbird Peter Rezant. They said, 'Of course he's different, you know!'

I said, 'So's my right foot from my left.' You can say what you like, man. Peter Rezant is a ruby of a ruddy blackbird. He's done this country good:

1942 – Johannesburg Cavalcade

1943 – Port Elizabeth Cavalcade

1944 – Cape Town Cavalcade

1954 – Peter Rezant keeps going and don't stop. Since 1919, he's been an outstanding entertainer. You can take me to court and I'll say to the judge, 'My Lord, since us blacks took to show business, comma, Peter Rezant has been the most outstanding of the whole bang shoot of us full stop.'

I remember 1919. My ma used to say to me, 'Yes my son, your elder brother was born during the Great Flu – 1919.'

Peter Rezant was on the stage in 1919, still today. He remembers the days when a band wouldn't play if they didn't have a four-gallon tin of beer standing by to keep them from falling! Whew.

It's great fun today. We've got lots of class fun . . . without the four-gallon tin of beer. Thanks to Peter Rezant. We've got Coronation balls, nurses' balls, dinky-winky kids' balls. Amen man. Then the Nxuma-los, the Campbells, the Rathebes, the Mpamas and the Ntshonas shine their Cadillacs and roll up for 'Another Evening with Peter Rezant'.

All the classy people turn out. Dr Woodie Matsie dusts up his white tie and tails, and he's the best-dressed man and partner on the floor.

Thanks a lot Peter Rezant. Your band has been a great civilising agent. My Cousin Joe says he felt real small at your last dance. You and your band turned out smart. Kitty bows, nugget shines, toothbrush smiles, gold cuff-links. And there he was, waltzing, waltzing . . . in brown shoes and grey pants. Heavens! Thanks. Firs' class, firs' class, Peter Rezant.

(September 1954)

Peter Rezant: We were all playing straight American jazz in the '50s. Now and then groups like the Jazz Maniacs played their own music in the deep townships, but we all played traditional jazz.

I liked Duke Ellington; I liked his music because it always had that African sound, that sound of a fellow coming across the veld playing this concertina underneath his blanket, repeating this thing for a long time and also humming there: hmmmm, ummmmmm. Now Duke Ellington was like that. Count Basie, too. Once, on the mines, it was a cold night, I remember playing 'The General Jumped at Dawn'. And we were hitting it. And the people were dancing. And when we finished playing I turned to the boys and said, 'You know if Duke Ellington had walked in here he would have complimented you tonight.' Oh it was a great night.

We used to play for the Communist Party, before they were banned. They gave fund-raising parties in their private homes in the northern suburbs [of Johannesburg]. There, on the tennis courts, in those beautiful gardens in summer when the flowers are at their best and the grass is lush. Those were our hunting grounds. The lawns of the northern suburbs. They loved it. They went wild. They really loved our music. These parties were often at Advocate [Bram] Fischer's, the famous advocate Fischer [who led the defence at the Rivonia Trial in 1963 when a number of ANC men, among them Nelson Mandela and Walter Sisulu, were sentenced to life imprisonment. In 1966 Fischer was found guilty of sabotage and the promotion of revolutionary activities and also sentenced to life imprisonment. He died in gaol in 1975]. He was a very fine fellow, ay, such a soft-spoken man, such a humble man. Sometimes God does things that only He knows. That man should have been living today to see what is happening because he gave his life for this. I remember the biggest party the SACP gave was an annual affair and everything flowed most lavishly. Then the law was amended to stop us blacks playing at any public or private function where whites were served liquor. After that it was very difficult for us. But never mind.

Once we were playing at Zonderwater hospital. This man introduces us. He says, 'The Americans have got their Duke Ellingtons and Count Basies but we've got our' – and he shouts – 'Merry Blackbirds.' The curtain went up and we struck up with the drummer going hell for a thing. Eh eh, oooh. Man, they thought they were dreaming. Eh, eh eh eh oooh. One of the other numbers that we rode for a long time was the 'Tiger Rag'. Aah, we went to town with that. Oh, we had our moments. And I started it from rock-bottom in Johannesburg. Rock-bottom. There was never anything like this. Ah, it was a hard life. You know life is very hard when you know what you want and you know it is difficult to get it and you strive to get it. That's hard.

The Merry Blackbirds were hard musicians. They liked to get into something that had meat on it. There wasn't anything above us. Todd Matshikiza adored us. In fact one night we were playing in the northern suburbs. The son of the general manager of the Chamber of Mines was having his twenty-first birthday party. We were playing for them. Todd played with us that night. He was a very good musician. You couldn't take a chance of playing in the Blackbirds unless you were very sure of yourself.

We put life into music. That's what the audience wanted. We were playing 'Jealousy is a Tango' and a couple comes on the floor, real ballroom dancers. After the tango had played they came up to the stage and said, 'I've heard that number being played before but I've never heard it like you played it tonight.' Now that is the type of thing that inspired you to get along. It must be in you. [He sings] You go to my head, ta dee da do de de de de de. It's a very slow number, hauntingly slow. This couple came up and said, 'What's that number you're playing?' I said, "You go to my Head".' They said, 'Well it went to our heads, I can tell you.' That is the fun of music, that's how I like it. That was my life. I don't play any more. I listen now. But I don't like the new music. You can't talk when the band plays. The singers just shout with the veins standing out in their necks. I say no. I'm in the wrong time, that's what I say to myself. And sooner or later I'll just take my hat and bow out. I saw the best of it.

18

HOW MUSICIANS DIE by Todd Matshikiza

> Some are stabbed
> Some are burned
> Some just vanish . . .

If you ever wished you were a famous musician, you might as well wish you were a circus clown. But of course you've never given a moment's thought to the private life of a circus clown.

If I tell you now that these people have great fears that stalk their puny lives like a hunter stalks a rabbit, you'd be surprised.

Take a musician. His greatest fear is the fear of dying violently and suddenly. The best of them die that way. Solomon Zulu Boy Cele, the famous leader of the Jazz Maniacs, died like a homeless hare. His mutilated body was found on a railway line near Nancefield, Johannesburg. His killer was never found.

Tiny Mbata, young, handsome, a singer of merit with the Diamond Horse Shoe and later with Ace Buya's Mordenaires, was stabbed to death at the Wemmer Municipal Compound, Johannesburg. Kitchener Sekese who sang with the popular UPC Lads also died by someone's knife. Some have been burned alive, like Bob Kwaza, the singing pianist of the Hot Lips. Someone poured fuel over his body while he lay peacefully asleep . . . and burned him to death. Another singer with the UPC Lads, Elliot Mabusela, was killed by the knife of a young dancer in a hall in Benoni.

Take the saxophonist Ally Pretorius, one of the young men that made the Harlem Swingsters famous. He dropped to his end from a skyscraper in Johannesburg. Did he slip? Did he jump? Or was he pushed over?

Why does death take them thus? Why can't they die like gentlemen – on a white bed, with white pillows and white surroundings that will comfort their dying moments?

Contrary to the popular belief, the life of a musician is full of hazards. He travels hundreds of miles to entertain you. He never knows perfect rest. He rehearses through the day and plays for you through the night and even works for a white boss to make rough ends almost meet. When next a touring musician comes to your little town, think of the miles and miles of cruel darkness that he has to cross to be with you. You will see him tonight at the show. His next appointment might be with death.

He might die in a car accident, like the two actors Sampuna and Sam of the Dixie Bing Boys or like Moffat Ndabula, well known in Johannesburg circles and trumpeter with Rhythm Clouds. He died in a motor-car accident under a railway bridge on his way to his home and family.

If you're a musician, your heart might just stand still and you die. Like Joe Setlogelo of that stormy, sensational troupe the Never Hivers. He collapsed in a train in 1941.

Sometimes fate is kinder and makes these pitiful creatures die more naturally.

One of the greatest actors I've ever known was Moses Ramailane. He and Koppie Masoleng were the idols in the Pitch Black Follies under Griffiths Motsieloa. Moses became insane. He died insane.

If it is a natural death, musicians die from 'chest troubles'. The powerful pianist Sullivan Mphahlele died of 'chest troubles'. So did Lazarus 'Snookie' Melk of the

Jazz Maniacs, the Synco Fans and the Merry Mischiefs. He was an alto-sax man. 'Chest trouble' also claimed the Harlem Swingsters drummer Isaac 'Zakes' Seabi in 1946. The many long hours of exposure, the dusty dingy places of entertainment, and many days without proper food and shelter must end in 'chest trouble'. Then you whisper the word around with a voice full of fear, for you dare not call this disease [TB] by any other name!

We musicians and clowns can never tell the manner of our death. The happiness of a secure and sheltered life is not for us. We die by your hand, by violence. Sometimes among friends, most times not. Like Stephen Monkoe, the champion trumpeter of the Merry Blackbirds, or Arrah Lefatula, the dancing star of the Pitch Black Follies. They both died in prison cells where fate had thrown them . . . far from friend or family.

The price of musical fame is the price of your life. So if you still want to be a famous musician, you know the price that many of us have paid.

(October 1953)

Back o' the Moon

19

Juby Mayet: I got sloshed with all the *Drum* guys in the shebeens. I did. I got sloshed. There was prohibition. And it was great fun going to shebeens and hearing on the grapevine that the gatters [police] were on the way, and everyone would dive through doorways and windows and leave glasses and things. There was an element of fun and excitement about it.

Esme Matshikiza: I never went to shebeens, but Todd certainly did. I don't think he ever played in a shebeen but he certainly would go there to drink and came back with wonderful stories which he wrote about. I mean life seemed to have happened in the shebeens.

Anthony Sampson: I was introduced to Sophiatown and its shebeens by Can Themba. If I remember rightly, the first one he took me to was called Back o' the Moon and run by a woman called Fatsy. We found our way through the back yards and alleyways of a part of Sophiatown known as 'Berlin'. Can knocked on the door and called the woman's name. She shot back the bolts, and this huge fleshy woman literally hauled us into the room. Another time I can remember watching a man hide under a table when word came that his wife was looking for him while his mistress was bundled out of the window. That was like watching an Elizabethan play.

Jean Hart: Bloke once gave a party in Alexandra township. Now Alexandra you could not enter as a white, it was much harder than anywhere else, unless you were on official business. You couldn't have a party there with the same degree of ease you could in Sophiatown. The entrance to the township was patrolled, sometimes by Afrikaans policemen, sometimes by black cops. There was a very real sense you were going into a controlled place. Literally you went in through a gatepost and if you were white you could be asked for a pass. That was a foretaste of what apartheid was to become. Bloke married Fiki, who was from a Cape coloured family, so he was moving up the social scale as people saw things in those days.

We had this huge party in Alexandra township to celebrate their wedding and we were really raving. Then suddenly a kid came running in and said the police were coming. In forty seconds you couldn't see a bottle or a glass anywhere. Everybody had their own way of dealing with this crisis. I remember John Goldblatt, who always wore a beret, had been drinking out of a quarter-bottle of gin. He was sitting there drunk as a skunk, and I thought, This time they've got you John. But that bottle just disappeared. It wasn't until afterwards that I realised he'd put the bottle on his head underneath the beret. We got away with that one.

There was prohibition. There was and there wasn't. As far as blacks were concerned there was; as far as whites were concerned there wasn't. 'White man's booze', 'European liquor', may have been forbidden but was available everywhere in shebeens and township back yards. As were some dangerous and potent home-made brews which always ruined, and often ended, their drinkers' lives. There was also 'kaffir beer', 'Bantu beer', 'municipal beer', 'pink gold' – call it what you will – being consumed in vast quantities in the township beer halls. These municipally run beer halls generated massive profits, supposedly destined for the creation of housing. It was a cynical way of raising revenue in a community beset by poverty, drunkenness and violence. But then it had many precedents. In South Africa liquor has often been used to exploit and control black labour.

The shebeens, however, were another story. Here was what Nat Nakasa called that 'noble institution', those 'hospitable homes'. Here was a place outside of apartheid as the names reflected: Back o' the Moon, Cabin in the Sky, Little Heaven, The Sanctuary, Kind Lady.

In the Bailey archives is a photograph of Can Themba in one of these shebeens. There's not a glass in sight, but there's a bright young girl on his knee and he's looking up at her from beneath those lizard eyes: mischievous, grinning with good times. Or is he . . .?

Es'kia Mphahlele: What was life worth? So few of us survived it just by sheer luck, simply because we had our interests elsewhere. If for instance I hadn't been a writer and a teacher I'd probably have just sunken into the same pit as so many of the people on *Drum* did. I resisted it all the time: the parties Bailey arranged and the shebeen subculture which I thought was a dead end. People had a kamikaze attitude towards drinking. When you saw Todd and Henry and Can trailing off to the shebeen down Polly Street for a drink every single day you knew they were destroying themselves. But they seemed to think it jacked them up, jacked up their spirits and gave them more drive for their journalistic careers. Also it highlighted them, it gave them a bigger profile because they were then street-wise and had the gift of the pen. This was the illusion, that drink gave them power, but at the same time ironically they knew that it was an escape from the pressures of life.

I would say that to a man their lives were a shambles. Henry's family life. Bloke's family life. Todd's, Casey's, Can's. They were all breaking down. Much of the drinking was to get away from a sense of failure. They were intelligent, sensitive men unable to cope.

Jurgen Schadeberg: There was a lot of money in supplying shebeens with liquor. In some cases the cops were involved. But also many poor whites made their living out of it. They would go to bottle stores and buy bottles to sell to blacks.

The liquor trade flourished. And then there were the police raids, which made it much more romantic. There were places called 'Sip and Fly' for obvious reasons. One popular drink was brandy with beer. A quart of beer and a jack of brandy and you mixed it. It tasted awful but it was very popular because it had an instant effect. Beer was too weak and brandy had to be mixed with something so you might as well mix it with something strong.

The *skokiaan* [an illegal brew] and other mixes were available mainly at the low dives.

I've been in shebeens where there were some extraordinary characters, like Black Diamond, who would make some extraordinary speeches.

I remember once following a police van to a place in Fordsburg. They jumped out, hammered on the doors, went in and found illegal liquor. They were pushing people around and emptying out the liquor. I was right there taking pictures. They asked me what I was doing. I told them I was taking pictures. They said Oh, and left me. Maybe they thought I was an official policeman.

Jean Hart: Guess who supplied the liquor? The Afrikaans police. The police obviously ran protection in Sophiatown and people paid very heavily for the police to cast their eyes somewhere else. In addition, the police had a very lucrative business supplying white liquor to the shebeens in the townships. It was part of the mafioso protection role that police play in those kind of situations.

Jim Bailey: The cops would raid a shebeen and pinch the liquor and either drink it themselves or send it off to other people. I've been drinking in a shebeen at midnight when a couple of white cops came in and looked sheepishly at me and I've looked sheepishly at them and then they'd go into the back room and would get a rake-off and free drink and then walk out again. The head of the liquor squad, I remember, was arrested for selling something like five million rands' worth of liquor in the black areas.

20

SHEBEENS I HAVE KNOWN by 'Skappie'

The liquor laws have failed hopelessly. The non-Europeans have not been saved from the evils of excess drinking. Liquor can be obtained with little difficulty at a certain price and sometimes under the very nose of the law. Liquor restrictions have only served to raise the price and lower the quality of liquor in shebeens. There has been no abatement in the liquor traffic. There are more shebeens today than ever before.

Native beer needs time to mature and tins of fermenting beer are often seized by raiding police. Because of the police danger, vicious concoctions, which take a convenient time to ferment, have been invented. Many stomach-turning ingredients are used to give the drinkers a 'special feeling of intoxication' and thus become custom to a particular shebeen.

There is big money in illicit liquor. The shebeen queens are very wealthy. Some have fine homes away from their places of business. Their husbands drive large American cars and their children receive a good education. It is not uncommon to see a relative of a shebeen queen place several hundred pounds on a post office counter.

There are two types of shebeens: the one already mentioned caters for the poorer type of non-European, chiefly African. In places where 'European' liquor (brandy, gin, wine and malt) is sold, the needs of all prohibited persons – Africans, coloureds, Indians and even some Europeans – are catered for.

These are of two types: one is a squalid 'joint' used exclusively for liquor-selling, not a very pleasant place to visit; the other is run in the owner's home and is usually very neat and 'respectable'. The latter is selective and one has to be introduced. Class distinctions are the rule once inside. A sherry drinker is served in a room of his sort. He often sits on hard benches at a bare table.

But more expensive tastes are catered for in the front room or the lounge, where one sits on comfortable Chesterfield suites and drinks are brought in on a tray and placed on a finely polished table. Every shebeen has a 'Ma': she may be small or big, light or fair, plain or handsome, but she is always very obliging to a good customer. Without allowing you any liberties she sees that your satisfaction is her concern.

Sometimes you are invited for a special meal or your first drink on a Monday morning is 'on the house', often known as a *'babalaas dop'*. 'Ma' may be very young, attractive and unattached. The attraction is now intensified but 'the atmosphere is a trifle electric', especially if more than one customer gets the idea that he is the cock o' the walk. Only utmost tact on the part of the woman prevents a rowdy climax.

Shebeens always depended upon the 'mail'. Before all liquor purchases were recorded, your mail was a white, or near-white, who supplied on a commission basis. He would spend the whole day riding from one bottle store to another to get the supplies. Sometimes he lived with the shebeen keeper in a back room. These mails had a dog's life. They invariably ended broken men or women. They often spent a considerable part of their lives in gaol.

A source of constant headache is the 'John' on the liquor staff. She has to have a 'possie', or hiding place, whose construction and planning is a tribute to the genius of 'Ma' and 'Pop'.

When hollow table-legs, false bottoms to drawers, unfixed flooring boards, holes in the ground and other tricks became hackneyed, new plans were made. When a plumber's job was completed, all the shebeen keeper had to do was turn on the hot-water tap for brandy and cold water for wine.

In some shops you were served over the counter with bottles of ginger-ale-cum-brandy. 'Boiled' eggs containing brandy were smuggled into the mines and bicycle tubes filled with liquor were wheeled in. An observant policeman observed a mine-boy playing a tune on a concertina which did not seem to be pressed very much. Investigation revealed a bottle of whisky!

One shebeen queen who had to fetch her own supplies from her mail wore wide dresses and was full of insouciance when on her transport duties. Once a little boy who was walking with her heard a mysterious clink and every time this happened 'Ma' would place a finger behind her to keep the offending bottle in place. She jokingly revealed, later, a specially made undergarment with pockets for as many as a dozen bottles of wine.

Another pushed her supplies home in a pram.

Alertness is essential. One liquor king sat on his stoep during business hours with his hand on a bell which gave a constant 'all-clear' signal and the appropriate warning when danger was imminent, in which case the liquor was hurriedly gulped down or the bottle emptied into the kitchen sink.

An intellectual discussion is a good ruse. At one shebeen a minute book would be kept close at hand and whenever necessary it would be fished out and 'business arising therefrom' would be discussed in a fashion which would put Charles Laughton to shame.

The headaches and inconveniences which the police subject them to are trivial. When raids are made, a stool-pigeon in the employ of the keeper is arrested, to be bailed out shortly after with business proceeding literally a few minutes later.

With the trouble given by police and the increases in fines, drinkers have been taxed in the form of concoctions and 'doping'; brandy is mixed with tobacco water and ginger ale; wine with tobacco water, and in some cases a weak solution of either tea or Condy's crystals. Of late, some Eastern folk have been brewing a very potent and harmful ersatz brandy which goes by the name of Korea.

The solution to the liquor problem in the Transvaal is very simple. Give everybody the franchise. Lourenço Marques, with a mixed population like ours, is an excellent example. If anything, the city is happier for it. At least the police do not have to be bothered with trivialities. Until the powers that be see the liquor question in its true perspective, then, like the poor, the illicit liquor traffic will always be with us.

(November 1952)

21

From THE GREAT DRINK RACKET:

. . . Most of us shebeen owners are women. The customers like it better. I have been on the job for years. I took it on partly because I was brought up to it, partly to educate my children.

I have learned a lot about people, their weaknesses and their craftiness. And I learned how to handle money.

Oddly enough, the greatest harassment is not so much the risk that I take. It is the protection money (often in kind) that I have to pay to keep going. Firstly there are the gangsters. These are two kinds. Those who just expect one to pay them sums of up to £2 a month for a protection that I don't see I need. And those who, after their 'jobs', want free refreshment at my shebeen. Then there are the type who expect me to go to bed with them just because a shebeen queen is thought to be easy.

I have a group of loafers [hole diggers to bury the illegal brews] who do all sorts of chores for me so long as I can keep them in free drinks throughout the day. I have one guy who is even prepared to do my laundry for me.

In my shebeen I find I cannot give up things like kaffir beer, Barberton and pineapple because now that the price of spirits has gone up many more people have taken to drinking these things.

I am not unduly worried about the threat that Africans may be allowed to have liquor legally. [Towards the end of the '50s a government commission recommended blacks be allowed light wine and beer.] Moreover, I understand that the government wants Africans to run these businesses themselves. I have a lot of experience in how to handle African customers, and if I could get a licence without protection fees, without toughs, without bullying policemen . . . OK! Meanwhile shebeening pays for the school fees of my children, and helps me to keep being respectable.

(January 1959)

22

BOOZERS, BEWARE OF BARBERTON! by Can Themba

No. 17, Marshall Street, Ferreirastown, Johannesburg, is just about the craziest address I've met. So many people who have lived there have gone mad, even as so many other people have stood in the slummy yard drinking that poisonous brew of shebeen invention – Barberton. There is an obvious connection. But the startling fact is that four of these people lived and went mad in the same room.

A South African neurologist has sent a paper to America on Barberton. He has found that it does drive certain people mad.

In the 1940s, they say, a coloured woman living in this yard and selling Barberton thought that her neighbours might want to take away from her profitable trade in shebeen liquor. So in the dead of night she decided to 'put the jinx' on this room and here and there in the yard by planting magic. Not long after this people began to behave strangely.

That's the story of how it all started, but the facts of what happened subsequently are hardly less startling. At about this time there lived in the fatal room Chris Tyssen, his wife and Willem Tyssen, his brother. Chris just suddenly found out that his wife was unhappy with him. They were always quarrelling and fighting, until one day she just deserted him to go and live in Pretoria. This affected Chris so badly that he became very ill, and sometimes would mutter delirious nonsense. Then suddenly his brother, Willem, started to act crazy. This was more serious than Chris's condition, which was described as having had 'just a touch'. Willem did mad things like collecting bits of paper, old tins, rubbish. Then suddenly he vanished. People looked for him everywhere. Not a sign of him. Not a sound about him. For over two months. Then came the rumour that an unidentified body had been found at Germiston. He had been drowned in a lake there. The police did not suspect foul play, but his friends are still uneasy. He was given a pauper's funeral.

Chris was ejected from the room, but he still stays in the yard, sleeping outside on a miserable mattress with the stars for a blanket. He wanders in and out like a lost, bewildered animal.

But just opposite to this notorious room is the Fourie room. Here lived Willie 'Oom Johnnie' Fourie and his wife, Maria. Unlike many of the other victims, Oom Johnnie did not get ill at all. He was completely healthy on the night of 17 March 1957 when he suddenly got it into his head that he wanted to make a great speech. He stripped himself stark naked, grabbed an axe and jumped on to the table to deliver his great oration. He made a magnificent figure standing there in his innocence and the light casting an enormous, distorted shadow on the wall and roof.

The people rushed out and sent for the flying squad. He was removed from there and taken to the 'mad cells' at Newlands Police Station where he was duly garbed in a blanket and left among the other mixed-ups. His wife, Maria, went to see him on the following Thursday. He seemed all right. But when she went to see him again, she heard that he had died.

'Those whom the gods wish to destroy, they first make mad.'

The wife is so distracted by the death of Oom Johnnie that she's a thin edge away herself from daylight-clear level-headedness. She moves about in a daze and mumbles, 'Me, I don't want to talk. I don't want to talk. I don't want to talk.'

But the yard in which she lives has become the talk of Malay Camp [Ferreirastown]. And in that Doom Room, now occupied by two brothers, it looks like violence plans to strike again. Now, these two brothers are very fond of each other. The other day they had been having a brotherly drink together. They got a little high. When they got home the older brother just suddenly attacked his kid brother. They had a wild fight, throwing in everything they could lay hands on, kicking, biting, fisting. They smashed two of the large window-panes of the Doom Room. By the following day when I got there they had contracted a sulky truce, but it was obvious there was no more as much bad blood between them. But the people in that yard intimated to me in hushed whispers that they knew it was the jinx over the room striking again.

I think, however, there is a much simpler explanation of the phenomenon. Next to Maria Fourie's room there's another room whose role in this business is much more ominous than people realise. This is the house where they sell Barberton in a big way. African men come from the neighbouring mines, the town and industrial concerns for their mugful of Mbamba (Barberton). But Barberton is a poison made in such a way as to give a quick kick. It is made of bread, yeast and sugar. It's main characteristic is that it is 'raw' (swiftly prepared) liquor. One of its commonest effects is against the skin, which it peels off and swallows. People get red lips and purulent black pimples on the face. But it has made those who have drunk it for a long time raging madmen, especially in fights. Here then may lie the answer to the mystery of the yard of lunatics. That the people have fed too long and too much on a poisonous concoction. It has made them sick and driven them mad.

(May 1957)

23

MR DRUM LOOKS AT THE TOT SYSTEM

What is the 'system'? In the Cape Province, particularly in the wine-growing areas, a large part of coloured farm workers have part of their wages paid in wine instead of money. The wine is given in 'tots' several times a day. Usually if a worker doesn't take his tot he gets nothing instead. Farmers say that the tot makes workers work better, and that they can't do without it.

This 'system' dates back to the first landing at the Cape, when Hottentots building Cape Town Castle were paid with wine. Today, many of the men who get the tot were born in 'tot families', and have never known of life without tots. Life on the vineyards revolves round the tot. One investigator comments: 'A habit-forming drug forms part of the wages of industry.'

The effect of the tot system is disastrous. Everyone who has investigated it has agreed about this. Government enquiries held in 1915, 1926, 1937 and 1945 all found that the tot caused drunkenness, demoralisation and disease among the coloured people. Dutch Reformed ministers have expressed their indignation against the corruption and immorality of the system.

Coloured leaders have repeatedly attacked a system that has degraded the people: in 1933 the first National Convention urged its abolition in the strongest terms, and five years later repeated their plea. The coloured leaders that Mr Drum interviewed without exception spoke against the system. Many independent individuals have added their protests . . . convinced that the

108

rate of crime, TB and early deaths in the wine-growing areas was largely caused by the tot system.

The most surprising thing about the tot system is that it is perfectly legal. Laws have attempted to control it, but have never recognised the system as an evil. In spite of the abundant evidence from every quarter, the giving of up to one and a half pints of wine a day is approved by law.

Not only this. A new Liquor Bill, which is awaiting a second reading in parliament, extends the tot system to apply to the whole of the Union, including the Transvaal and Natal, and permits the giving of tots to Africans. The same Bill takes drastic steps to prevent the sale and brewing of liquor by Africans. As one institute points out: 'The absurd position arises that one section of the law enables the man to form a habit which another section of the same law altogether prohibits him from indulging.'

Mr Drum made a tour of the wine-growing areas of the Cape – Paarl, Worcester, Stellenbosch, Constantia – where the tot is most frequently given. He talked to labourers on the farms, to farmers and to public men in the district who come in close contact with the working of the system.

Mr Drum found that workers on the vineyards are nearly all coloureds, who have been on the farms often for generations. The tot system has made them a class apart, and for many it is true to say that their lives revolve round the drinks which are given to them five times a day, with an extra tot before going home – one at 9 a.m., 11 a.m., 2 p.m., 4 p.m. and two at 6 p.m. At work they are apathetic and half-dazed, watching the farmhouse and slackening off when it gets near tot-time. They work a long day and some farmers say that they must have their tots to keep them going. When there is extra work or they have to work at weekends, they are given an extra tot, or 'overdop', as an incentive.

In the evenings you can see them walking along together, slouching drink-sodden to their homes, and sometimes they even come drunk into church.

Families usually live on the farms, in one-room hovels. Often the farmers themselves admitted that they were disgraceful. In a typical hovel, a husband and wife and four children live in one small room. The husband's tot-sodden existence is shown all too clearly by the grim bareness of the rooms – often with no furniture at all, only one bed, and a broken box with bottles on it.

'*Pandokkies*' – self-built shelters of scraps of corrugated iron – are common in the tot districts and breed their own race of addicts, who cannot face being sober to their world. Workers who are not given free housing by their farmer often have to pay high rents for *pandokkies* on wasteland. For some shacks of iron sheeting that Mr Drum saw, the rent was £2 a month.

The children are born and bred to the world of tots. Many of the people who protested most strongly to Mr Drum had their childhood overshadowed by the tot. They remember how their father came home with no thought of anything but drink, and spent any money he had on weekend bottles and drinks at the bar. Often the men go straight from work to the bar each night to down as much as they can before closing time.

The workers care more for drink than for food or their families. The children are often all too clearly underfed, and the schoolmasters complain that they sometimes get nothing to eat except what they are given at school.

One farmer was quoted as saying: 'If I stop giving my men tots, they'll send their children to school and I'll lose them from the farm.' Nine- and ten-year-old children go to work on the vineyards: many people told Mr Drum they had seen ten-year-olds given tots with the rest, although the law insists on an age limit of twenty-one.

As a result of hard drinking and bad feeding, disease is rampant. TB is rife and a special hospital, Sonstraal, deals with the great number of cases in the Paarl area. Cases of TB and venereal disease are most common among farm workers, and the dirty communal drinking tins spread infection quickly.

. . . What can be said in defence of the tot system? Why is it tolerated at all by honest, Christian people? Many of the farmers are upright and respected men who have no wish to degrade and demoralise their workers. How do they permit the system to continue?

The tot system is deeply embedded in the lives of the vineyard workers. For generations they have been bred and raised on liquor. It is a part, and the major part, of their way of life. So farmers maintain that it cannot be done away with unless, perhaps, by gradual stages.

Farmers say that the tot does no harm, that the wine provided is clean and pure, and that if they stopped tots their workers would simply buy stronger 'fortified' wine at the bottle stores. One farmer described how, when he ran out of tot wine, it simply led to more drunkenness in the pub. Farmers say that the tot is not part of wages, but merely an extra gift for those who want it.

But many farmers have put an end to tots on their farms, and have still got men to work for them: they are usually paid 1s. to 1s. 6d. extra instead. Normal wages without tots are 5s. to 6s. a day, with tots 3s. 6d. to 5s. Some farmers instead of tots provide free facilities – better housing, education, free boots and clothes. Mr Drum was told of one farmer in the Paarl district who takes the children of his farm workers to school by car every day. The reports of farmers who have done away with the tot differ; obviously it takes a long time before the effects of so old a system wear off, but they all agree that the workers can quite well do without their tots, and in most cases work better.

. . . Many arguments have been produced in defence of the tot system: some people say simply that their workers are happier that way, others that if the tot were stopped they would drink more dangerously, and that the tot never makes them drunk. Their state has been described by a magistrate as 'never drunk, but never sober'.

One justification of the tot system given by an MP was that 'I can give two hundred texts out of the Bible where the use of wine in the form of rations or otherwise is praised . . . Even the Great Master made wine.'

. . . Why, after the overwhelming evidence against the system, should a Bill be put forward not to abolish but to extend it?

The answer is admitted by many farmers. Faced with a diminishing overseas market after the post-war boom and expanding production on the vineyards, the wine farmers will have a serious surplus of their wines. The tot system provides an easy, cheap and reliable method of disposing of the excess. By extending the system to the whole of the Union, this market would be greatly increased, and the prosperity of the wine trade assured for some time to come.

There are other reasons, of course. For the farmer it provides a cheap way of paying labour, since the wine costs him less than it would cost his labourer – if he could buy it at all. In the case of Africans, who cannot buy wine, it puts the farmer in a very strong position. Also, there is no doubt that the tot in many ways simplifies labour troubles, and makes the workers more content with their lot.

. . . In a country which strictly limits the sale of wine and spirits and prohibits it entirely to the greatest section of the people, it is the more astonishing to find liquor being urged on the same people. If the tot system is right, then so is drinking anywhere, anytime, by anybody: if drinking is limited, then the tot system must be abolished. To say to someone, 'You cannot under any circumstances drink, unless you go and work for Mr X,' is surely one of the most corrupt forms of bribery ever devised.

(June 1952)

The Complete Hollywood Journalist

24

Early in 1952 a young man with a passion for journalism became *Drum*'s first cub reporter. His name was Arthur Maimane. He was just out of St Peter's, the 'Eton of South Africa', as Father Trevor Huddleston's school in Sophiatown was known.

Anthony Sampson describes him as the 'complete Hollywood journalist', with bow-tie, dark shirt, light suit and white shoes, but for all that 'the most natural journalist we had'. In many photographs he has a cynical look on his face and a cigarette stuck in the corner of his mouth. Unlike the others he didn't drink.

In later years Maimane became a mentor for Obed Musi, who'd also come out of 'Eton'. But these days Musi is inclined to see through the cult when talking about Maimane: 'He was another guy with pretensions. He used to call himself J. Arthur Maimane after J. Arthur Rank, the movie house. His first name was Jay. He didn't want to speak English like a black man, he wanted to give the impression he had a cultured accent. He was a perfect gentleman and many of us owe our successes to him. He always seemed to be a level-headed guy.

'I remember one time Bob Gosani, the photographer, was being harassed just outside our offices by two white cops. They wanted to know where he'd got the camera from. They wanted to see a receipt for it. I was then a copy-boy, I saw the situation and called Arthur. He stormed downstairs and went up to these cops and asked them: "Have you got a receipt for that gun you're carrying?" The cops were very embarrassed. Obviously they were hassling Bob because of

1. Henry Nxumalo

2. Jim Bailey

3. ANC president Albert Luthuli with Anthony Sampson

4. *Drum* staff in March 1955. *From left:* Henry Nxumalo, Es'kia Mphahlele, Casey Motsisi, Can Themba, Jerry Ntsipe, Arthur Maimane, Victor Xashimba, Dan Chocho. *Squatting:* Benson Dyantyi, Ken Mtetwa, Bob Gosani

5. A gangster lies dead beneath a poster
advertising the movie *The Great Sinner*

6. Members of the Russian gang

7. Todd Matshikiza

with the Manhattan Brothers

9. (*above*) Nathan 'Dam-dam' Mdledle of the Manhattan Brothers

10. A shebeen queen mixing an illegal brew called *skokiaan* in a Sophiatown back yard

11. Arthur Maimane

12. Arthur Maimane's detective character, the Chief, in action

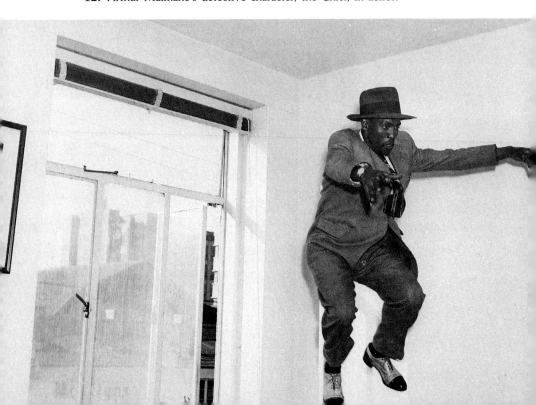

his trade, because black journalists were unheard of. Nor was it heard of for a black guy, a small guy like Arthur, to confront two burly white cops, and his stock rose among us from that point onwards.

'He had a sardonic look, he would treat cops as idiots and forgive them because they didn't know what they were doing. Very tolerant he was.'

Arthur Maimane was a good journalist. He could turn his hand to anything, as everyone had to on *Drum*: sport, beauty queens, picture captions, racy fiction, but he did so with a lot less fuss, a lot less of the dilettante than some of the others. One of his creations – often under the by-line of Arthur Mogale – was a long-running series featuring a detective called the Chief. It was part Raymond Chandler, part Peter Cheyney. Maimane says it was one way of writing all the gangster stories he picked up in the shebeens but couldn't report factually for fear of his life. Well maybe, maybe not: it was a lot of stories to come across so conveniently.

Part of the legend – or is it the myth? – around Maimane is that he was on a gang's hit-list. According to Don Mattera it's legend.

'Maimane was among the most serious of the young men on *Drum*; we called him one of the "favourites" of Father Huddleston. But that didn't get him any special protection. We all knew he was Arthur Mogale and I can tell you the Berliners especially were pissed off with him. Maimane was very scared and very afraid. I remember there was word out once that we should wipe this guy off. This guy was reporting shit about the Americans, the Vultures, the Berliners. I tell you, there was a hit ticket on this man. And this guy had to flee Sophiatown to live in Alexandra township, and he had to flee from there as well.'

Perhaps, perhaps not; but Maimane is on record thus: 'I left South Africa because I knew I would be killed by the gangsters if I lived there any longer. I was fairly safe at the beginning but after I had done one story on one of them they put a contract out for my life and I decided that I had stuck my neck out enough times for *Drum* . . . I must get out of here . . .'

So at the end of the '50s he left, drifted north to Tanzania and eventually ended up in London, where over the last three decades he's worked for both the BBC and ITV. In 1990 he returned to South Africa to a position as features editor on *The Weekly Mail*.

25

THE WHITE DAHLIA by Arthur Mogale

Last month I was telling you blokes about how the police got me out of gaol whilst serving a term for my movie-making misdeeds. They wanted me to stop a gang of diamond smugglers working from Durban. Their undercover man, Detective-Sergeant Joe Moloi, had only found out that the leader was called the 'White Dahlia'. I come down here, I see Joe killed, and I follow a lady who drives a car I recognise as the one that carried Joe's killers. And what does she do? She leads me into a trap!

I come up for air like a drowning hippo.

'What's the game, Big Boy?' she asks in a theatrical whisper.

'Say, lady, what's the matter now?' I act surprised.

'You think you are a clever one, don't you? Maybe you don't think I know you've been following me since I left my car, hey? You snoopy bas –'

'Now wait a minute!' I say, acting relieved, though the point of the gun hidden by my open jacket isn't very comforting. 'You've got me all wrong – though I'm flattered by your noticing my following you. Why I did is because with the big bag you're carrying, I thought you might be going for a swim – and I wanted to see if those curves are real. And I thought we might have an interesting chat after the smile you gave me. You know lady, I've seen plenty pieces of Eve's flesh but not one to touch you. I remember when I was in –' I'm getting set for the usual boring success-of-a-wolf story when she cuts me short.

'On your way, sailor! I don't come tickey-a-dozen. I'm awfully expensive – and even then not for punks like you who think they own all the cheesecake they're allowed to see!' she says in a not-so-good American accent. I watch the graceful retreat of her swaying curves.

I'm interested. Professionally and otherwise. I go to the nearest phone and put a call through to Cassim at his lounge. I give him the Buick's licence number and describe the expensive lady. He tells me she's Lillian and I shouldn't touch her. She's poison. Her present boyfriend is a tough egg from Jo'burg called Moollah. I'm wondering if it's the Moollah I knew. He doesn't know where she lives, but knows she'll be at a party given by some rich Moonsamy Loogat tomorrow night. If I want to know more about her, he says I must come round and see him. He doesn't trust the phone.

I have nothing to do, so I go and see him. With the encouragement of a few pounds he tells me a bit about her; not anything definite.

'And who's the White Dahlia?' I ask him as I leave.

'The White Dah –' his face turns grey and his voice fades off. I know he won't be much use, so I leave him.

I'm pretty busy the next twenty-four hours, verifying Cassim's suggestions.

He arranges for me to get an invitation to Loogat's party, and even supplies me with a quite pretty partner. He almost knows his way around here.

When we get to the big and over-furnished house I find the 'cream' of Durban society: African, coloured and Indian. Not the type of cream I'd use in my coffee, though; the type that's only good for the rubbish bin.

And she's there.

It's about elevenish when I get a chance to speak to her. She's standing to one side, dressed like a Christmas tree with all the lights on and looking at the crowd like they were already in the rubbish bin I've been associating it with.

'Hello Annie-get-your-gun!' I say to her with my best smile.

'Hello yourself Mr Follow-me-around!' she says with a smile brighter than a searchlight.

'I'd prefer you calling me "Sailor" like you did the other day. 'Cos if you do, you'll give me an opening to tell you about my amorous adventures on the Seven Seas – the ones you so rudely stopped me from telling the other day.'

'Oh stop that nonsense, Chester!' she says with a little laugh that looks like it's been practised in front of a mirror. 'Why don't you tell me instead about your, shall I say, pleasant though short residence under His Excellency the Governor-General's hospitality?'

'Oh that! You surprise me, Lillian. I didn't think you'd take so much interest in a peanut-boy like me.'

'And perhaps I should be equally surprised that you know my name? Don't try and pull that one over on me, Chief; I've heard a lot about you. You are too clever to speak like that,' she says with a knowing look. And I reckon she's very very clever herself.

After that we have quite a nice time together, dancing, talking and laughing like old friends. I notice when we dance she tries to get close enough to feel if I'm carrying a gun. I don't let her 'cos I am.

Everything stops about two.

'Will you drive me home?' she asks prettily. 'You can see I'm an unwanted lady without an escort. But perhaps you brought a lady-friend?'

'Friend?' I query quickly, looking round and seeing my partner has vanished like a good girl. 'You're the first lady I've met in this town – and I don't care to meet any others.' We look deep into each other's eyes.

As we drive off in the Buick I quickly slip my Mauser

from its special pocket under my left armpit into the glove compartment next to my thigh. Now I let her snuggle into me. She really puts on the pressure, and I'm enjoying myself – what with driving a souped-up car that can do 130 miles per hour and being caressed by a lady like this Delilah here.

'Which way do we go, Sweets?' I ask softly.

'Anywhere you please,' she answers dreamily.

After searching a bit I get on to a road that leads into the hilly and deserted hinterlands. I notice a car following us. She is clever all right. I park near the top of a steep hill. It parks farther back where I don't see it.

We have a grand necking session. And as she caresses me, she makes sure that I'm not carrying a gun. I make as if I don't notice it.

When I've had enough of her, I come to business. I reckon I better start asking questions before she does – in the Delilah fashion.

'Look, Sweets,' I say, 'I've got some business to talk to you. I don't know which gang's boss you're running around with, but he must be making a packet to satisfy all your awfully expensive tastes. Though I've got my idea about him and his racket, you're going to tell me everything. And I mean everything! And you're going to like it; 'cos if you don't I'll get you a few years on Robben Island – I know all about you and the joint in Cato Manor!'

She gasps – and I can hear you too – 'cos I haven't told you what Cassim suggested and what I verified, eh? I didn't 'cos I wasn't sure till now that she gasps.

'Surprised, eh? Here's another surprise: I'm a cop! Specially imported from Jo'burg to crack this town wide open. I reckon you don't believe it 'cos everybody who knows me here thinks I escaped from prison? Well, Sweets, here's another surprise: I never was in prison! Anyway, that's beside the point. Say your pie – ' She gives a loud honk on the hooter.

As I hear a self-starter whine a hundred yards back, I switch on the ignition and kick down the accelerator. She's been looked after good; she roars to life, and I let her roll. I forget about Diamond Lil for a minute. She slams down the footbrake when we get to forty m.p.h. and I almost kiss the windshield as the car jerks to a stop.

I give her a judo-chop with my hand on the back of her neck and start the engine up. The Buick jumps forward and she slumps on to the floorboards, paralysed from the neck downwards.

I don't know the curving road, so I drive slow and they catch up on me. They draw level.

You blokes ought to know that I mean for them to catch up with me soon. But I want to give them a run for their money first – even if it means ducking bullets. What I'm thinking now is that if they get me, maybe I can get a bit nearer this character they call 'White Dahlia'.

'Stop! Stop or we shoot!' a gratey voice commands.

I look out the far window and only see blackness. I can see a gun barrel pointing at me from their car. I pull out my Mauser and throw a shot at them. They slacken and I lead again.

Not for long, though. They draw level again. I look out my window again. I have a fleeting glimpse of the top of a tree in mid-air ahead and to my side.

As they try to stop me by edging in front of me I swing the Buick to my right. The engines collide with a loud tearing sound. As if in a dream I watch the Buick engine rise into the air, turn to the left and the dark void . . . Then it comes down, down, down, down until I can see my feet straight under me.

A last resounding crash and all is blackness.

(May 1953)

The House of God

26

As the first anniversary of the magazine approached, in March 1952, Jim Bailey, Anthony Sampson, Henry Nxumalo, Jurgen Schadeberg and Arthur Maimane sat down to decide on a big story to celebrate the occasion. The junior reporter Maimane came up with the goods.

He had a cousin in Pretoria who had ended up on a potato farm in the Bethal district, an area notorious for the murder and ill-treatment of labourers. The court records dating back to 1929 revealed a history of violence. In that early trial a farmer was found guilty of tying a labourer by his feet from a tree and flogging him to death. During the ordeal the victim had begged for water, a request which was answered by the farmer pouring scalding water into his mouth. And so the litany of crimes continued: guilty of beating a labourer to death; guilty of assaulting two labourers and getting a dog to savage them; guilty of chaining a man to a tree all night and whipping him; guilty of sjambokking; guilty . . . guilty . . . guilty . . .

Bethal – which ironically means the house of God – was a name that struck terror into black hearts. Such terror that farmers 'collecting' labourers at the border with Rhodesia had to change their Bethal number plates. One labourer, Frank Phivi, on learning he was on a train bound for Bethal, not Germiston as he had been told, jumped out of the window, killing himself.

Behind all this terror lay the contract system and the special employment agencies that exploited it. They would trick men walking city streets in search of work into signing a contract; they picked up others crossing into South Africa in the hopes of employment and bound them all to six months' farm labour. And there was no getting out of it: the law saw to that by severely punishing blacks who broke their contracts.

The story Maimane's cousin told said it all:

'I had been looking for work for two months in the city of Pretoria when I met this white man. He asked me if I wanted work. I said Yes. Any type? I again said Yes. He told me that he knew of a baas who wanted boys to work on his lorry that carried produce between the market at Johannesburg and Pretoria. I eagerly asked him where I could find the baas; for this, I thought, would be wonderful work and I would see the City of Gold! He directed me to the office in Church Street.

'There I found this baas. He told me that he did not have any more work for lorry-boys, but he had work on his farm and in his mine. I had to choose between those two. I did not take long; for after you walk the streets for nine weeks you are glad for any work. I told him I would work for him on the farm.

'I was sent to the yard behind where I found six other men. We spent three days there and were not allowed to go out for the baas said we would be leaving at any moment.

'On the fourth day we were marched into an office, and after some writing by the white men we were told to hold a pen in the hand. After we had all done this we were told that we had signed a contract for six months' work on this white man's farm. This alarmed us and three of us asked for it to be cancelled. The baas said we could rub our signatures off with money only. We had no money so we also climbed into the canvas-covered lorry with the others. We climbed out of it with cramped legs that night in Leslie [near Bethal]. We were led into a compound surrounded by a high stone wall, given a blanket each, and told to sleep in one of the low, dirty, mud-walled long rooms by a black foreman.

'At dawn on the Monday we were herded into the fields by horse-riding, sjambok-carrying black and white men. The fields were flat, wide, treeless plains planted with potatoes. The black guards were telling us, "*Le jele nama ea Kalajane, kajeno l tla e patela*" (You have eaten the meat of a cheat and today you will pay for it'. We did not understand that we were to pay for the meat of Kalajane with burning stripes on our backs.

'We strung out in a straight line from one end of the potato field to the other, holding bags and big baskets between us. We were not to break the line or we would be whipped by the guards. We were not to leave any potatoes behind or we would be whipped. It was difficult for us to keep in line without leaving some potatoes behind, and our backs were not used to this prolonged bending, so we were constantly whipped and cursed.

'At midday we had a meal of dry, stiff porridge that looked like white clods of earth. In the morning we had liquid fermented porridge and in the evening we had the same dry porridge. The veterans had improved on this heart-sickening diet by privately preparing a concoction of boiled potatoes and bits of meat in jam-tins.

'In the evening we were herded back to the compound, walking on tired feet, with bent backs. After the porridge we lay down on the blocks of cement or on the floor and slept like the dead must sleep.'

Further on he describes how one day the police came to the farm. 'We were called together before them, and they asked us if we were satisfied with the conditions. For a moment nobody answered . . . then some said "*Yebo Nkosi*" (Yes, my lord). My heart filled with anger at this untruth; but I knew why they had said it. They hoped to curry favour with the white men. Nobody could dare to contradict what they had said for they would have paid most sorely for that moment of boldness.'

Some months later, with a limp arm damaged accidentally by a white guard, Maimane's cousin breaks a plough. He is ordered to pick up pumpkins to pay for his carelessness. When he tries to lift the bag his weak shoulder gives way and the pumpkins roll all over the ground. Livid with an 'unholy rage', the guard jumps off his horse and 'set to kicking me till my trousers became a ragged skirt'. He survives the beating and after working three months longer than his contract manages to save enough money to pay his train fare back to Pretoria.

'It was obvious,' recalls Sampson, 'that we also needed to visit Bethal. I discussed this with Jim and Henry, who had visited the district some years previously with a churchman, and they both agreed. Henry's only words were, "I'd better go and have another look."'

'There was really no other way to do the Bethal story,' says Jurgen Schadeberg. 'Henry had to discard his suit, dress in tattered clothes like a farm labourer and go and find work on the farm. Which he did. And then after a few days picking potatoes he escaped at night. It was a dangerous situation to run away at night: he could have been shot, killed, but there was no other way to do it. Then the two of us went back and we drove around the district interviewing people and taking photographs. He was my "boy" whenever farmers stopped us, which they often did. At the time I had a very heavy German accent and my English wasn't very good so that helped. I pretended to be a tourist. Some farmers were suspicious but they couldn't pin us down. One farmer, who I remember had quite a reputation as a slave driver, was so friendly he even gave Henry a sack of potatoes for being such a good native. Most times though Henry would stay in the car and I got out to talk to them. Not that there was much risk of Henry being recognised because for one thing he had a suit on now. We went back to the same farm where he worked and in the compound took pictures of a fourteen-year-old boy's hands bleeding from digging up potatoes. Apart from the state of his hands, the boy was under age, but little matters like that didn't worry the farmers. We were lucky on that occasion because the farmer wasn't there. Otherwise we just went around from farm to farm being tourists and taking pictures.'

125

Those pictures show compounds that, as Nxumalo described them, looked much like gaols, with barbed wire round the top of the walls. 'They have high walls,' he wrote, 'they are dirty and are often so closely attached to a cattle kraal that the labourers breathe nearly the same air as the cattle.' The beds were concrete ledges with a row of loose bricks separating one man's space from another's. Old sacks were used as blankets. For many labourers they were also clothes. As Nxumalo found, 'Labourers admitted that farmers are always willing to give them credit when their clothes give in. [Most] farmers keep large supplies of khaki clothes which they sell to their labourers on credit at the exorbitant price of £1. 12s. shirt and £2. 10s. a pair of trousers. Older men prefer to wear sacks in which holes have been cut for head and arms and sleep on sacks instead of blankets rather than incur more debt.' Out of a monthly wage of £3, £2.10s. was a heavy price to pay.

The story was illustrated by other pictures of black prisoners sitting in cages on open lorries, being taken to the farms to serve their sentences. It turned out that when contract labour was scarce the farmers had an inexhaustible supply from the nearby prisons. Officialdom thought the system an ideal rehabilitation scheme but, as *Drum* commented, 'When farmers can use prison labour, there is obviously less incentive to attract voluntary labour by better conditions and pay.'

Nxumalo interviewed more than fifty labourers. He was told stories of labourers flogged to death, of others who died of the cold, of repeated beatings, of farmers known as 'Mabulala' (the Killer) and 'Fakefutheni' (Hit him in the marrow). Everyone had a story of atrocity; most had been conned into coming to Bethal.

Just how they were conned Nxumalo went to find out, this time by standing in the Johannesburg pass office queue. Here were hundreds of hopefuls, in a queue that each day went right round the building as men tried to get passes which would allow them to stay and work in Johannesburg.

These queues were worked by the agency touts who were paid a per-head commission for anybody naïve enough to think he was being offered a straight chance. Soon enough Nxumalo was taken to a baas who could fix him up. He gave his name as George Magwaza and spent the night in a stinking compound with a group of men.

Next morning Nxumalo was signed on. A black clerk called their names and said, 'You're going to work on a farm in the Middelburg district; you're on a six-months' contract. You will be paid £3 a month plus food and quarters. When you leave here you will be given an advance of 5s. for pocket money, 10s. 5d. for food, and 14s. 5d. for train fare. The total amount is £1. 9s. 5d., and this amount will be deducted from your first month's wages. Have you got that?'

Everyone answered Yes.

'You will now proceed to touch the pencil,' said the clerk.

'But I was told before that I was going to be sent to a farm in Springs. Why am I now going to Middelburg?' asked Nxumalo.

'I'm telling you where you're going, according to your contract sheet, and nothing else,' replied the clerk.

Nxumalo refused to touch the pencil when he reached the attesting officer and was told to wait outside. The other fifty recruits then ran past and touched the pencil.

They didn't know it but they had just signed a contract which read: 'The above Contract of Service was read aloud, interpreted and fully explained to the above-mentioned Natives, who acknowledged that they understood the same and voluntarily affixed their signatures (or marks) thereto in my presence and in the presence of . . . The provisions of the Native Service Contract Act, 1932, have been complied with. The consent of parents or guardians of Natives aged between sixteen and eighteen years recruited for agricultural purposes has been produced to me.'

While the recruits were loaded into lorries, Henry Nxumalo was shoved back into the street.

'I went back to the recruiting office with Henry the next

morning,' says Jurgen Schadeberg. 'Fortunately we found an open window into the room where the pencil-touching procedure was again taking place. I think I stood on some bricks to see in, or maybe I was jumping up and down, anyway I clicked off a few shots and ran. Nobody chased us but we could hear them shouting in the room.'

In March 1952 *Drum* published the story under the head-line BETHAL TODAY – *DRUM'S* FEARLESS EXPOSURE OF HUMAN EXPLOITATION.

Happily, in a country that has a history of being blind and deaf to the exploitation of black workers, the story was noticed by a Nationalist morning newspaper, *Die Transvaler*. 'The article is written to stir up trouble and cause ill-feeling,' it whined.

Questions were asked the next day in parliament and the government appointed a small committee to investigate conditions in Bethal. Needless to say their report was never published and, although conditions may have softened for a while on the Bethal farms, by the following year the courts were once again hearing cases of floggings and beatings and chained labourers.

But on the magazine and for its readers, Mr Drum, Henry Nxumalo, had become a hero. Readers wrote in:

'Who is this wonderful Mr Drum?' 'Because of your bravery I suggest calling you Dr Drum instead of Mr Drum. In fact, Dr Bravery would be the most appropriate name for you.'

A Story of Defiance

27

In the archives is a photograph which shows the crowd massing in Freedom Square, Fordsburg, not far from the centre of Johannesburg. It is 6 April 1952 and the ANC and the Indian Congress are exhorting people to a campaign of defiance. Defiance against the pass laws, against group areas legislation, against separate representation on the electoral roll. Defiance against all discriminatory legislation. On a platform at the far end of the square, just visible through the autumn trees, stand Dr J. S. Moroka, president of the ANC, and Yusuf Dadoo, president of the Indian Congress. 'I am glad to see you in such large numbers . . .' begins Moroka as he looks out over the raised faces, the flags, the placards.

Elsewhere whites are celebrating the third centenary of Jan van Riebeeck's landing at the Cape.

Another photograph shows the Boksburg contingent of the ANC marching towards the square beneath a banner portraying Moroka and Dadoo. But there is one taken from the platform over the crowd which is most arresting. There are few young faces and hardly anyone is smiling. The women are tight-lipped, the men frowning. There are ANC flags and demands like AWAY WITH PASSES and VOTES FOR ALL roughly written on makeshift cardboard posters, but curiously there seems a lack of energy. At least when compared with the slogan and T-shirt demonstrations of today there seems to be something almost gentle here.

Although, of course, the state was anything but gentle in its treatment of protest. Strikes and protests in the first two years of the '50s – starting with the Communist-Party-inspired work stay-away on May Day 1950 – had often ended in violent clashes with the police that inevitably left demonstrators dead. And the Prime Minister had warned the ANC, when they wrote to him urging parliament to repeal the pass laws, the Group Areas Act of 1950 and the Bantu Authorities Act of 1951, that the government would 'make full use of the machinery at its disposal to quell any disturbances'. It did. As the Defiance Campaign gathered momentum, the police reacted harshly and people died.

And yet the campaign had been conceived, not as a violent reaction to apartheid, but as a means of embarrassing the state. Campaigners, singing, 'Hey, Malan, open the gaol doors, we want to get in . . .' simply defied the laws of white privilege. Arrests led to sentences and imprisonment in an attempt to overcrowd the prisons. However, as the months passed the punishment became harsher and some resisters were sentenced to be whipped.

In October, at the height of the campaign, *Drum* wrote THE STORY OF 'DEFIANCE':

> Three months ago the first groups in the Defiance Campaign went into action, after a year of planning and preparation. The campaign, which aims to defy six laws of the country, has been denounced in the strongest terms by the Prime Minister, Dr Malan, and by the leader of the Opposition. Since last December, when Dr Moroka, president of the African National Congress, demanded the repeal of the 'unjust laws' at Bloemfontein, events have moved swiftly.
>
> The Defiance Campaign was born over a year ago in Johannesburg, on 29 July 1951, when non-white leaders met together and decided to form a Joint Planning Council to co-ordinate Africans, Indians and coloureds and 'to embark upon an immediate mass campaign for the repeal of oppressive measures'. The 'oppressive measures' which the Council were pledged to attack

were, and still are, limited to the pass laws, stock limitation, the Group Areas Act, the Separate Voters' Representation Act, the Bantu Authorities Act and the Suppression of Communism Act.

The Joint Planning Council was formed, and consisted of Moroka, Marks and Sisulu of the African National Congress, and Dadoo and Y. Cachalia of the Indian Congress. They issued a report, to be put before the African Congress: the government should be called on to repeal the unjust laws. If they refused, mass demonstrations were to be held, followed by defiance of the laws.

On 17 December, the report was approved by the African National Congress at Bloemfontein and the campaign had begun. Dr Moroka demanded the Prime Minister repeal the laws; in reply Dr Malan stated: 'The government has no intention of repealing the long-existing laws between Europeans and Bantu.'

The first mass demonstration was planned for 6 April 1952, exactly three hundred years after van Riebeeck with the first white settlers landed at the Cape.

On 6 April a mass meeting was held in Red Square, Fordsburg, Johannesburg (now called 'Freedom Square'), and in other main centres of the Union. The Johannesburg meeting was attended by units marching in from the locations and outlying towns; a large number of overseas pressmen and photographers were also present. The meeting was addressed by Dr Moroka, president of the African Congress, Dr Dadoo, president of the SA Indian Congress, and many other African, Indian and coloured leaders. They protested against the 'oppressive measures' and called for ten thousand volunteers to defy the laws.

The date fixed for the first defiance of the laws was 26 June, commemorating the protest strike by non-whites two years ago against living conditions.

But the first actual cases of defiance, as it happened,

occurred before that. On 10 May, the government, under the Suppression of Communism Act, called on four 'named' non-white ex-Communists to resign from all organisations – Dadoo, Marks, Bopape and Kotane. All four leaders were closely involved in the Defiance Campaign, and both Dadoo and Marks were members of the original Joint Planning Council.

The four leaders defied the order from the Minister of Justice, and continued to address meetings. With others, they were each in turn arrested and awaited trial.

In the mean time volunteers were enlisted from all parts of the Union and from all the non-white races to take part in acts of defiance. Men and women from all walks of life signed on, to be later organised into batches to defy the laws together.

On 9 June the 'named' non-white leaders who had defied the ban came before the Magistrate's Court in Johannesburg. The week of the trial, or 'Leaders' Week' as it was called, was the occasion for more protesting, with the crowds squeezing in and around the courts, and volunteers signing on in hundreds. All over the Union, in the towns and in the locations, the leaders made speeches for the campaign.

The four principal banned leaders, together with others, were found guilty. They were sentenced to four to six months' imprisonment. They were granted leave to appeal and await second trial.

On 26 June, bands of volunteers went into action for the first time. Without violence or disorder, a small group led by Nana Sita, an old-stager of passive resistance, insisted on entering Boksburg location, close to Johannesburg, without the necessary permits. After an argument with the police, they were arrested and without resistance entered the police lorry which took them to gaol. The first group was shortly followed by others, and Walter Sisulu, secretary-general of the African Congress, was one of the leaders arrested.

On the same evening a meeting was held at Garment Workers' Hall in Anderson Street, Johannesburg. After the meeting, attended by picked bands of volunteers and a number of pressmen, a group of Africans left the building after the official curfew time. They came into the street to find a row of armed police lining the street on both sides. After brief questioning by the police chief, the groups were arrested and, singing 'Africa' and with thumbs uplifted to the 'Afrika' sign, they climbed into the waiting lorry. With them to the gaol went Defiance leaders Yusuf Cachalia and Nelson Mandela.

The first groups of Defiers came up before the magistrate and were sentenced to periods from four to six weeks, with option of a fine. The fine was refused, and the Defiers served their full sentence.

This was the pattern of all the Defiance groups which followed. There was no violence, no resistance to arrest. The groups marched off and were taken to the gaol without incident.

The campaign spread over the country, to Port Elizabeth, East London, Cape Town, and then to Durban. Prominent people of all races joined the Defiers. And volunteers continued to sign on as the gaols became fuller and fuller.

A month after the acts of defiance had begun, on 30 July, the police made sudden surprise searches of Congress. Searching for evidence of Communist connections to the campaign, they entered the offices of the African Congress in Johannesburg and – after a twenty-four-hour wait for the keys – of the Indian Congress. They entered the homes of several leaders, including Dr Moroka's house at Thaba Nchu. They collected a large mass of correspondence and documents for inspection.

As a result, three weeks later, warrants were issued for the arrest, under the Suppression of Communism Act, of twenty non-white leaders involved in the campaign, including Moroka, Sisulu, Marks, Mandela, Bopape, Thloome, Phillips of the African Congress; and Dadoo, Thandray, Kathrada, Sita, Desai and the Cachalias of the Indian Congress. They were arrested and let out on bail awaiting trial.

In the mean time the centre of the Defiance Campaign had shifted for the time to the Cape Province, where, at Port Elizabeth, groups of volunteers in hundreds were defying apartheid regulations in stations and elsewhere.

On 24 August the Joint Executives of the African National Congress met again, and advocated intensified action to coincide with the beginning of the trial of the twenty leaders. In the next forty-eight hours 461 people defied the law in Johannesburg, Port Elizabeth and Cape Town, and were arrested.

On the 26th the twenty leaders appeared at the Johannesburg Magistrate's Court on a charge of contravening the Suppression of Communism Act. A crowd of thousands assembled outside the courts, including eight hundred Indian schoolchildren from a nearby school. People sang and shouted outside the courtroom and were only quietened when Moroka, at the request of the court, came out and asked them to be silent and disperse: they did so immediately.

On the same day Indian and African women, including two cripples and an eighteen-year-old girl, defied the permit regulations at Germiston, followed by more batches of volunteers at Boksburg and Benoni. At New Brighton Station, Port Elizabeth, a crowd of 245 volunteers defied apartheid regulations and were arrested.

And so the campaign continued, and still goes on. In increasing numbers, and in spite of longer sentences and caning, Defiers continue to oppose the law in all parts of the Union. Where and when will it end?

(October 1952)

28

Among the photographic files in the Bailey Archives is one of ANC veteran Walter Sisulu. It mostly contains group shots, taken during the Defiance Campaign trial, or shots of him talking with Nelson Mandela later in the decade at the Treason Trial. His pictures seldom appear in *Drum* and when they do they're usually tightly cropped mug shots. One thing that's striking, though, is the strength in his face at forty, which over the years of incarceration has turned into dignity. And another detail: how frequently he is smiling to reveal the gap between his front teeth. He is smiling in the Defiance Campaign portrait and in most of the photographs *Drum* ran. Or he is speaking: a short dapper man in dark glasses with a thumb hooked into the pocket of his double-breasted jacket. The occasion is a Youth League meeting at Sophiatown in 1953. Only in a photograph taken in 1956 during the Treason Trial is he contemplative: his head resting lightly on the fingers of his left hand, mouth pursed, lines cut into his forehead like scars, and his eyes concerned, worried. It was this picture I took with me to Soweto. This picture I looked at in the car outside his house: what would the years and prison have done to the face and the man? I placed it upside-down on the passenger seat and climbed out into the humidity trapped below a close grey sky. Wind whipped dust and litter about the street, and that evening the thunderstorm which was threatening now would break with highveld magnificence. The road in front of Sisulu's house was roped off and children from the kindergarten opposite played within its protection. Over the roof an ANC flag, tacked to a makeshift pole, tore through the wind.

Despite the humidity, Sisulu wore a thick jersey, and in the small room where we talked burned a single-bar electric heater. He had been out of gaol three weeks by then. Three weeks of freedom after twenty-six years in prison serving a sentence that might only have ended with his death. I searched his face for the young image that lay outside in the car and found it there, in the eyes and the set of the mouth. Certainly he had aged, but the years in prison had not broken the strength in his face.

When a great deal had changed, and yet stayed the same, in the country beyond the Island; when ever more was being asked of Walter Sisulu: be leader, be hero, be figure of wonder, be man, be myth – was there a line, a continuous man from the photograph to the person before me?

'What do you mean?'

And then: 'Remember, I have been a leading official of the organisation since 1949. That hasn't changed. People haven't had to exaggerate my role because I was already in a senior position then. I was active. I was the first full-time official.'

Yes, you've been a political and public figure all your life . . .

'. . . Yes . . .'

. . . would you ever have had it any other way?

'No. No, I wouldn't have. It is something which has always been in my mind. In my early days, even when I was too young to know what politics was, I had this fighting capacity in me.'

All right, given that . . . but when you set foot on Robben Island, what thoughts were going through your mind then, when suddenly the whole being you had created couldn't work any more?

'No. Absolute confidence. I have never once lost confidence. I didn't know whether I would ever leave the Island, ever come out of gaol, but I knew that the start we had made was unstoppable . . .'

But not knowing whether you were going to come out of gaol . . .

'. . . Not knowing . . .'

. . . surely that is an unbearable thought, a terrible thought. You have only one life.

'Yes. No. You see . . . one life. But I think because of the confidence I had, even though I were to die in gaol that death in prison would be part of my duty. It was not anything to be regretted.'

And not to be bitter about?

'No. I . . . It was something I expected. It was what I had been, what I was made of.'

29

Walter Sisulu: There was a strong sense of optimism at the time of the Defiance Campaign, but I think there was optimism because the spirit, our morale, was high. Certainly, though, liberation wasn't next door. For us in Congress there was no feeling that the government could topple at any moment. There was no indication of that. But there was great optimism for the future, the distant future, for twenty years' time. At least that's my recollection. You know, when the spirit is high, the tendency of the people is to think of tomorrow. But I don't think that optimism was anything like what it was in the '80s.

The '50s opened with a number of strikes. The May Day strike and the shooting of fifty people, the 26 June strike. The struggle in the '50s was more a matter of preparing the people for days to come. That was the object of the Defiance Campaign itself. Its aim was not to overthrow the government but to stimulate a spirit of resistance – that was really the point.

We from the Youth League wanted to create our own image, we didn't want to take the course set by the ANC leadership in the '40s, we wanted to stimulate something for ourselves and to this extent there was a bit of a clash within the Party. We had a particular programme, but the old guard were holding things back, they seemed to be unable to move things quickly and that is what led to lack of support for the May Day strike. But when the authorities reacted the way they did, by shooting, we felt we had to express our anger quickly.

I was the secretary-general and I called an emergency

meeting without even consulting the leadership. I merely called the emergency meeting and said we had to consider what was to be done now, not tomorrow, not any other day. That meeting led to the strike of 26 June, a day of protest. It hadn't originally been part of our programme of action, but it fitted in with the concept. I was also feeling a bit guilty that some of us had not taken a positive line with the strike in May, so I was now very determined that this strike take place. I wasn't at one with all my colleagues on this. Nelson [Mandela] was the closest to me at the time, and although he disagreed personally, he supported me. So I forced things. I precipitated 26 June.

At that meeting were the national executives of the African National Congress, the Indian Congress, the Communist Party, the African People's Organisation. It was a historic meeting. Initially there wasn't agreement but at that conference we decided on the strike approach, not only to protest the shootings but also the Act which was going to suppress the Communist Party. Despite a lack of accord with the Communist Party and even hostility towards it, that meeting consolidated the leadership: we closed ranks, we would do something.

Moroka was merely a figurehead, so much of the organisation settled on me as the secretary-general. Fortunately there was a great friendship between Nelson and I no matter what differences we had. We were more or less like family. There was never any question of his not helping, of letting me down. So although Nelson didn't see eye to eye with me as I took these steps, he was the key man in the office and he was absolutely excellent in running it. It was a source of strength to be working closely with a man like that, who I liked very much. I was appearing all round the country organising the Party. At the time he was not yet an executive member. We had proposed him but he still needed to be accepted. Even so, I don't think there was anyone as vigorous in bringing about the situation on 26 June.

That closes the chapter of '51, yet it was really the

starting point. We now started preparing for the Defiance Campaign.

My arrest after the Defiance Campaign didn't come as a surprise. We were engaged in a campaign and expected harassment and arrest. It was, however, my first arrest, except for those under the pass laws. I think we were given a suspended sentence because Judge Rumpff was a remarkably intelligent man. He had initiative, he wasn't a stooge of the Nationalists, he did what he thought was law.

I'm sure the government was hoping we would be imprisoned, but I don't think the sentence caused them too much concern because they were now using other methods, bannings, to harass people. I, together with Nelson and others, was placed under a banning order for six months. When we had our conference in December 1953 I couldn't attend it openly so I would merely deliver my secretary's address and then get out. In terms of what was to come later that was minor harassment.

30

From an interview in *Drum* with newly elected ANC president, Albert Luthuli:

Do you consider that Communism is a serious menace to South Africa?

Albert Luthuli: No, I do not. The nature of our own movement at present is nationalist rather than Communist. There should be room for all political parties among us. At the moment we are only concerned with rescuing ourselves out of the mire, and we cannot yet say which direction we shall follow after that. For myself, I would wish for socialism, in the British sense – if I were in England I would vote for Attlee. But in Congress we have people of many different political beliefs – capitalists, socialists, and the rest . . .

Is there a danger of extreme nationalism in Congress?

There is no sign of it at present, and the fact that we have welcomed co-operation with other races shows that it is being avoided. We recognise the danger and are guarding against it.

Do you think there is a hope for South Africa?

Yes, I do. But a bitter conflict can only be avoided if those in power can adjust their thinking to accept the sharing of power with others. Otherwise there will be no real peace in this country.

I firmly believe that the different races can live together amicably; but first they must abandon selfishness and fear. Most of the difficulties that the Europeans are now facing are the result of selfishness. We are like members of a family, who cannot live together if they are selfish or jealous of one another.

Are Africans still prepared to accept leadership from the whites?

Since the 1936 Hertzog Bills the African people have lost faith in the good intentions of the whites to improve their conditions, and the Congress movement has become more and more a liberatory one. It is no longer possible for an African leader to appeal for better conditions only: what the people demand is political rights. By joining the Natives' Representative Council the African leaders gave the whites a last chance to prove their good faith, but they have not done so.

(May 1953)

Love and Hot Dames

31

'Hot dames'. *Drum* was big on hot dames. The first cover girl that showed more than just her pretty face adorned the issue of February 1952. She wore a bikini, lay on a beach with a hat on her backside and gave readers a wonderful smile. From then on it was a rare cover that wasn't graced by a similar beauty. Inside there would be more photographs: girls in swimming costumes, girls in summer dresses, girls posing in whatever inventive way the photographer could dream up. As Sylvester Stein, who introduced a demure centre-fold spread during his editorship, argues, 'Cover girls sold that magazine. It wasn't a matter of demeaning anybody. It wasn't a meat market. Men like to look at women and women want to see what they could be.'

During his editorship Tom Hopkinson defended it in similar terms. On a rare visit from Johannesburg to London he was cornered by a television reporter who pointed at a number of *Drum* 'dolly bird' covers and indignantly asked: 'Is that the best you can do for the African in South Africa? Putting glamour girls on the cover when there is so much in the country that ought to be criticised and attacked?' Hopkinson replied: 'But the readers like glamour girls. Their own glamour girls. D'you think that because they live under tough conditions they're different from you? Or want anything different from you?'

For the *Drum* writers the cover girls were an occasion for eulogy. Under the heading HOT BABE, Todd Matshikiza launched into this adulation:

> Her first name is Amaren. Her second is locked up in her bosom . . . just in case fans start writing endlessly.

Her story is as deep as her dark eyes. Her grandpa was an Arab craftsman, sailor, musician and trader who sold black people to white people for calico! He sold mostly tall black people, because the taller you were the more calico he got for you. She lives her own young life among a closed circle of unknown [undivulged] friends. But she's a breeze of an actress, and what a voice! She loves the Rand like liquorice and wants to write a big book . . . Amaren was dancing, singing and acting professionally at sixteen. She has written a number of 'jungle' songs based on themes from East Africa, which she remembers from childhood. She has sung some of these over the air. Very emotional, yes, and easily upset; but brimful of life when occasion arises. Amaren is an unabashed actress.

(December 1952)

Years later, Can Themba, infatuated with a pin-up girl called Dolly Rathebe who later became a blues singer, a film star and the most sought-after woman of the '50s, devoted three long articles to her. *The Life and Love of Dolly Rathebe*, the series was called. The last one ended like this:

It is true that she has had a tempestuous life. Men have floated in and out of it, some as gloomy spectres, some as rogues, some as vital, effervescent boilers. She has known and lived the violence and sordidness and stink of township life. She has drunk, even, and has found *in vino veritas*, the tot of truth. People have called her all sorts of names, those who thought they were entitled to cast the first stone. But somehow none of these things stuck. Out of the mire has emerged a queen, on the compost heap has grown a flower to perfume the township air. But there are moments when we feel her character doesn't matter. Exactly the moment when she slithers on to the stage and sings to us. Like the way she has taken life and given back to it with a vengeance, so has she taken her screeching audiences and given back to them with interest. That furry, breath-hot, sexy voice of hers has soothed away the cares of thousands of concert-goers countrywide.

If she has been a she-devil, that's because she's a helluva woman!

(February 1957)

Jurgen Schadeberg: There is no doubt about it, Dolly was a helluva woman. I think it was in about 1952 I took pictures of her. First we went to Zoo Lake and took some photographs there, then we drove out to the mine dumps because I needed a picture of her in a bikini against a background that looked like a beach. Now as you know, there's nobody out on the mine dumps, it's desolate. So anyway we drive out there and we're laughing and talking and at some stage this police van must have started tailing us. We got to the mine dump and Dolly changed in the car and then I took the pictures. Afterwards, when Dolly's getting dressed again, these policemen appear and want to know what's going on. They said we were lovers and that we'd broken the Immorality Act. We tried to explain what we were doing but they couldn't understand why a white man would be with a black woman unless it was for sex. So we had to go back to the police station with them. They questioned us for a long time, then they warned us that if they caught us breaking the Act we would be for it.

As Can Themba wrote in his series: '. . . it could not be proved that anything more than the camera's eye had peeked at Dolly's luscious figure'.

Nadine Gordimer: The nice thing about the men on *Drum* is that they really loved women. I think when men really love women the idea of women being objects doesn't arise. For them it was a real appreciation and joy to see a curvaceous woman in a bathing suit. The way they presented it, it wasn't offensive, it wasn't a *Playboy* spread. It wasn't sexual harassment, it was meant in the nicest way possible.

145

Juby Mayet: I can't remember there being any discrimination against me or any of the other women who worked on *Drum* or *Golden City Post*. I would say we got paid the same salary as the men. But then I don't think that at that stage I thought about money. It didn't hassle me and it doesn't hassle me to this day, unless I haven't got it. But I can't say there was any discrimination. The way I remember the magazine, it didn't matter who you were, it was your writing that counted. If you were good you got in. If you could do the job well then you got in.

Unfortunately they didn't only want me to write for them, they also wanted to make me a cover girl. Initially I refused. I wanted to be a serious reporter, I wanted to be a journalist. I didn't think being a cover girl went along with that. But they insisted and said that it wouldn't affect my career as a journalist. And I don't think it did. I can't remember how I actually came to agree; I probably said, OK let's have a bit of fun, and I did it in that spirit. I don't think being a cover girl made an object of me. Initially I thought it was trivialising me but I don't think it made a sex object of me, just as it didn't of any of the other girls.

If I thought about running 'dolly birds' on the cover, I probably thought that we needed a cover picture, that a pretty cover catches the eye, and I felt it was fair to have a girl on the front. The other girls thought it was great fun, they didn't think it was a meat market. A lot of them thought it was quite a prestigious thing to be on the cover. I mean *Drum* was *the* magazine.

There was quite a lot of resistance from my parents to me joining the magazine. Perhaps not so much from my mother because she'd known for a long time that I wanted to write. She thought I was weird because in that day and age for a middle-class Malay girl to want to write was just weird. Which is why she first insisted I get a teaching certificate. As for my daddy, well, I made it quite clear to him when I finished my teacher training that either I went to Nelspruit [a small town four hundred kilometres from Johannesburg] where I'd been offered a job, or I stay at home and work for *Drum*. They had already offered me a position by then. I think he felt it was the lesser of two evils for me to stay here because at least I would be at home. Even so he almost had a heart attack when he saw my picture on the cover, but I don't think there was any other reaction from my family.

Despite *Drum*'s 'love of women', readers didn't always share this view: '. . . I'm filled with gratitude for those readers who have written attacking women. As one who has known and associated with women on different occasions, here are my findings: 1. They are people with sugar-coated love. 2. They are always proud of their own qualities. 3. They are fickle and unable to respond immediately. 4. They shuttle off from one partner to another, ever seeking new thrills. – Joe Toboo, Koegasburg.' To which the editor responded in true *Drum* fashion: 'Let's get this straight! You're talking about those delicious things with the shapely curves!'

Although *Drum* was largely staffed by males – with the exception of Dolly of the *Heartbreak* column – and could see no harm in advertising the female form at every possible occasion, they were prepared to give women writers a chance. Juby Mayet is a case in point. On the strength of a letter she wrote as a teenager to *Drum*, a deputation made up of the editor of *Golden City Post* and Casey Motsisi tried to persuade her to join the magazine immediately she'd finished school. In those days women journalists were a rarity. Those who did have positions on newspapers would be white; for a 'middle-class Malay girl' to be solicited was unheard of. Yet in other small ways *Drum* had given women writers a forum.

Dinah Lefakane: Looking back now, as a publisher, it seems to me that *Drum* became the vehicle for women writers. At the time, women's writing was hardly a new phenomenon, there had been a few who had published works, but by and large they didn't have a vehicle and they didn't have the time. Yet somehow there is a lot that came out of the '50s as against the '60s, when it died down, and only came up again in the '70s with magazines like *Staffrider*.

Drum published the work of more than twenty female contributors. One or two even won prizes for their stories. So it seems that *Drum* was open to receiving fiction from women.

Yet there's a paradox here, because it was a male paper which looked at dolly birds, ran sexist letters from males and even in the broken-hearts columns placed women squarely in traditional roles. Maybe that's why it's understandable that most of the stories by women are along the lines of 'I broke their hearts'. But I think you have to look below the narrative, you have to look deeper, because I believe the statement they were making is: we, too, can take our place. We, too, can be strong. On the surface it's just a story, 'I broke their hearts', 'My husband was a flirt', but what was she actually saying? What was she reflecting of the time? I don't think it was an acceptance of norms, it was a critical look at the role the men were playing.

So the very act of writing becomes important. Sure the stories don't mean very much compared with the articles Henry Nxumalo was writing, but the very fact that they were written and appeared is significant. Also they were describing social situations which had to be talked about; in their own way they were reassessing the urban roles of men and women.

You must remember that in the township the black man has no kingdom, no area of authority. I've got my home where I'm boss, and that gives me strength. Where is the black man boss? He's not boss in the workplace, not boss at home. Where is his area of authority? It has been taken away from him so that he becomes weak and ineffectual. Even in the home he is merely a figurehead.

What I'm saying is that his moral strength is waning because he doesn't have an area of authority any more. At home the woman's the boss: the children defer to her first, and she may as a matter of courtesy tell their father. When children ask their father if they can go out he will reply, Yes, I think it's all right, but ask your mother. She will say, Yes, it's all right. I will tell your father. She makes the decisions. She decides what's to be bought, what cooked. He just fits in. He's a cog.

So we can now look at the *Drum* writers as examples of their time, and see why they were cut off from their families. Why they drank and destroyed themselves. And why it is now that the present journalists are kicking the drinking idea and saying you've got to take a part. There's something bigger than us.

A cautionary note: if one counts the names one finds more than twenty female contributors, but names do not necessarily tell all. Maybe knowing that many of the 'true-love confessions' were written by men using female pseudonyms will make the male attitudes seem even more ambiguous than they were before. And in many of these romances women are depicted as stereotypes: the helpless wife, the fickle lover, the alluring vamp.

32

MY HUSBAND WAS A FLIRT by Joan Mokwena

'Yes. Yes, you've said it often enough for me to remember it that these girls force themselves on you, and you have to satisfy them a little. Yes, you love me. But please. Please darling! Stop it. For my sake.'

'Now, now, Sweets! You know I'm in a tough spot!' he said with a smile, holding me in his arms. 'If I stop now, some woman might poison me. You know the old saying: "Hell hath no fury like a woman scorned". And I'm scared of hell in the first place.'

'But where is it all going to end?' I said tearfully, looking into his smiling and loving eyes. 'When our children begin understanding. What will they think of all the gossip they hear about your goings-on? You've got to stop it! And,' I continued, trying to smile bravely, 'I'm jealous you know. Sometimes you do it so realistically I begin to get doubts. One day I'm going to make a scene!'

'But Sweets! You know you're the only one I love – and will ever love. Remember the old days? They should have proved to you that I really and truly love you.'

Yes, I remember those old days. I remember the first time I met him. He was – and still is – so handsome. The salesman at the wholesalers I worked for had hired a new driver. I didn't see him during his first week. But I heard about him from the girls I worked with. They were all crazy about this 'tall, dark and handsome' guy.

They all agreed he looked like Cesar Romero, the film star. And he was jolly, they said. Very jolly. And Emma kept talking about the day he took her to lunch at a Boom Street restaurant – Mooloo's – in the car. He lived in Cape Location, Pretoria's coloured reserve. He wasn't coloured, though. And I wasn't, too, though I also lived there.

Then I met him. There was some trouble about the samples the salesman was taking out that day. Francis walked into the dispatch department, where I worked, in a rage. My back was turned as he walked up to the counter, grumbling that the slip said he had two more trunks of samples than he really had.

I turned round. With an 'Oh!' he stopped in mid-sentence. He looked at me for a few moments without speaking. I did better. I concealed my surprise, joy, embarrassment, or whatever it was, well. I looked at him enquiringly with my pencil poised. We fixed up the difficulty. Then he tried to date me for the lunch hour. He made elaborate explanations about leaving that afternoon for a week in the north, and that this date would keep him going for the week away from civilisation, and his being sorry that he'd never met me before . . . With a smile I told him I was meeting my boyfriend, Robert.

He was so disappointed I felt some pity for him. He was trying to make one for the following week when the car hooter called him away. I didn't see him again before he left. But I thought about him. I was surprised and rather excited when Emma told me the following day as we walked to work that he had asked her my name and where I lived.

During the following week, until he came back, I thought a lot about him. And I think my imagination ran away with my reason. Though he was unusually handsome and well dressed, my imagination made him grow into a still more handsome and pretty man.

I think it was then I fell in love with him. What made me think I had was that every time I met Robert I compared him with Francis. And Robert came off worse.

The following Tuesday morning I was walking towards town, intending to pick up Emma on the way as usual, when I heard a hooter behind me. I moved off the street. I still heard it. This time next to me. I looked round. It was Francis! My heart missed a few beats.

With a big smile he leaned over, opened the door, and invited me in. The next moment I was sitting by his side. He began telling me about the trip and why he had the car that morning. They had returned late the night before, and the boss had told him he could drive home.

When we came to Emma's corner I asked him to turn left so we could pick her up. Against all my reasons and pleas he refused, saying he wanted to see me alone. I couldn't go out to lunch with him as Robert was meeting me again. He didn't complain.

When I told Emma why I didn't pick her up, she wasn't very pleased. She had booked Cisco, as they called Francis, for herself; but she only complained about my having made her late for work. I liked her very much and didn't want Francis to spoil our friendship. So I poured as much oil as I could on the troubled waters. She was happier at two, for Cisco had taken her out to lunch.

I asked her why they called him Cisco.

'Well, his name ends with "cis"; and anyway, can't you see he looks and acts like Cesar Romero – the Cisco Kid? He's a great romantic!' she finished dreamily.

A flirt, I thought.

And I was justified. It wasn't necessary for him to come into my department, but he made it a point to do so every morning – if he hadn't walked me and Emma to work. Emma was a nice kid. When she saw that 'three was a crowd', she dodged these walks to the office. We saw a lot of each other, Francis and I. Robert was jealous and, after a quarrel, we split.

Fran took me to parties, bioscopes, dances; and we had a lot of fun. Going to the bioscope every Saturday afternoon became so regular he didn't ask me any more; and we had a permanent booking for our favourite seats at the Empire. Even if the picture was dull we went. We didn't see much of the pictures though, as time went on.

It was at the parties and dances that I knew I had lots of competition. He was very popular in Cape Location, and all the girls were after him. And he carried on a mild flirtation with all the pretty ones. At first these amused me; but as time went on I grew jealous.

We'd been going regular for a year or so when I had my first trouble. Lisa took Fran's flirtation seriously, and tried to push me out of the way at the parties. Fran was quick to notice this, and made it very obvious to her that he didn't like it. Neither did she like it. We almost had a fight. And this time it was more serious than the other quarrels I'd had with his flirts.

After this one he was most considerate. He said the only way to stop all this was to get married. And, with a song in my heart, we were married a month later.

But that wasn't the end. It seemed more like the beginning. Women take more pleasure trying to steal a husband than a boyfriend. Some even told me that I had the ring and they had the man! And flirting was already in his blood. I didn't tell him about all I was told by his more brassy girls; nor did I complain about what I heard from the gossip-mongers.

But I was troubled, especially when he was away for a week or so with the salesman. He always told me about the girls who tried to steal him in all the towns he went to; and again, when I was alone, my imagination would enlarge these to great proportions.

153

It became worse during the later months of my pregnancy. I couldn't go out with him and he got so many invitations he couldn't refuse them all.

Now our baby boy, just as handsome as him, was three years old. I was beginning to fear that soon he would begin to understand all that was going on. That is why I was telling him to stop at the beginning of the story.

He did try to stop, but it only seemed to increase the number of girls who ran after him. Some were so shameless they even came to our home to ask for him. One day Jean came. She was a pretty coloured girl with curling brown hair and soft, perfectly rounded curves. She was bewitching. And I'd heard a lot about her goings-on with my man. And funnily enough, he never said anything about her to me, as he did about the others. They'd all been a joke to him. But Jean didn't seem to be.

She sat down on the settee. She was most casual and proud in her manners. I had a foreboding of evil to come. She didn't waste much time with formalities.

'You love Cisco?' she asked me.

'If you mean my husband – yes, I do!' I answered, on the defensive. I felt very angry with her. And angry with myself for being so uneasy.

'He doesn't love you any more,' she said with a smile. 'He loves me. And you must divorce him!'

I felt weak and cold.

'Wha – what – what do you mean he doesn't love me? How do you know that? And why must I divorce him?' the questions fell off my tongue in a stream.

'You ask too many questions,' she answered with a pitying, but exultant, smile. 'First I know he doesn't love you because he told me so. He's like a child, you know, I almost had to put the words in his mouth. Surely you aren't surprised that he loves me and not you? Look at me.' She had her slim legs crossed, and

154

her dress showed too much thigh. I didn't think any man would be able to resist that. I was very cold and collected now. Listening most calmly. She didn't seem to like this. She'd hoped to make me angry.

'And secondly,' she continued with a glint in her eye, 'I'm carrying his baby! I've been to the doctor today. And that gives you your grounds for divorce! I seduced him! And he'll marry me when I tell him about it.'

She looked at my son – I don't know why I didn't think of him as our son any more. 'I'll give him a prettier boy than that!'

It was then that he walked in through the kitchen door. He was furious.

'Hello, darling,' she said, standing up . . . She moved close up to him: 'I was just telling your wife . . .'

'Enough of that!' he almost shouted, pushing her violently away. 'I've had enough of that and heard enough of what you were saying to my wife! If it is my child you are carrying, I'll pay whatever the law demands; but I won't marry you or anybody else. I'm not leaving Jo . . . if she'll have me.' His voice softened with this last bit. He looked at me with pleading eyes. He walked up to me, knelt down next to my chair . . . and I fell into his arms to hide those pleading sad eyes. We only heard the door bang shut.

Yes, I had forgiven him. I wouldn't even listen to his story. His flirting days were all over, he said. And I believed him. She was right. He had been a baby.

That wasn't the end though. A week later our son was taken to hospital suffering from poisoned food.

Yes. Hell hath no fury like a woman scorned.

(May 1953)

Nothing Worth Believing In

33

Fiction played a big part in the early *Drum*. In June 1951 an editorial announced the magazine's intention of discovering and encouraging writers, and from then on the stories flooded in. Certainly in the first five or six years *Drum* stood by this declaration and it is likely many short-story writers would never have surfaced, let alone developed, without it. The range of stories was eclectic, from downright slushy love dramas with no literary merit to work by such people as Peter Abrahams, Richard Rive and Es'kia Mphahlele who were later to acquire international reputations for their novels and short stories – although Mphahlele felt he made it in spite of, rather than because of, *Drum*.

Nevertheless, township life came alive in fiction: *tsotsis*, gangsters, small-time crooks, colour prejudice, shebeen life, non-racialism, the hard, funny grind of daily living where the best of human values – love and trust – still survived flourished alongside 'real' stories on the same topics. In fact where non-fiction ended and fiction began seemed often to be of small concern to the writer/journalists of *Drum*. All that mattered was the urban world they inhabited.

'People like Can and Todd and Lewis Nkosi were essentially products of Johannesburg urbanism,' says Nadine Gordimer. 'In my experience of other parts of Africa, with the possible exception of Lagos, there is nothing to compare with this kind of African, these urbane men and women. What is amazing is that they flourished in those brief ten years, mostly in one place – Sophiatown – and that it has never happened again. A lot of credit has to go to Sampson for this writing. He saw the kind of life in the townships wasn't being written about and he was concerned to encourage black writers to capture that experience. Some of his writers showed a wonderful command of English. Today young writers are struggling to use a language that they know very poorly: they haven't got the vocabulary, they haven't got a sense of structure, they're battling to express themselves. There is supposed to be something called a '*Drum* style'; but if you look at Can's work, for instance, you'll see he is well read, he quotes very naturally. These days young black writers don't understand the quotations in Can Themba's work, they don't know where they come from.

'Nor did the *Drum* writers suffer from any inhibitions. For instance they would write about whites. There are a lot of whites in their stories and books dealt with in a humorous, ironic way, sometimes in a bitter way but there they are. Humour was a big thing then; it's gone now except in black theatre. To paraphrase Brecht, people feel – writers feel – to laugh is treason. In general the trouble is that aspiring writers don't read fiction. They want to write it but they think they can do that without reading. Just look at the books people are reading in the Cosaw [Congress of South African Writers] library [ironically named the Can Themba library]. You'll see they're struggling through Lukacs, never mind Karl Marx, in fact any political tract. Then they want to write stories. Of course they also watch television so they come up with standard bathetic plots and don't reflect their own lives as the *Drum* writers did.'

Those lives found frequent expression in short stories, yet none of the writers ever turned to the novel, for reasons they have been quick to advance.

Es'kia Mphahlele: It is impossible for a writer who lives in oppression to organise his whole personality into creating a novel.

Bloke Modisane: The short story is used as a short cut [to get] some things off one's chest in quick time . . . Everything is always in a state of such violent change in human relationships – a man is not sure where he will be next month or next week or even for that matter next day – he wants to put all down in a short story. The situation is so vast and the best way to communicate is to pin-point the incidents.

Lewis Nkosi: Johannesburg . . . was also dense, rhythmic: it was swaggering and wasteful, totally without an inner life. People loved quickly, they lived fitfully; so profligate were they with emotion, so wasteful with their vitality, that it was very often difficult for them to pause and reflect on the passing scene. This I think partly explains why so many black South African writers have concentrated on the jour-nalistic prose, more often on the short story but rarely on the long reflective novel. It is not so much the intense suffering (though this helped a great deal) which makes it impossible for black writers to produce long and complex works of literary genius as it is the very absorbing, violent and immediate nature of experience which impinges upon individual life. Unless literature is assumed to be important in itself, for its own sake, unless it is assumed to be its own justification, there was no reason whatever why anyone in our generation should have wanted to write. It seems to me that literature begins where life fails. In Johannesburg there was much too much of this direct experience to be had: there was no privacy in which to reflect; people called on you early in the morning bringing bottles or asking you out to a shebeen; police raided you at night for permits and identity documents; parties were too numerous and sprang up too arbitrarily in the middle of some important work; and if one wasn't sure which gaol one was going to be in on the morrow, or even whether one was going to be alive or cut down by a police bullet or perhaps by the knife of a thug, there was no reason not to grab at this life, at this gift, eagerly, without waiting even for the mediating intervention of art and literature.

'I think if the *Drum* writers had stayed there would have been more novels, more fiction,' says Nadine Gordimer. 'But perhaps we have to look at their autobiographical works [Todd Matshikiza's *Chocolates For My Wife*, Bloke Modisane's *Blame Me On History*] as their first novels. Certainly when they went into exile it seemed to disorientate them. Only two writers I know kept on writing, [the poet] Dennis Brutus and Zeke [Mphahlele]. Almost all the others dried up. Maybe it's because they had to adjust to living such different lives. In a way Lewis Nkosi is an exception because somehow there was a resurrection a few years ago [with the publication of the novel *Mating Birds* in 1986]. But for those years in between, all he did was keep that job at the Africa Service of the BBC, which was a double-edged affair because, while it provided bread and butter, it also somehow was just enough to keep him going so that he wasn't pushed into writing. It was stultifying in a sense.'

But in the '50s the words poured out. In 1952 *Drum* ran its first short-story competition. The response was overwhelming. One thousand stories came in. Peter Abrahams was one of the judges. Of the winning entry he said: 'I should say that we have in this story notice of unusual literary promise and I can think of nothing more encouraging than that such promise should be rewarded with the *Drum* prize.' The author was a twenty-eight-year-old bachelor who initially called himself D. Can Themba.

Henry Nxumalo went off to Sophiatown to give him his £50 award:

> At the top of a noisy street in Sophiatown, sitting reading on the stoep of his home, we found *Drum*'s winning author Dorsay Can Themba. He took us into his tiny bed-sitting room which he shares with an old friend. Books of poetry, short stories, reference books

and half-typed-over sheets of paper were piled high on a table at the end of his bed.

When his work as a schoolteacher is over for the day, Themba seeks the peace of his room, where he can work. But peace rarely comes until after midnight.

'I must wait until they're all asleep,' Themba remarked patiently. 'I don't start writing until after twelve sometimes, and then my room-mate snores. If I'm to get anything done, I must work on until three and often four in the morning. It's the best time to work here. But it's tiring on the eyes working by lamplight.'

One of a family of four, his mother and father had a hard struggle finding the money to educate them all.

'But I was lucky,' he went on. 'I was the first boy to be awarded the Mendi Scholarship to Fort Hare [now a university]. It has been a wonderful help.'

After college he took a job in the Western Native Bantu School, where he has been ever since, teaching English and in his spare time reading, writing and studying for a degree in Political Philosophy. Almost his only relaxation from work is walking.

'I walk up and down the streets of Sophiatown for hours, forming stories in the back of my mind. Then when I come to plan them – to write them down – they are in one piece ready to be written. But don't think that I'm a believer in writing by inspiration only – no, it's just plain hard work all the way. As for hobbies, I have none other than my reading and writing. I don't drink, but smoke heavily, and of course . . .' he looked shy, smiling: 'I like women, although I'm still a bachelor. But all my love affairs until now have been tragic ones. But at last I'm lucky, my girlfriend – she's a twenty-two-year-old nurse – is one of the prettiest girls on the Reef. At least I think so!'

And what of his future in writing? It was only a year ago that he first took up short-story writing. 'Mob

Passion', the winning *Drum* story, was Themba's first attempt at a short story.

'And now,' he said, 'winning the *Drum* contest, I feel inspired to go on writing and writing until one day, perhaps I'll be a really famous author.'

(March 1953)

34

MOB PASSION by Can Themba

There was a thick crowd on Platform 2, rushing for the 'all stations' Randfontein train. Men, women and children were pushing madly to board the train. They were heaving and pressing, elbows in faces, bundles bursting, weak ones kneaded. Even at the opposite side people were balancing precariously to escape being shoved off the platform. Somewhere an outraged dignity was shrieking stridently, vilely cursing someone's parentage. Fuller and fuller the carriages became. With a jerk the electric train moved out of the station.

'Whew!' blew Linga Sakwe. He gathered his few parcels upon his lap, pressing his elbows to his side pockets. He did not really have any valuables in these pockets; only long habit was working instinctively now.

Linga was a tall, slender fellow, more man than boy. He was not particularly handsome, but he had those tense eyes of the young student who was ever innerly protesting against some wrong or other. In fact at the moment he was not a student at all. He was working for a firm of lawyers in Market Street. He hoped to save enough money in a year or two to return to university to complete an arts degree which he had been forced by 'circumstances' to abandon.

People were still heaving about in the train, but Linga was not annoyed. He knew that by Langlaagte, or perhaps Westbury, most of these folk would be gone and he would be able to breathe again. At Braamfontein many

162

people alighted: but he was not thinking of his discomfort any more. He was thinking of Mapula now. She had promised that she would be in time for this train. That depended, of course, on whether she succeeded to persuade the staff nurse in charge of the ward in which she worked to let her off a few minutes before time.

The train slowed down: Industria. Linga anxiously looked outside. Sure enough, there she was! He gave a wolf-whistle, as if he was admiring some girl he did not know. She hurried to his carriage, stepped in and sat beside him. They did not seem to know each other from Adam. An old man nearby was giving a lively narration in the grimmest terms of the murders committed in Newclare.

At Westbury the atmosphere was tense. Everybody crowded at the windows to see. Everywhere there were white policemen, heavily armed. The situation was 'under control', but everyone knew that in the soul of almost every being in this area raved a seething madness, wild and passionate, with the causes lying deep. No cursory measures can remedy; no superficial explanation can illuminate. These jovial faces that can change into masks of blood-lust and destruction with no warning, on the smallest provocation! There is a vicious technique faithfully applied in these riots. Each morning these people quietly rise, and with a business-like manner hurry to their work. Each evening they return to a devil's party, uncontrollably drawn into hideous orgies. Sometimes the violence would subside for weeks or months and then suddenly would flare up at some unexpected spot, on some unexpected pretext.

At Newclare, too, from the train all seemed quiet. But Linga and Mapula knew the deceptive quiet meant the same even here. The train skimmed on, emptier. Only when they had passed Maraisburg did these two venture to speak to each other. Linga was Xhosa and Mapula Sotho. A Letebele and a Russian! They had to be very careful. Love in its mysterious, often ill-starred ways had flung them together.

Linga spoke first:

'Sure you saw no one who might know you?' he asked softly.

'Eh-eh,' she replied.

She fidgeted uneasily with the strap of her handbag. His hand went out and closed over her fingers. They turned simultaneously to look at each other.

A sympathetic understanding came into Linga's eyes. He smiled.

'Rather tense, isn't it?' he said.

She looked past him through the window.

'Witpoortje!' she exclaimed. 'Come let's go.'

They rose and went to the door. The train stopped and they went out. Together they walked to a bridge, went over the line and out by a little gate. For some two hundred yards they walked over flat, stubbly ground. Then they went down a mountain cleft at the bottom of which ran a streamlet. They found a shady spot and sat down on the green grass. Then suddenly they fled into each other's arms like frightened children. The time-old ritual, ancient almost as the hills, always novel as the ever changing skies. Long they clung to each other, long and silent. Only the little stream gurgled its nonsense; these two daring hearts were lost in each other. The world, too – good, bad or indifferent – was forgotten in the glorious flux of their souls' meeting and mingling.

At last Mapula spoke – half cried: 'Oh Linga! I'm afraid.'

'"Here where the world is quiet"?' he quoted, with infinite softness. 'No, dear, nothing can reach and harm us here.' Then with a sigh: 'Still, the cruellest thing they do is to drive two young people like guilty things to sneak off only to see each other. What is wrong with our people, Mapula?'

She did not answer. He lay musing for a long time. She could see that he was slowly getting angry. Sometimes she wished she could understand the strange indignations of his spirit and the great arguments by which he explained life. Most times she only yearned for his love.

'They do not see! They do not see!' he continued vehemently. 'They butcher one another, and they seem to like it. Where there should be brotherhood and love, there are bitter animosities. Where there should be co-operation in common adversity, there are barriers of hostility, steeling a brother's heart against a brother's misery. Sometimes, 'Pule, I understand it. We have had so many dishonest leaders, and we have so often had our true leaders left in the lurch by weak-kneed colleagues and lukewarm followers, that no one wishes to stick his neck out too far. Where is the courage to weld these suicidal factions into a nation? The trouble is, very few of us have a vision comprehensive enough of our destiny! I believe God has a few of us to whom he whispers in the ear! Our true history is before us, for we yet have to build, to create, to achieve. Our very oppression is the flower of opportunity. If not for history's grand finale, why then does God hold us back? Hell! And here we are, feuding in God's dressing room even before the curtain rises. Oh!' He covered his face and fell into her lap unable to say any more.

Instinctively, Mapula fingered his hair. '*In God's dressing room.*' she thought. What does it mean? But his anguish stabbed at her heart. Trying to forget herself she only sought within her a tenderness to quell the bitter wretchedness she had heard in his voice.

'Linga, no! Let me show you something else – something that I understand. It is no more so long before you and I can marry. I dream about the home that we are going to have. I . . . I want that home, Linga. You

165

taught me that woman's greatest contribution to civilisation so far has been to furnish homes where great men
and great ideas have developed. Moreover, there's our
problem. Let us rather think of ways of handling my
father. No, no; not now. Let us think now of now.'

Thabo was running faster now that he was nearing
home. His mind was in a whirl; but he knew that he
had to tell his father. The lopsided gate was in the far
corner, so he smartly leaped over the fence where it
was slack. He stopped abruptly at the door. He always
did when there were people. But now, he soon realised,
these people were his two uncles – Uncle Alpheus and
Uncle Frans. Somehow great news always brings a
glory of prestige on the head of the bringer. Thabo felt
himself almost a hero now, for these two men were die-
hard stalwarts in the Russian cause. Uncle Alpheus was
a romantic firebrand. Uncle Frans was a scheming
character of the power-behind-the-throne variety. They
were complementary to each other: together, a formi-
dable team.

  'Father, where is he?' hissed Thabo, breathing hard.
The excitement in his voice aroused everyone.

  'Holy Shepherd! What's the matter, boy?' cried Uncle
Alpheus.

  'Mapula. Mapula. She loves a Letebele.'

  'What!' exploded Uncle Alpheus. 'Where is she?'
Then, more calmly: 'Come'n, boy. Tell us everything
more quietly; your father is out there?'

  'J-J-Jonas t-t-tells me – J-Jonas is a boy who works
with me – Jonas tells me that Mapula loves with a
Letebele. They always meet at the hospital; but never in
the sitting room. He hopes to marry her.'

  'Never!' barked Alpheus. Just then the door burst
open. A party of men carried in the limp form of
Thabo's father. He was unconscious, and blood
streamed all over his face. Beyond them, just outside

the door, a crowd had gathered. Everyone was at once asking what had happened. As the news spread, ugly moods swept the crowd. Ra-Thabo was carried into the bedroom and tended by the women. Alpheus and Frans returned to the fore room and conferred.

'What now?' Alpheus asked Frans.

'Of course, we must revenge. You will talk to the people – the women. Talk fire into them. Connect it with the Mapula business – that'll warm them. Suggest drugs – a Letebele must use drugs, mustn't he? I'll be in the house. Just when they begin to get excited I'll arrange to carry Ra-Thabo out – to the hospital, you know. See if we can't get them bad!' He smiled cheerlessly.

Outside, the crowd – mostly women – was thickening. Even in the streets they could be seen coming along in groups, blanketed men and women. From the house Thabo and his little sister, Martha, joined the crowd. It was obvious that their uncles were going to do something about it.

Alpheus stepped on to the little mud wall. He raised his left hand and the blanket over it rose with it. That movement was most dramatic. In a few moments the crowd moved closer to him and became silent. Then he began to speak. He began in a matter-of-fact voice, giving the bare fact that Ra-Thabo, their leader, had been hurt. Warming gradually, he discussed the virtues of this man. Then he went on to tell of how this man had actually been hurt. Not confused fighting nor cowardly brutalities rose in the mind as this man spoke, but a glorious picture of crusaders charging on in a holy cause behind their lion-hearted leader. Oh, what a clash was there! The Matabele were pushed beyond Westbury Station. There the heroes met a rested, reinforced enemy. For a moment all that could be seen was the head of Ra-Thabo going down among them. The clang of battle could be heard; the furious charge could be seen, in the words of this man who was not there. The Basothos fought desperately and won so much ground that their all-but-lost leader could be rescued and carried back home. And what finds he there? Alpheus's voice went down, softer and heavier, touching strings of pathos, rousing tragic emotions which the hearts present had never before experienced. There was an automatic movement in the crowd as everybody strained forward to hear. In awful, horror-filled whispers he told of Ra-Thabo's daughter giving herself to a Letebele. 'The thing is not possible!' he hissed. 'It would not have happened if the maid had not been bewitched with drugs. Are they going to brook it?' he cracked. 'No!' all the throats roared. 'Are they ready for vengeance?' 'Now!' thundered the mob. Someone in the crowd shouted 'Mule!' Then the women took up their famous war-cry, chilling to a stranger, but driving the last doubting spirit there to frenzy and fury.

'Ee!-le!-le!-le!-le!-le! Eu! Eu! Eu!'

Now they were prancing and swaying in uninterpretable rhythms. A possessed bard in their midst was chattering the praises of the dead, the living and the unborn, his words clattering like the drumsticks of a fiend.

'Let us go past Maraisburg and attack them from the rear!' yelled Alpheus over the din.

At that moment the door of the house went open. The mob, which had been on the point of dashing out, recoiled. The sight they saw stunned them. Frans and two other men were carrying out Ra-Thabo, besmeared with blood. Thabo saw Uncle Alpheus leaping with trailing blanket and yelling, 'To Maraisburg!' Again he leaped over the fence into the street. The mob followed hard on his heels.

As the last blanket swept round the corner, Frans turned back to the injured man. His two helpers had also been drawn in by the irresistible suction of mob feeling. With a smile, he said to the unhearing Ra-Thabo: 'I'll have to get a taxi to take you to hospital, brother.' Then he carried him back into the house.

Late in the afternoon the train from Randfontein suddenly stopped at Maraisburg. Everybody was surprised. Something must be wrong. This train never stops at Maraisburg. Then suddenly;

'All change! All change!' And more brusquely: 'Come'n puma! Puma!'

Linga and Mapula hurried out. News had arrived that trouble had started again at Newclare, more seriously than usual. All trains from Randfontein were being stopped here and sent back.

Shrugging his shoulders, Linga drew Mapula away, and arm-in-arm they strolled along the platform out by the little gate, into some suburban area. For a time they walked on in silence. Then Mapula spoke.

'I hope I'll get back in time,' she said.

'Let's walk faster, then. We might get a lift outside the suburb.'

They walked into the open country. Linga knew that if he could only find a certain golf course somewhere around here, he would know where the road was. Meanwhile, they had to stumble on over rough country and Mapula's cork-heel shoes were tormenting her toes. She limped on as stoically as she could. Linga did not notice her suffering, as he was looking out for familiar landmarks. Those trees looked suspiciously like the golf course to him.

When they reached the trees Mapula said: 'Linga, let us rest here; my toes are suffering.'

'All right,' he replied. 'But I must look for the road. Let's look for a cool place where you may rest, while I search for the golf course.'

'Mm.'

He led her amongst the trees. She sat down and

169

pulled off her shoes. When he thought he saw a shadow of distress flit across her brow, he bent down, took her hand, pressed it, and then muttered, 'Back in a moment, sweet.' He rose slowly, looked at her indecisively, then turned away slowly and walked off.

He did not search far before he noticed a torn and faded flag. The hole was nearby. Suddenly he emerged from the cluster of trees, and came upon the road. But his attention was caught by a horde of Russians pursuing a woman who came flying towards Linga. Should he chance it? he wondered. He spoke fluent Sesotho and believed he could pass as a Mosotho, possibly as a Russian. He quickly drew a white handkerchief from his trouser pocket and tied it round his head. This made him, he knew, an active supporter of the Russian cause. Skirts flying, the woman sped past him. Facing the mob, he shouted:

'Helele!'

All its wrath spent, the mob crowded round out of sheer curiosity. Some were even in a jocular mood now, one playing lustily on a concertina. But here and there Linga could see deadly weapons, snatched up in their hasty exodus from Newclare. He spoke to them in fluent Sesotho, taking his idiom from Teya-teyaneng. He asked if that was the road to Newclare; he said that he worked in Roodepoort, but was going to Newclare because his uncle there wanted more manpower in the house. Won't they please tell him where this road is?

'Che! It is no Letebele this; this is a child of at home,' remarked Alpheus.

'Kgele! You speak it, man,' said a burly fellow. Then everyone directed Linga how to get to Newclare.

As fate would have it, just then Mapula came running, shoes in hand and stockings twisted round her neck.

'Linga! Linga, darling mine. What are they doing to you?' she screamed, as she forced her way through the crowd. Linga stiffened. When she came to him she flung her arm around him and clung to him with all her strength, crying all the time. Then she saw her uncle, stupefied like the rest of them standing there. She fled to him and begged him to save her lover. He pushed her aside and walked up to Linga. He stood before him, arms akimbo.

'Ehe! So you are a Letebele after all. You lie so sleekly that I can understand why my daughter thinks she loves you.' Then he swung round, his blanket trailing in an arc. 'Friends, we need go no further. This is the dog that bewitched my brother's child. Let's waste no time with him. Tear him to pieces!' The mob rushed upon Linga: 'Mmate! Mmate!'

'Uncle! Uncle!' cried Mapula. But even as she cried she knew that nothing could be done. She had courted the contempt of her people, and she understood now that all her entreaties were falling upon deaf ears. Whether from convenience or superstition – it did not matter which – she was considered a victim of the Letebele's root-craft.

From the scuffling mob suddenly flew an axe, which fell at her feet. In a flash she knew her fate. Love, frustrated beyond bearing, bent her mind to the horrible deed.

Mapula acted. Quickly she picked up the axe whilst the mob was withdrawing from the prey, several of them bespattered with blood. With the axe in her hand, Mapula pressed through them until she reached the inner, sparser group. She saw Alpheus spitting upon Linga's battered body. He turned with a guttural cackle – 'He-he-he! He-he-he!' – into the descending axe. It sank into his neck and down he went. She stepped on his chest and pulled out the axe. The blood gushed out all over her face and clothing. That evil-looking countenance she gradually turned to the stunned crowd, half lifting the axe and moving slowly but menacingly towards the largest group. They retreated – 170 men and women retreated before this Devil-possessed woman with the ghastly appearance. But then she saw the mangled body of the man she loved and her nerve snapped. The axe slipped from her hand and she dropped on Linga's body, crying piteously:

'Jo-o! Jo-o! Jo-na-jo! Jo-na-jo!'

Someone came and lifted her up. Someone else was dragging Alpheus's bleeding corpse by the collar so that his shoes sprang out one after the other.

The crowd was going back now. All the bravado gone, they were quiet and sulky. Only the agonised wailing of Mapula. Every breast was quelled by a sense of something deeply wrong, a sense of outrage. The tumult in every heart, feeling individually now, was a human protest insistently seeking expression, and then that persistent wail of the anguished girl, torturing the innermost core of even the rudest conscience there. The men felt themselves before God; the women heard the denunciations of thwarted love. Within they were all crying bitterly: 'Jo-o! Jo-o! Jo-nana-jo!'

(April 1953)

35

The first photograph of Can Themba used by *Drum* was the one announcing his winning story. It's a highly romantic picture, almost a stock writer's picture, with books piled up on the desk, some open as if for reference, sheets of manuscript topping the pile, an ashtray with dog ends, a paraffin lamp and the writer: young, bespectacled, in his shirt-sleeves with his tie undone, fingers poised above the typewriter keys, a blank sheet of paper turned round the platen. It's a serious photograph to back Themba's contention that writing is 'sheer hard work'. Not too many serious photographs of Themba follow it.

After that there are photographs of Can Themba clowning with blues singer and *Drum* cover girl Dolly Rathebe; Themba with his arm round another ravishing beauty, Dotty Tiyo; Themba with his back to the camera chatting up two girls and a notice pinned to his jacket which reads: NOT NOW THE MISSUS IS AROUND PHONE 351240; Themba fooling with a jazzman's drums; Themba holding forth in a shebeen; Themba in floral shirt and straw hat looking quizzical; and then another serious portrait: Themba, his tie knotted, his head in his hands, his mouth slightly distorted, the skin pulled tight across his chin from the pressure of his hands. But it's the eyes that catch you: they're staring into such a deep distance and there's so much sadness in them.

The thing about Themba is that he had talent and he also had the learning and the reading. Yet he squandered it. He turned his hand to a journalism which sparkled but was as thin as tissue paper.

This sort of thing:

The last bus to Sophiatown. About the eleven o'clock before midnight. Peter was waiting for the fish-tin to rattle off.

Then she came in.

'Hello, beautiful! Come sit with me,' someone called. Then a chorus of amateur wolves called, inviting her to come and sit with them. And Peter noticed how she glanced round uneasily. She was looking for a safe seat near a gentleman. But he did not feel gallant. In Sophiatown you don't get gallant.

Then he saw a thug coming up from the back to take her hand. Suddenly she saw Peter and made up her mind.

'Hello, Jerry!' she exclaimed, and went to sit by his side. Peter did not know her from Adam and Eve, and he felt sick. The thug hesitated a moment. Then he, too, decided. He was going to get tough. But she addressed herself to Peter again.

'When did you get out of gaol for murder, Jerry darling?' she cooed.

'Last week,' Peter muttered unhappily.

The thug shuffled past to the door discreetly. Peter did not know whether his reputation had risen or fallen. But some girls do think fast, don't they?

(March 1958)

Admittedly Themba didn't only stick with the light-hearted column; he wrote some searing reports of gangster terror, illegal brews that were killing the unwary in the cut-throat shebeens, and he was the grim witness of Sophiatown's destruction. But it's almost as if he deliberately misused and neglected his real abilities, in fact with an ironic malice made sure he'd never produce anything of worth. Perhaps it was *Drum*'s fault. Perhaps the crime-sex-sport cycle got to him. Perhaps the 'island' made him think he was doing great things. Perhaps, perhaps, perhaps.

But it's too easy to blame *Drum*. There are all kinds of

other factors, social and personal. He wallowed in township life: the shebeens, the shebeen queens, the good-time girls, the singers, the gangsters. He saw in Sophiatown a celebration of life, a magnificent defiance against the forces of oppression, a vitality, a demand for existence which triumphed over the degrading slum.

'It is true,' wrote Lewis Nkosi in an obituary, 'that Can Themba's romanticism drove him in the end to admire more and more the ingenious methods of that survival – the illicit shebeens and illicit traffic, the lawlessness, the everyday street drama in which violence was enacted as a supreme test that one was willing to gamble one's life away for one moment of truth. Such moments of intensity and extreme self-awareness in the face of danger are what the white suburb will never know in its dull bourgeois regularity. In this respect he echoed Ernest Hemingway's romanticism of violence.'

Romanticism, irony, booze. They were Themba's way of life. He called his home in Sophiatown the House of Truth and made everyone welcome, provided they didn't tell lies under his roof. Here he formed a court of friends, each with his own title: the Kabaka, P-Boy, the Chief and himself, Can von Themba.

'Can,' remembers Schadeberg, 'had that rare ability of throwing an idea into the air to look at it from all sides, fascinated by its unexpected possibilities. Not for him the crude certainty of the political fanatic. He was far too intrigued by the human comedy to drop his position of amused observer, far too civilised, too kind, too sceptical and detached.'

When he was not discoursing in the House of Truth, Themba could be found at the Back o' the Moon, one of his favourite Sophiatown shebeens. Here, drinking illegal beer, smoking endless cigarettes, he would talk on into the night, pausing only to listen to Miriam Makeba singing:

'Back o' the Moon is where the folks let go
Friday night at the Back o' the Moon.'

Then in the maudlin small hours a bleary-eyed, slur-voiced Themba would have been brought to the black depths of his philosophy: 'There is absolutely nothing worth believing in. Absolutely nothing. Human nature stinks.'

Romanticism, irony, booze. Those were the three things Themba used to cope with himself, with the townships, whites, *Drum* and South Africa. In the end they also killed him.

Themba was taken on by Bailey right after he won the short-story competition because 'he seemed such a likely chap'. At the time Themba claimed not to be drinking. If that's so he must have started fairly soon after he joined the magazine, because it seems to have been part and parcel of the job.

So much so that Jurgen Schadeberg recollects that Themba and others used to disappear regularly and return with bottles of Coke which they'd sip through straws.

'Then suddenly, they were all giggling and shiny-eyed. Of course what was happening was they'd been up to the shebeen on the roof of our Troye Street office to fill up their bottles with brandy and Coke. And now they were getting pissed while they worked. Definitely Henry, Can and Casey were boozing like this.

'There was a form of alcoholic decay in Can which I thought was very sad, because he was bright, an intellectual. He was obviously well read and loved philosophising. Quite brilliant and also a good writer. It's really tragic when you think that when we presented Can with his short-story prize he was living in a very respectable-looking place. He was a teacher, there were books on the wall. About five or six years later, by 1958 at any rate, he looked terrible: he was puffed up with drink, he slept in a room on a mattress on the floor with dirty blankets and other people sleeping all over the place, empty bottles everywhere.'

There seems to have been an inevitability about Themba's life, that he had a hard destiny which he couldn't escape. Nadine Gordimer doesn't use the word 'fatalism', but it's implicit in her opinions and it is difficult to imagine his life going any other way. 'I think what happened to Can would have happened no matter where he'd been living. Writing is a very hazardous profession and none of us is well balanced because otherwise we wouldn't be writing. Some of us fall by the wayside, many writers drink themselves to death.

'I don't think you can argue that Can lived the life he did because of the frustrations here. He was never involved politically, he was never harassed politically, but because he was the personality he was he suffered terribly from the ordinary daily limitations that other blacks took for granted. So I think that he was almost a natural for what happened. Certainly I don't think that *Drum* is to blame because he didn't become a great writer. I think that newspaper or magazine journalism can be dangerous for a writer, because the style can be inhibiting. For instance, someone like Zeke couldn't take it at all, but he had an alternative because he was qualified for academic life. Yet imagine Can as a white American – he would perhaps have led much the same kind of life. In the end he didn't have the self-discipline necessary to write. In his last years the only other thing he could do was teach, but he must have died of boredom in that little backwater in Swaziland because he was such a city person.'

Anthony Sampson has an image of Themba chewing a pin, shifting it around in his mouth while he considered his next ironic statement. 'He was one of the most brilliant of the early *Drum* writers. A magnetic personality who lived off his irony, his cynical posture, and was always ready to construct an elaborate new theory about women or politics. He once said, with his usual sarcasm, that if he'd gone in for politics he'd have been ruthless and cunning. When asked why he didn't, he'd reply that he had sold out for a salary.'

Sylvester Stein remembers Themba as a 'very powerful presence, an existentialist, he was my hero. During my time

he was an assistant editor. He was a leader but unfortunately there was the drink, possibly a way of coping with a
frustrated future through being a black man and banging
your head constantly with no result. In my ignorance, I saw
him as becoming one of the leaders of Africa. I think he
could have become a close friend. He had charisma, a good
brain, a good education, but I didn't think he was such an
artist.

'Can was a very difficult man to employ. He wouldn't
turn up, he would have days off. So what do you do when
the number two isn't there? How do you manage and how
do you explain it away? Can would go on a drunken spree
and that would be it for days.'

'I know Can once went off to Pretoria at the time when he
was acting editor to do a story and he didn't come back for
two weeks,' says Schadeberg. 'Even Henry disappeared like
this occasionally. Eventually they'd come back and say, Hi,
I had problems. I remember looking for Can all over Sophiatown once after he'd been missing for a couple of days.'

Sampson and Stein understood and tolerated Themba's
erratic behaviour, but when Tom Hopkinson became editor
he was outraged by what he saw as such gross irresponsibil-
ity. Hopkinson tells of a number of occasions when Themba
was either too drunk to go to work, or after a long Friday's
boozing session would crawl back to the offices and pass
out. Sometime on the weekend he would wake up, find
himself locked in, and phone his editor for a lift home. He
was never refused. But what did rouse Hopkinson's ire was
not having an assistant editor he could rely on. He acknow-
ledges that the *Drum* journalists probably drank as a gesture
of defiance, but to have them drunk and absent just when
they were needed most ran absolutely against the grain.

So he fired Themba.

'I had made a rule regarding drunkenness and Can
Themba ignored it twice. Then he got so drunk while away
from the office with a cameraman that he was arrested by
two cops and imprisoned. I must stress, he was at this time

13. The title page of Henry Nxumalo's investigation into farm labour conditions in the Bethal region

BETHAL TODAY

DRUM'S FEARLESS EXPOSURE OF HUMAN EXPLOITATION

HOEING MEALIES AT BETHAL—Picture taken on Mr. DRUM'S visit a month ago.

14. Walter Sisulu during the 1956 Treason Trial

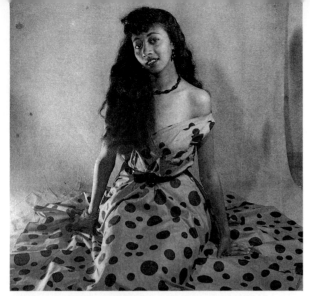

15. Juby Mayet, cover girl, April 1958

16. Dolly Rathebe on a mine dump shortly before she and the photographer, Jurgen Schadeberg, were questioned for a possible infringement of the Immorality Act

17. Can Themba and Arthur Maimane with two beauty queens, Dottie Tiyo and Selina Kolae

18. Can Themba

19. & 20. Prisoners in the Johannesburg gaol doing the *tausa*, or 'monkey dance', meant to dislodge anything hidden in the rectum

21. Casey Motsisi

22. Dancing at
the Ritz, a famous
Johannesburg venue
for black ball-
room dancers

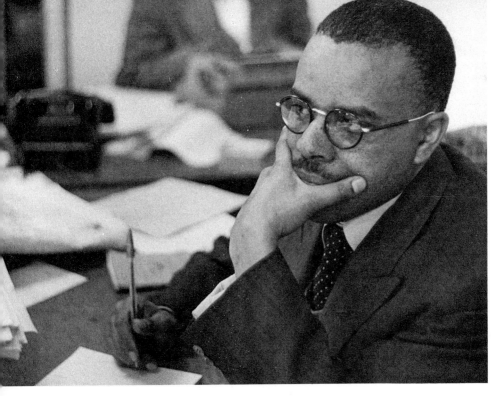

23. (*above*) Es'kia Mphahlele **24.** (*below*) Bloke Modisane

25. Sophiatown in February 1955, when the first families were moved under the Native Resettlement Act of 1954

26. Father Trevor Huddleston in Sophiatown

Drum's assistant editor! According to the rule, a third offence meant his being sacked.'

By all accounts, Can Themba, suffering from a suddenly broken love affair, was drinking heavily. He was, as Nadine Gordimer describes it, 'impossible', and Hopkinson had very little choice. Yet understandably the staff's confidence in their editor dropped to rock-bottom and this lack of morale is reflected in the editions of that time.

'You must understand,' says Obed Musi, 'that Can was a guru to most of us young reporters. But bear in mind that Can was more of a teacher than a journalist, more of an intellectual than a hard scribe, more of a pedagogue, but he made people feel at home and you enjoyed his company. Can could talk to a professor in the morning, a beauty queen at lunch-time and a gangster in the afternoon. And have everyone laughing and eating out of his hand. He was a master of the English language. But not a master of his own life. Can was a very ebullient man, larger than life in a way. There was a bit of loneliness one could detect under the hard-drinking Can. Because to this day I've never met anybody who says, I'm Can's brother or Can's cousin. And I don't think there was ever an occasion when Can spoke a single line in an African language. He either spoke English or township lingo. The reason was probably because Can's surname was actually Tembe, a Shangaan name, and he had his roots in Pretoria. There was a rivalry between the guys from Johannesburg and those from Pretoria: the Johannesburg people considered themselves superior and vice versa. Can did not want to identify with Pretoria, he wanted to be one of the slick guys from Johannesburg, and this also made him live in two worlds. He wanted to be all things to all men.'

Being all things to all men takes nerve and self-control. Lewis Nkosi felt that the only time he saw Themba's nerve nearly snap, despite the prodigious quantities of alcohol which held it together, was when the beautiful young Englishwoman he was in love with was told by the security police to leave the country. She was going – she had to – but he was staying trapped in the land of apartheid. Nkosi was given a glimpse into someone's suffering and he recoiled horrified. Nadine Gordimer admits that her novel *Occasion for Loving* parallels that period of Themba's life.

'The basis for *Occasion for Loving*, the idea, not the characters, was taken from Can's love affair with a white woman, but that sort of thing was happening to lots of people. It could have been half a dozen others. There was someone else I knew who came out here and had a flaming affair with a black friend of mine, a prominent person in the youth movement of Congress. The outcome was that they were caught under the Immorality Act, the Swedish embassy stepped in and promptly put her on a plane back to Sweden. There was such an outcry about the case being pursued against him, not her, that it was dropped. But the fact is that he was someone with a high political profile. In a sense he was "disgraced" because he was seen to be wasting his time philandering. Somehow it always happened that the black person – whether man or woman – was always left high and dry. It was never just the normal end of an affair. So yes, Can suffered very badly from the end of that affair and whenever he suffered he always turned to the bottle. He got to the stage where he couldn't work any more. You should have seen the condition he was in in those days, often in this house. You just didn't know what to do with him. It was tragic to see someone of his intellect, wit and charm so wasted.'

The woman concerned was Jean Hart.

She and her husband Malcolm had come out in 1957 and been caught up in the *Drum*-Sophiatown-Alexandra shebeen life.

'I remember the first time I met Can Themba was at a party organised by Ma-Bloke [Bloke Modisane's mother] in Sophiatown. It was actually a party to welcome me, as Malcolm had already been in South Africa for some months. Can came up to me and looked at me and said: "Before we begin, just remember there are twelve million of us and three million of you, and if we kill one of you and die ourselves there are still enough of us to carry on. That's how you must remember your position in South Africa."

'This was a bit heavy, especially from him, because he turned out to be quite the opposite. I fell in love with him and we had an affair eventually. Apart from that introduction though, he turned out to be a most gentle and tolerant and humane person, not a heavy politico at all. I think what he was telling me was that this was all jolly and fun but the reality was different and you must never forget the reality. It was a rather hysterical, over-elaborate way of describing it, but I think that was what the intention was. We can now be friends but . . .

'After that, in most of the conversations we had he would talk about how the reality of being a black and a white in South Africa tortured relationships. And because he was a poet and not a politico, I think it was constantly a great pain for him, but at the same time he had to recognise it and keep reminding me. So we had an affair and we lived together, as far as you can live together under those circumstances, at friends' houses and so on, but there was always a point at which he would do a similar thing and shut the gate and say, Look, we are involved in a nonsense here, we can't be real people in this situation.

'I think he was the only person of the *Drum* group who knew that. Bloke didn't know that, because Bloke was much more party-party and optimistic and didn't think things through. Can, who was very analytical as well as being fun, thought things through and I think saw that you couldn't indulge in love and friendship without constantly remembering that those things were going to get distorted by the environment. It was a great pain to him because he was a very open, loving, amiable man.

'As you know he was also an alcoholic and that I think is where he buried that clarity of vision of what was possible in the society in which he was living. I think it was true of

Can that he drank to stop it hurting. He drank most of the time.'

After the Hopkinson episode he quit journalism, went on the wagon and took a teaching post near Manzini in Swaziland. Not long after that, in 1962, the South African government declared him a banned person who could not be quoted and whose writings could not be published. Only in 1982 did the government condescend to allow his voice to be heard once more, but by that time he'd been dead for fourteen years. He died in exile. As Lewis Nkosi heard the news, 'His heart just stopped.'

Jim Bailey saw Themba shortly before his death. He remembers Themba kept on talking about the oppressors. 'Given the South African context you would have thought you knew who he was talking about, but actually you didn't. By the oppressors, Can meant his wife and his girlfriend. I asked him how he enjoyed teaching at a mixed school, as he had only taught at a boys' school before. He replied, "You have to taste the pot to see if the cooking is done."'

Number Four

36

March 1954, the magazine's third anniversary, was approaching. As the Bethal exposé had set the tone of how to celebrate these occasions, something big, and grim, was again needed. Not that there was any shortage of scandals, but laws were beginning to be pushed through parliament curtailing what the government saw as 'irresponsible' reporting. As Anthony Sampson complained, editors could be 'flogged for publishing any article "calculated to cause any person to comit an offence by way of protest"'.

One subject that kept coming up was the gaols. There were stories of beatings, bad food, appalling conditions and the notorious '*tausa* dance' – a way of searching naked prisoners for tobacco, dagga or anything else hidden in their rectums. With an annual prison population of more than a quarter of a million blacks, many of whom were serving time for such trivial offences as forgetting to carry their passes, it seemed a good story.

A lawyer told Sampson that provided he didn't commission a reporter to get an inside story he wouldn't be breaking the law.

'So I told Henry to take a holiday,' says Sampson. 'And I added something like if he did get arrested I would be interested to hear about it.'

Nxumalo went off, but believe it or not, in a city where every black person could be expected to be behind bars sometime or other in his life he had difficulty getting arrested.

Three times he tried. On the first occasion he visited Boksburg township without a permit, and although he had someone tip off the police they weren't interested in a native without a pass that day. Then he refused to pay for a train ticket, was arrested, but discharged when the officer who had arrested him failed to appear for the court case. Next he got drunk, was involved in a fight, and arrested. The magistrate fined him five days or 10s. but a friend paid his fine. Finally he was arrested in Johannesburg after curfew without his pass and sentenced to five days in the Fort, Johannesburg's prison, or 'Number Four' as it was known to inmates.

When Nxumalo got out he wrote this story:

I served five days' imprisonment at the Johannesburg Central Prison from 20 to 24 January. My crime was being found without a night pass five minutes before midnight, and I was charged under the curfew regulations. I was sentenced to a fine of 10s. or five days' imprisonment.

Two constables arrested me at the corner of Rissik and Plein Streets. I was taken to Marshall Square Police Station, charged, searched, given two blankets and locked up in the cells together with thirty-seven others. The night was long. The prison doors kept clanging as more prisoners trickled in during the night. The cell itself was dark. I couldn't tell the day from the night. Only the familiar shout of the young constable carrying a noisy bunch of prison keys told us it was morning.

We had roll-call, breakfast, got back our personal effects and were packed like sardines – over forty of us – in a truck, and delivered to the cells below the magistrate's court. When we got off the truck into the cells below the courts, one elderly-looking prisoner was a little slow to climb off. The prisoners were jostling to get off at once and blocking the way, and when the old man reached the ground he nearly missed the direction the other prisoners were taking. He looked about and S. saw him. He hit him with his open hand on the temples and told him to wake up.

Before we appeared in court I asked one of the black constables to allow me to phone my employers and my family.

He said: 'Go on, *voetsek*! [Get away!]'

Meanwhile white prisoners in the opposite cells were phoning their families and their employers without trouble from a wall telephone near the warder.

After our cases had been heard by the magistrate, we were sent back to the cells. Convicted prisoners who couldn't raise enough money to pay their fines employed various methods to get money. They either borrowed or bartered their clothes, promising to release their benefactors as soon as they were out. Discharged prisoners took messages to relatives of convicted prisoners.

This lasted about two hours; we were checked and taken to Johannesburg Central Prison by truck. We arrived at the prison immediately after one o'clock. From the truck we were given orders to '*shayisa*' (close up), fall in twos and 'sharp shoot' (run) to the prison reception office. From then on, 'Come on, kaffir' was the operative phrase from both black and white prison officials, and in all languages.

Many of us who were going to prison for the first time didn't know exactly where the reception office was. Although the prison officials were with us, no one was directing us. But if a prisoner hesitated, slackened his half-running pace and looked round, he got a hard boot kick on the buttocks, a slap on his face or a whipping from the warders. Fortunately there were some second offenders with us who knew where to go. We followed them through the prison's many zig-zagging corridors until we reached the reception office.

The reception office had a terrifyingly brutal atmosphere. It was full of foul language. A number of khaki-uniformed white officials stood behind a long, cement, bar-like, curved counter. They wore the initials PSDG on their shoulders. When they were not joking about prisoners, they were swearing at them and taking down their particulars. Two were taking fingerprints and hitting the prisoners in the face when they made mistakes.

Five long-term prisoners attended us. One came up to me and said he knew me. I didn't know him. He asked for cigarettes, but I didn't have any. Another told us to take off our watches and money and hold them in our hands. These were to be kept separate from our other possessions. Another asked me for 2s. 6d., but I had 5d. only and he wasn't interested. He noticed I had a copy of *Time* magazine in my hand and asked for it. I gave it to him. He hid it under the counter so the warders couldn't see it. Later he asked me what paper it was, how old it was and whether it was interesting. After we had undressed, one long-term prisoner demanded my fountain pen.

'That's a fine pen you've got, eh?' he said. 'How about giving it to me?'

I said: 'I'm afraid I can't; it's not my pen, it's my boss's pen.'

'Hi, don't tell me lies, you bastard,' he said. 'What the hell are you doing with your boss's pen in prison? Did you steal it?'

I said I hadn't stolen it. I was using it and had it in my possession when I was arrested.

'Give it here, I want it for my work here; if you refuse you'll see blood streaming down your dirty mouth soon!'

I was nervous, but didn't reply.

'Look, you little fool, I'll see that you are well treated in prison if you give me that pen.'

The other prisoners looked at me anxiously. I didn't know whether they approved of my giving my pen or not; but their anxious look seemed to suggest that their fate in prison lay in that pen. I gave it away.

We were called up to have our fingerprints taken by a white warder. Before taking the impression the warder made a loud complaint that the glove he uses when taking impressions was missing. He swore at the long-term prisoner who assists him and told him to find it. The other white prison officials helped him find the glove. He was a stout, middle-aged man, apparently a senior official. He took my impression, examined it and then complained that my hands were wet. He hit me on the mouth with the back of his gloved hand. I rubbed my right thumb on my hair and he took another impression.

From there I ran down to the end of the wide curved desk to have my height taken, and stood beside the measuring rod, naked. The long-term prisoner taking my height asked for my name and checked it against my ticket. He asked for my address and tribe. He then recited something very long to the white official who was writing in a big book opposite him.

My surname and address were wrong. But I dared not complain at that stage for fear of getting more blows. The only words I recognised throughout the recitation was my first name and 'five foot, *bassie* [boss]', which is three inches below my actual height. Though I was near the measuring stick, he hadn't measured me, nor did he measure the other prisoners. He merely looked at them and assessed their height at sight. When finished with a prisoner, he would throw his ticket on the floor for the prisoner to pick up and get on with the next one.

We were then taken to the showers in another room. There was neither soap nor a towel. After a few minutes under water we were told to get out, and skip to get dry. Then our prison clothes were thrown at us – a red shirt and a torn white pair of short pants. They looked clean, but the cap and the white jacket which were issued to me later were filthy. The jacket had dry sweat on the neck.

From then on we were barefoot, and were marched to the hospital for a medical examination in double time. Another long-term prisoner lined us up, ordered us to undress and turn our faces to the wall, so that we would not pollute the medical officer with our breath when he came to examine us. While we were being inoculated, another prisoner, apparently being hit by someone for some reason, suddenly ran into the others at the end of the queue and there was a general shuffling-round of places. We were then told to face forward and make urine. Three prisoners were detained and sent to the hospital as VD suspects. Whether the white official in khaki uniform was a doctor or not, I was unable to tell. He didn't examine me. There was a mix-up of prison clothes after that shuffling-round and changing of places, so that many prisoners couldn't find their clothes. Everyone picked up the clothes nearest to him. Some said the clothes they were wearing had been worn by the prisoners detained for VD.

After this we were marched down to the main court of the prison in double time. Here we found different white and black warders and long-term prisoners, who took charge of us. Again we undressed and had our second shower in thirty minutes. I was unable to make out my own clothes after the shower and skipping. The African warder kicked me in the stomach with the toe of his boot. I tried to hold the boot to protect myself, and fell on my face. He asked if I had had an operation to my stomach. I said no. He looked at me scornfully. I got up, picked up the clothes in front of me and ran to join the others squatting on the floor.

After another roll-call we were marched to the top of the court to collect our food. The dishes were lined in rows and each prisoner picked up the dish nearest to him. The zinc dishes containing the food were rusty.

The top of my dish was broken in three places. The food itself was boiled whole mielies with fat. We were marched to No. 7 cell, given blankets and a sleeping mat and locked in. We ate. The time was about 4.30 p.m. Clean water and toilet buckets were installed. But that water wasn't enough for sixty people. The long-term prisoners warned us not to use the water as if we were at our own homes. An old man went to fetch water with his dish at one stage and the long-term prisoner in charge of the cell swore at him. The old man insisted that he was thirsty and continued scooping the water. The long-term prisoner took the water away from him and threw it all over the old man's face.

There was a stinking smell when prisoners used the toilet bucket at night without toilet paper. At 8 p.m. the bell rang and we were ordered to be quiet and sleep. Some prisoners who had smuggled dagga and matches into the cell started conversing in whispers and smoking. The blankets were full of bugs; I turned round and round during the night without being able to sleep and kept my prison clothes on for protection against bugs.

We were up at about six o'clock the following morning. I tried to get some water to wash my dish and drink. The dish was full of the previous night's fat, and I didn't know how I was going to do it. But the long-term prisoner shouted at me and ordered me to leave the water alone. I obeyed. He swore at me in Afrikaans and ordered me to wipe the urine which was overflowing from the toilet bucket with a small sack cloth. I did so. He said I must wipe it dry but the cloth was so small that the floor remained wet.

He told me to find two other prisoners to help me carry the toilet bucket out, empty it and clean it. It was full of the night's excrement. There were no volunteers, so I slipped to a corner and waited. He saw me and rushed at me.

'What did I tell you, damn it, what did I say?'

He slapped me on my left cheek with his open right hand as he spoke. He said he could have me put in solitary confinement if he wished. He could tell the chief warder that I had messed the floor and I would get an additional punishment. I kept quiet. I had done nothing of the sort. Finally he ordered two other prisoners to help me.

We emptied the bucket and washed it as the other prisoners were being lined up in readiness for breakfast. One of my colleagues tried to wash his hands after we had emptied the bucket. The white warder saw him and slashed him with the strap part of his baton. The dish containing my porridge – and many others – still had the previous night's fat. It had been washed in cold water. The breakfast itself was yellow porridge with half-cooked pieces of turnips, potatoes, carrots and other vegetables I could not recognise. No spoons are provided, so I had my breakfast with my stinking soiled hands. I didn't feel like eating, but feared that I would be inviting further trouble.

After breakfast we were divided into many work spans. I spent my first day with a span cutting grass, pulling out weeds with my hands and pushing wheelbarrows at the Johannesburg Training College in Parktown. We walked for about half a mile to our place of work, and I was one of two prisoners carrying a heavy steel food-can which contained lunch porridge for a party of sixteen. Two warders escorted us, one white and one black. Once I slacked because we were going down a precipice; my fingers were sore and the burden was heavy.

The old white warder, who was carrying a big rifle, slashed me on my bare legs with the strap of his baton and said, '*Ek donder jou* [I'll beat you], kaffir.'

We returned to gaol at four. We were ordered to undress and '*tausa*', a common routine of undressing prisoners when they return from work searching their clothes, their mouths, armpits and rectum for hidden articles. I didn't know how it was done. I opened my mouth, turned round and didn't jump and clap my hands. The white warder conducting the search hit me with his fist on my left jaw, threw my clothes at me and went on searching the others. I ran off and joined the food queue.

One night I didn't have a mat to sleep on. Long-term prisoners in charge of the cells sometimes took a bundle of mats to make themselves comfortable beds, to the discomfort of other prisoners. In practice, a prisoner never knows where he will sleep the next day. It is all determined by your speed in *tausa*, food and blanket queues. Invariably a prisoner is always using another prisoner's dirty blankets every night.

In the four days I was in prison – I got a remission of one day – I was kicked or thrashed every day. I saw many other prisoners being thrashed daily. I was never told what was expected of me but had to guess. Sometimes I guessed wrong and got into trouble.

Long-term and short-term prisoners mixed freely at the prison. For example, the famous 'Tiger' of Alexandra township, who is doing a ten-year sentence for various crimes, was one of the most important persons in prison during my time. He was responsible for the in- and out-movements of other prisoners and was respected by prisoners and warders. Though I was a short-term prisoner, I too took orders from Tiger.

It was a common practice for short-term prisoners to give their small piece of meat to long-term prisoners on meat days for small favours such as tobacco, dagga, shoes (which are supposed to be supplied to coloured prisoners only), wooden spoons – or to ensure that they were always supplied with sleeping mats.

Many other prisoners shared the same fate. There are no directions or rules read or posted in prison. At least

I didn't see any. Thrashing-time for warders was roll-call and breakfast-time as well as supper-time. For long-term prisoners it was inside the cells at all times. Long-term prisoners thrashed more prisoners more severely and much oftener than the prison officials themselves, and often in the presence of either white or black warders. All prisoners were called kaffirs at all times.

On the day of our discharge we were mustered in a big hall at breakfast and checked. There was an open lavatory at the corner of the hall. Six men used it and when the seventh one went a long-term prisoner swore at him and told him to keep his stomach full until he reached home. He said the man belonged to a tribe he detested, a tribe which killed his brother. After that none of us could use the latrine.

We were then marched to the reception office for our personal effects and checking out. The long-term prisoners officiating there told us not to think that we were already out of prison. They kicked and slapped prisoners for the slightest mistake and sometimes for no mistake at all; and promised them additional sentences if they complained. In the office there was a notice warning prisoners to see that their personal belongings were recorded in the prison's books correctly and exactly as they had brought them. But I dared not complain about my pen that was commandeered on my arrival, lest I be detained. Even the prisoner who took it pretended not to know me.

Before we left prison we were told the superintendent would address us. We could make complaints to him if we had any. But the fat Zulu warder who paraded us to the yard for the superintendent's inspection said we must tell him everything was all right if we wanted to leave prison.

'This is a court of law,' he said. 'You are about to go home, but before you leave this prison the big boss of the prison will address you. He will ask you if you have any complaints. Now I take it that you all want to go to your homes, to your wives and children – you don't want to stay here. So if the big boss asks you if everything is all right, say, "Yes sir." If he says Have you any complaints, say, "No sir." You hear?'

In a chorus we said, 'Yes.'

Just then one prisoner complained that his Kliptown train ticket was missing from his things. It was a season ticket. The Zulu warder pulled him aside and said: 'You think you're clever, eh? You'll see.' He put him at the tail end of the parade. The superintendent came and we answered him as instructed. Most of us were seeing him for the first time. The Zulu warder said nothing about the complaint of the man from Kliptown. Later as we were going to collect our monies from the pay office, the man from Kliptown was escorted to the reception office to see the famous fierce discharge officer, C.

C. said the man's papers showed that he was charged at Fordsburg and not at Kliptown. He was not entitled to any ticket. But the man insisted that he was arrested at Kliptown, charged at Fordsburg and appeared in Johannesburg.

The fat Zulu warder said in Afrikaans, 'He's mad, sir.'

He gave the man a hard slap in the face with his open hand and said: 'You're just wasting the boss's time, eh? On your way . . . *voetsek*!'

And the man sneaked out.

One by one we zigzagged our way out of the prison's many doors and gates and lined up in twos in front of the main and final gate. We were ordered to leave prison quietly and in pairs when the small gate was open. If we blocked the gate we would be thrashed. We were to come out in the order of the line. The man on the left would go out first and the one on the right would follow. The gate was opened. We saw freedom

and blocked the gate in our anxiety. If they thrashed us
we couldn't feel it . . . we didn't look back.

(March 1954)

Henry Nxumalo's story was published under the headline
MR DRUM GOES TO GAOL. Opposite it was a half-page picture
of a naked prisoner doing the *tausa* dance which Nxumalo
had been forced to learn. The headline under it was: SEEMLY
AND DECENT? Below that was an extract from the prison
regulations of 1911: 'The searching of a convict shall be
conducted with due regard to decency and self-respect, and
in as seemly a manner as is consistent with the necessity of
discovering any concealed article on or in any part of his
body or clothing.'

'I think one of my most exciting times on *Drum* was going
to the dark-room and watching those pictures of the prisoners in the Fort doing the *tausa*, the monkey dance, being
developed,' says Sampson. 'Of course we were accused of
getting them by all sorts of devious means, like smuggling a
camera into the prison, bribing a warder, using a helicopter
or simply faking them.'

Actually the way they got them was by exploiting white
arrogance.

Arthur Maimane recalls that he and photographer Bob
Gosani were assigned to take the pictures. Gosani and
Sampson had already identified a block of flats overlooking
the Fort as the ideal vantage point and Gosani had built a
four-foot-long lens.

'The idea,' says Maimane, 'was to get on to the roof of the
flats posing as boys helping a white woman, actually Sampson's secretary, Deborah Duncan, who was supposed to be
a photographer taking panoramic shots of Johannesburg.
Well, the superintendent took us up and while Deborah
kept him occupied taking pictures and talking about the
view, Bob and I quickly put together his home-made camera
and took photographs of the prisoners doing the dance.'

The result once again earned Nxumalo and *Drum* high

praise. Conditions in the prisons improved, if only for a time, and Henry was given a party by the Orlando *tsotsis* for cleaning up Number Four. As one of Can Themba's friends put it: 'This Mr Drum fellow is going bang into history.'

Going Native

37

In the shebeens, church halls, rooms and township back-yards the jazzman Dollar Brand used to sing:

If you're white
You're all right
If you're brown
Stay around, but
If you're black
Get away you nigger
Get back.

The sentiments were hardly new. But the laws being enacted to enforce those words were. And if there had been hurt and hate before, it was now compounded by an absurdity that went beyond laughter. As officials diligently sought to separate black from coloured, coloured from Indian and everybody from white, they sometimes had to resort to such ludicrous methods as the hair-and-pencil test. If a pencil slipped easily through a head of hair the subject was at least not black. And that arbitrary stroke could separate lovers, destroy families. Even whites had their homes shattered when suddenly a child was declared 'coloured'.

So a story like that of Regina Brooks was very much a story of the time.

The headline said it all: CAN WHITE BE BLACK? *Charged under Immorality Act, white woman claims to have 'gone native'.*

In court was a twenty-two-year-old and her policeman lover. She was white; he was black. They had a daughter and lived in his Orlando home. By way of defence their attorney argued that she had 'gone native' – in dress (wasn't she wearing a *doek*?) and in manner (didn't she carry her baby strapped round her waist?). But having 'gone native' wasn't enough for the public prosecutor, because that didn't make her 'a native'. So they were found guilty under the Immorality Act of 1927, which had made it an offence for black and white to cohabit.

The sentence was four months' imprisonment. The attorney appealed and in the ensuing court action Regina Brooks was reclassified non-white. Legally she had become a 'native'. The integrity of the Immorality Act was once again unsullied.

By now Regina Brooks was a folk hero. *Drum* rushed to get her story.

38

MY LIFE STORY by Regina Brooks

I was born twenty-two years ago on a farm called
Rooipoort near the little town of Vrede in the Orange
Free State. I am the tenth of eleven children, all of
whom are living as Europeans in different parts of the
Union. My father was an Englishman and a farmer, but
he didn't live long enough for me to know him well: I
was only two when he died.

I have five brothers and five sisters, but since I was
nine I haven't seen them again. All I know about them
now is that one is a farmer in the Free State; another is
a miner at Germiston; and another is a clerk in Durban.
My eldest sister, Anna, was married to a Mr Viljoen,
but was divorced by him after she had given birth to
two children whose father was African.

I spent more of my early childhood days in the
company of my father's black servants than with my
white brothers and sisters. I played with the servants,
ate and slept with them in the kitchen of my home, and
visited their homes frequently.

I learned to speak Sesotho and Zulu; and these
languages I spoke more often and more fluently than I
spoke my mother tongue, English.

I attended a white school at Vrede. But I was not
used to white children and did not understand their
habits; I couldn't work and play with them. I was most
unhappy in their company. So after two years I left that
school. My sister Anna took me from home to live with

her on her husband's farm. I lived with the Viljoens until they divorced two years later.

When I was nine my sister Anna gave birth to her only daughter by Mr Viljoen. After this Anna fell in love with an African, Alpheus Mlilo, and gave birth to a black boy, who is now working at Melville, Johannesburg. She was charged and fined £50, and Mlilo was ordered to leave the district for three years. Mr Viljoen paid her fine. But when Mlilo returned Anna gave birth to another black child, this time a daughter, now living in Durban. Mlilo and my sister were each sentenced to six months' imprisonment. Mlilo served his sentence and Anna served hers at Pretoria prison. After this Mr Viljoen divorced my sister and gave her £1,000.

I then returned to my mother and lived with her on the farm. I attended an African school and spent more and more of my time with local Africans until Zulu came to me more naturally than my mother tongue, English or Afrikaans, which I learned when I lived with the Viljoens.

I never really got on with white people. I did not feel at ease with the way they behaved and lived among themselves. But I loved the Africans and felt like one of them. I was far happier in their company; I felt that they were like brothers and sisters.

My first boyfriend was an African, Thomas Mdakane. He was a taxi driver. I went out with him often in his car but our white neighbours didn't like it. They spoke about it disapprovingly in the shops, in the pubs and in public places. One night Mdakane came to my room drunk and I avoided him. I went to sleep with the servants in their quarters. At midnight the police raided my room; but they found Mdakane alone and left him there. I was terribly frightened the next day.

I rejected him for his powerful drinking. I then went to live with an African family, the Makubus. They were on a neighbouring farm.

I was very happy there. The white farmer didn't mind my living with the Zulu family. I became one of the family and was generally accepted by the Africans as one of themselves. It was here that I met the second man in my life, Paulus Hlokoma. I was in love with him for nearly two years. He gave me the name of Linda Malinga. Most people at Rooipoort still know me by that name. I have never been in love with a white man.

When I was twenty I met Richard Kumalo, a Johannesburg police sergeant. We met at a wedding on the farm. I knew that he had been married two years earlier, but still I loved him. He was one of the race I loved. He couldn't marry because he was already married; anyhow, even if he hadn't been married the laws of the country wouldn't have allowed it.

In March 1953 I gave birth to my daughter Tandi. I lived with her at the Makubus' until last year, when Kumalo asked me to come and join him in Johannesburg. He said he had bought a house at the new municipal-sponsored township of Dube, near Orlando, and I would be happy with him there.

Last September I came to Johannesburg to join the man I loved. I lived at Dube township and everyone was kind to me. Some said I was coloured, but they were surprised to see me carrying my baby on my back and speaking Zulu. But I didn't care what race or nationality they thought I was, so long as they were nice and kind to me.

But our happiness was not fated to last long. Kumalo's wife, who still lived at the police barracks in the city, found out about me and informed the police. So one night the police raided our house at Dube. We were charged at Marshall Square and I appeared the following week in court with Kumalo. Since then we have appeared in court several times. We were sentenced to four months' imprisonment each but we are now out on £25 bail each pending an appeal. I do not know what the outcome of the appeal will be.

But one thing is certain: I couldn't be happy living among whites. I am not used to them. I can't speak their language. If I lived among them I don't know what would happen to my daughter, Tandi. She wouldn't be allowed to live as a white person! When the case is over I would like to work in Johannesburg, but I cannot imagine myself being employed as a white woman because I can't behave like a white woman. The children of the people I grew up with and lived with most of my life are, to me, more my brothers and sisters than my mother's children.

There are a few of them living in Johannesburg, and with them I would be quite happy.

Mrs Kumalo herself, I must say, has not been unsympathetic towards me. When we were in prison she was kind enough to send us money and food. I am grateful to her for this. One of my brothers, and my sister Anna, are the only two members of my own family who are concerned about my welfare. The others have given me up.

I find Johannesburg's citizens very kind people. They have done a lot for us and even contributed towards legal expenses. Even the white police are obliging and friendly. Sometimes they argue among themselves whether I am white or coloured, but they always end up by calling me Linda Malinga!

(January 1955)

39

Today Regina Brooks lives in a neat little house in Eldorado Park, a suburb some way out of Johannesburg. It is a suburb for those classified by the Population Registration Act as 'coloured'. A toy Pomeranian snaps at my ankles and barks as I make my way down the side of the house towards the back yard where Regina Brooks, in dressing-gown and slippers, her hair in curlers, has suddenly appeared. She asks me what I want. I tell her I'd like to talk to her.

'Why have you come so early?' she says. 'It's too early.'

It is ten-thirty.

She is not happy about my request to interview her. 'I don't want any more scandal. That's all in the past. I don't want to bring it up again.'

Nevertheless she suggests I come inside. We enter through the kitchen where a black woman stands at the sink washing dishes. In the small narrow lounge, packed with heavy furniture and dominated by a large grey television screen, I outline my proposal.

'I never liked what they wrote about me in *Drum*,' she says.

'If you feel you've been wronged . . .' I begin, but she doesn't let me finish.

'They said that when I had no money I was taking in washing from Indians. I never took in washing from Indians. That was lies.'

We sit in awkward silence until she says: 'I must talk to my children about it.'

She tells me her telephone number and I agree to phone in a week's time. When I do, I discover she's given me a wrong number. In the following weeks I hear through the grape-vine that she is angry and won't be interviewed, even though someone has generously suggested I would pay R1,000 for her story.

40

CONFESSIONS OF A PLAYWHITE

I am a Playwhite. Before you condemn me, let me explain why I denied my people – and even my own flesh and blood.

Coming to Johannesburg from the Cape thirty years ago, I tried to find a job. There were none . . . for a coloured man. I didn't think of playing white then. The idea was put into me by a friend. We had arranged for a party, but he couldn't get enough liquor for it, so he suggested I go and buy it from the bottle store. I asked him why he didn't do it himself, like we did in the Cape. Very tersely he explained the Transvaal liquor law to me.

'But you can get it without the permit,' he told me. 'You are as white as any supposed-to-be European.'

I had no difficulty at all. From that day on I became a regular customer for the bottle stores with all the liquor I had to buy for my friends.

To the second step, too, I was led by my friends – not that I want to lay the blame on them. After weeks of seeking jobs I was told about one with good wages – but for whites only.

'Why worry about how and where you work? You are as white as any of them!' my friends urged me.

I took the job. There were only whites there; everybody was very pleasant to me, but I refused all invitations to their homes for fear they would expect me to invite them to my home, too.

But there was one fellow whose friendliness was hard to resist. He was a tall, fine-featured, blond giant. I grew very friendly with him during our beer drinks after work. One Saturday afternoon he found me in my favourite bar. We had a few drinks together and became so jolly I couldn't refuse his offer to go home with him and meet his 'mum'.

When I climbed out of his car I saw a chubby coloured woman sitting on the verandah. This must be the cook, I thought. You can imagine my surprise when he called her 'Granny'! Another coloured woman joined us and he introduced her as his 'mum'!

We had a most pleasant afternoon and evening. The time came for me to go home; I was in a fix. Though my friend had revealed himself to me, I wasn't sure I should do the same. I took the bold course and let him drive me home. I introduced him to my light- and dark-coloured relatives.

He slapped me on the back with a laugh: 'Hell!' he said, 'I see you're just as Irish as I am, hey?'

He is still a friend of mine, now. And not just because we are 'birds of a feather', but for his spirit. He has inherited all the stubbornness of his Scots father and isn't going to stand down to any 'white' South African!

With the passing years I adjusted myself to my two-faced life. With my three kids growing, the wife and I decided we should live in a bigger place. The only coloured townships where I could buy a house were far out of town, and the houses more expensive than those in a European area. At the end I bought a house in a quiet 'white' suburb. I say 'white' with a qualification. After a few weeks there I discovered that my neighbours had quite a sprinkling of 'Irish'!

With this change of residence my coloured friends thought we were going completely 'white'. We were hurt. To show them we were still the same we invited them often to our home and visited them, too, acting like we'd always done.

Our kids were reaching the school-going age now. Like all other parents, we wanted the best for them. They were passably white by South African standards – and opportunities were limited to them as coloureds. So we sent them to white schools. The only thing we feared was that at these schools they might be given the wrong ideas about non-Europeans and thus not be able to live the life we led.

My eldest son qualified as a motor mechanic years back, and is now running a business of his own where he employs Europeans, coloureds and Africans. None of his workers know of his 'Irish' blood.

My daughter is a well-paid shorthand typist in a 'desk-job-for-Europeans-only' company.

My youngest son, though, set us a problem. After applying for a government job, they asked for his birth certificate – which classes him as coloured. He was accepted without one on an affidavit sworn by an old friend of ours stating our son was of white parentage. Incidentally, the friend was a fine old 'Irish' gentleman!

During the war I enlisted in a famous Transvaal regiment. The number of 'Irish' soldiers in it was most surprising! Some of those who knew I'd seen through them, and had also seen through me, were inclined to be stand-offish with me. I didn't blame them.

While on duty 'up north', I noticed a Cape Corps truck stop in the desert and the coloureds in it climb out to look for souvenirs. It was my duty, as a white soldier, to stop them. I scolded them in the best white tradition. I was most embarrassed to find that the coloured driver was an old friend of mine.

In private life I've done my coloured friends, who can only 'pass' in the evenings, a lot of favours in buying them tickets to theatres, cinemas and other shows that aren't open to non-Europeans. But in spite of my advantage over them and all other darker-skinned people, life is not a bed of roses. There are many complications and situations arising that sometimes tempt me to stop playing white. The feeling of an impostor is too strong in me when I'm faced with a situation where I have to assert my rights as a white man.

I found a coloured man in a bottle store once. He was ordering liquor without a permit and the manager doubted him. An obviously coloured man the manager knew walked in. The manager called him aside and asked him if he didn't think the man was coloured.

'I think he's a Greek. I know where he lives, and only Europeans live in that area,' answered the coloured man, who I'm sure didn't know the 'Greek' from Adam.

Meanwhile the man in question was easily leaning on his stick and not a bit worried. I wouldn't have wished to be him for all the money in the world just then!

When one knows coloured people as only we who are coloured know them, then one can see the extent to which our light-skinned brothers are infiltrating into the white community. We see them in theatre queues, bars, railway coaches, and even the public services and higher places! Every place where a coloured is segregated against, there you'll find my 'Irish' brethren. The resultant effect on the supposed purity of the white people of this country is already evident: there are so many dark white people that it is very difficult for any person in a responsible position to dare challenge their bona fides in any place for 'Europeans Only'.

(April 1953)

41

'Hello. I want to speak to the editor.'

'I'm afraid he's not in, sir. Would you care to speak to the associate editor?'

'Who's he?'

'Mr. Themba.'

'Er . . . T-H-I-M-B-A?'

'No. T-H-E-M-B-A.'

'Oh, I see. A native.'

'Mr Themba is an African, sir.'

'I see. Well, I really wanted to speak to the editor. No discredit on Mr Themba, you know.'

(May 1956)

In his *Talk o' the Rand* column George Magwaza (alias Henry Nxumalo) puzzled: 'Each time I write about Africans I'm misunderstood. There are Africans, South Africans and South African Africans; but when you translate "African" into Afrikaans you get "Afrikaner". Indians, too, nowadays are Africans, and so are mixed-blood Africans who are generally called "coloureds". I've tried a couple of collective nouns for the lot: non-Europeans, non-whites and whatnot. I'm fed up with these negatives. "Natives" is meaningless and "coons" stinks. I'm now toying with blacks and non-blacks. So dry am I for ideas at this juncture that unless you customers of this column can give me a word, I'm going back to the old positive contemptibles: kaffirs, coolies, and Hot'nots. How's that?'

Although much has been made of *Drum* as an island of normality, a non-racial enclave, the outside world penetrated all too frequently. Not only in the office but also in the adjacent corridors of the liberal *Rand Daily Mail*.

Nobody can remember what Labuschagne's first name was but there was a time when he was *Drum*'s circulation manager. Assistant circulation manager was the sax man Gwigwi Mrwebi. 'Oh his first day this white guy thought Gwigwi was a messenger or something,' tells Obed Musi, 'and at lunch-time he said to Gwigwi: "Benjamin" – that, at least, was his name – "go and buy fish and chips," and he gave him two bob. Gwigwi thought, Well, fine, this is a nice guy, so he went out and bought fish and chips and came back eating them. This white guy says, "Hey, I sent you to buy fish and chips. Not only do you take your own bloody sweet time about getting them but you eat them as well." So Gwigwi says, "I thought you were a nice white guy and it was very generous of you to give me two bob for chips. But listen here laddie" – he called everybody laddie – he says, "listen here laddie, get this straight. I'm assistant circulation manager; if you want fish and chips you get them yourself." The white guy says he won't accept this and goes storming in to Bailey who told him how things were done in the office. Of course the white guy didn't last long.'

About the *Rand Daily Mail*, Arthur Maimane has a story of teacups and white superiority: 'I was friendly with some of the whites on the *Rand Daily Mail* and got on all right with the rest of them. Certainly with the immigrant whites, who were more actively liberal, we were friends, while the rest just kept their views to themselves and made sure they had separate teacups.

'We were ignored by some people in the *Rand Daily Mail* offices because as far as they were concerned there was no such thing as a black journalist, let alone one who could possibly know what he was doing.

'At one stage I was doing a lot of last-minute subbing in the printing works. Obviously while I was on the factory floor I would talk to the foreman and the printers who were all white, working-class Afrikaners. But I handled them in such a manner that they didn't resent my telling them what to do, giving them orders. All my life in South Africa I'd had to be polite just to survive. In a white world you have to be polite, but not crawl. And because I knew my job they accepted me for what I was rather than thinking of me as a stereotype, a kaffir.

'Then one day the general manager of the *RDM* walked into the press room and saw me there. Half an hour later I learned that he told my bosses that I should never ever again give instructions to his white employees. The next day I met the foreman, the head printer, who said, "Look, forget all this stupidity, you can come back any time you like. We'll work with you, we don't mind taking orders from you."

'Obviously we had to deal with these issues philosophically. The basic thing was to bite the bullet. Whether you bit it and laughed at them for making you bite it, or you bit it and choked on your own humiliation, was a matter of individual temperament. It had to do with your expectations.

'I think there were two kinds of Africans: educated Africans, the ones who desperately wanted to be accepted by the white liberal world as equals – Todd was one of those; so was Bloke – and then there were others. I think I was, Lewis [Nkosi] was, Can was. We had a way of saying to the white liberals, "Look, here's what I am, I'm not going to dance to your music, you take me as I am. Take it or leave it, this is me." But Todd and Bloke and others were trying to aspire to standards set for them by the white liberals. "You mean you've never heard Beethoven's fifth symphony?" – you go down a few rungs on the ladder. "Oh you've read Sartre!" – you go up two more rungs. That kind of patronising attitude that "we whites are the arbitrators of civilisation, we set the standards and you must live up to them". Or else. So they became bitter because they could never make it. The goalposts moved all the time.'

Those were workplace issues, but what happened in the shebeens or at mixed parties?

Nadine Gordimer: Most of those people on *Drum*, early on in the '50s, had an aversion to politics so there was no question of political tensions between us. There was no question of barriers. That business of if-you-were-black-you-couldn't-have-white-friends-because-it-was-politically-unac-ceptable was way off in the future. I enjoyed an easy and intimate kind of relationship with the *Drum* people. I never found barriers developing with Can or Todd. We had our little enclave and the rest of the world was outside. It was an illusion: we had chosen to ignore the facts of life here, but because it was so small it seemed to be natural. Nat wrote a very amusing little piece about a telephone conver-sation he had with a white man who was very friendly while he thought Nakasa was white.

[Nakasa's story begins when he telephones to reserve a seat on a night train.

> Booking Clerk: Certainly, sir, will you hold the line a minute?
> Me: Yes.
> BC (after a while): Are you there, sir? I'm afraid the Wednesday train is fully booked, sir.
> Me: What about Thursday morning?
> BC: I'll go and see, sir. Will you hold on again?
> Me: Yes.
> BC: Are you there, sir? Yes, I can put you on the Thursday morning train. What is the name, sir?
> Me: Nathaniel Nakasa.
> BC: Did you say MacArthur, sir? Could you spell it please?
> Me: N-A-K-A-S-A, Nakasa.
> BC: What nationality would that be?
> Me: African.
> BC: Damn it! Why the hell didn't you tell me in the beginning that you are a native?

> Me: I'm sorry, sir, I didn't . . .
> BC: Shut up! *Jy lieg!* (You lie!)]

The way he tells it, it's a funny story. But it's an awful, disgraceful incident that's related. And this is a key to the way things were. They hid behind a lot of irony, a lot of partying, a lot of drinking. The attitude was ironic. Humour was the release.

You must remember too that the solution people looked to then was to leave, to get out. The business of staying and fighting was for the politicians. But the artists felt frustrated and that is why so many of them went. And that is why in the case of Nat Nakasa it was such a tragedy. I think as white friends we were very much to blame because we encouraged the exodus and found ways of getting them out. We felt it was a wonderful thing that they should get out into the open world, not realising what it meant to leave on an exit permit. When we went to see Nat off we were celebrating, but it wasn't wonderful at all.

Jurgen Schadeberg: I don't think there were many whites going into shebeens in the early '50s. Later on it became a trendy thing to do. Everybody was terribly polite and terribly friendly to me. But it was very rare that you'd find a white who could handle it at that time. Although apartheid was being introduced, most of the social barriers had existed long before the Afrikaner government came into power.

For instance, we had a white advertising manager who would not leave copies of *Drum* on his table at home because he was too embarrassed. Nor would he walk down the street with a copy of *Drum* under his arm. In public he was ashamed and embarrassed about working for *Drum*. Socially, any form of involvement with blacks was shameful. They were garden-boys or kitchen-girls: it was socially unaccepted to mix with them, although there were a few liberals who had blacks as pets.

Esme Matshikiza: For blacks, whites were people you didn't have any contact with except at worker–manager level or in the churches, or at the level of the policeman, train conductor, magistrate or school inspector. And that was only because it was a necessary contact. Otherwise the black communities were virtually self-contained. Of course there was resentment and bitterness and hatred at the circumstances under which we had to live, but at the same time we had our lives to lead, which were very interesting lives, and life was fun. Even within the confines of the system we could still live extremely happy lives. There was a society within a society that actually functioned.

It was this society that *Drum* exposed. It became an attraction for certain whites. Before that, white people knew nothing about blacks. There was no contact, except perhaps at the level of the Communist Party. At that level there was genuine contact between black and white which had been going on for quite a long time. But really I think only with the advent of *Drum* did white people hear about black people who were not servants and were actually able to articulate their experiences.

Es'kia Mphahlele: I think it was a kind of diversion for whites to go to Sophiatown. It was something unusual for a white man to do. I don't think they thought they were pioneering any kind of movement which would result in back-and-forth traffic between black and white. They were just bored. It was much the same as the way white people would go into Harlem in the United States and fraternise with the blacks and feel they wanted to be normal in that kind of strange environment.

Esme Matshikiza: I think there was a sense of voyeurism about whites going to shebeens in the townships, and it still happens now in a way. It's exciting.

Nadine Gordimer: Our meeting ground to get rid of all the inhibitions between black and white was always the parties. The easiest way to feel at ease is to drink together, so no doubt whites didn't discourage people like Can from drinking. There was also the shebeen culture, which many whites found romantic. I am sure there may have been an element of voyeurism among some whites, but for most it was just a party and they became as foolish as anyone does under those circumstances.

Jean Hart: A lot of whites did go slumming in Sophiatown and other townships and did have black friends and used to vie with one another. You really couldn't go anywhere in good left-wing society without a black on each arm. Sons and daughters of the English upper-middle class – the old colonial diplomatic people – would go there and sow their wild oats, have wild times that they could never ever afford to have in their own homes. I was aware of this and hated it at the time. They would come round to Sophiatown and flirt and have sexual scenes with some of the black women, not because they liked them but because they were . . . what's that lovely quote?: "Thou hast committed fornication. Ay but that was in another country, besides the wench is dead." There was a lot of that kind of thing, and a lot of it from the middle-class South African whites as well. You could go to Sophiatown and let your rocks off. It was a bit like sin city in a way, or how uptown New Yorkers used Harlem in the '20s and '30s. Much the same sort of thing. Because life was warmer and more bubbling and funnier. The shebeens were wonderful. There was one called the Seven Steps, which was the best, there was a party there every night.

Arthur Maimane: Without a doubt the liberal whites who went to Sophiatown, to the shebeens in the townships, were slumming. Slumming is an old thing. We all saw it as that. Or at least some of us did. Others were flattered to have some white people there, fell over themselves to invite whites to their houses for a meal and were flattered when these whites accepted their invitation. You just have to read Sampson, Nadine Gordimer and others on the shebeens to see they are there as tourists who are amazed at their own bravery, at their own liberalism in sinking to these levels. They did not see the people in the shebeens as fellow South

Africans; they saw them as oddities who improved one's party stories.

I remember Sampson once invited us round to his flat for a drink, and when we got there we were confronted by a whole lot of whites in cocktail dresses and suits. When some of them left they shook our hands and said, 'I'll never call a black person "boy" again.' Now these were the liberals. The only response was to laugh and cry. Laugh at them, be angry at ourselves for accepting this kind of thing. But you've got to live in the system so you do the best you can.

We went to a lot of parties: parties in the northern suburbs, parties in the townships, parties at Jim Bailey's place with the Immorality Act being broken left right and centre for reasons that had more to do with lust than love.

Esme Matshikiza: This is complex ground. I think that when blacks rationalised their motives to make white conquests they might have said it was retribution, but I would also say it had to do with a curiosity, that it was a reaction to the system. People wanted to prove that they were equal. Nor would I rule out the possibility that it was due to an inferiority complex. It's a possibility that some did it so that they could crow over their conquests, but it is also possible that it was done out of a feeling of inferiority which they had to overcome.

As for white women . . . Was it curiosity? Yes, I think so.

Shakespeare of the Shebeens

42

KID HANGOVER

One of my pet hates is going to a midnite party – you know, those riotous money-making affairs which begin on Friday and follow through right up to the impossible hours on Sunday.

But I guess I'll have to go to this here midnite party 'cause the bizarro who's throwing it happens to be my pal, with the name of 'Kid Hangover'. And besides I reckon he'll need the boodle he charges guests, since he's been out of a job for a mile of a time and spending the better part of it in the gaolhouse on account he didn't square up with the maintenance of his two bambinos – not that he's wedded.

It's about eight bells, and the bright Saturday moon makes me feel somewhat romantic and adventurous. I leave my Sophiatown shanty and head for Western, which is the place where this here midnite party is participating.

When I reach Western I find the place spilling over with humans, and I reckon Kid Hangover is going to make himself a good screw. There's enough booze to keep Mr Khrushchev blotto for weeks on end.

I go to the back of the house, where there's a tent pitched for 'rockagers' who now and again want to shake a leg.

Benches are supplied for those who are tired or can't get partners, and those – like myself – who want to battle with the bottles.

A busty young girl in jeans slides a disc on the battered gramophone, and some rockagers begin to dance while the Elvis of Presley accuses each and everyone of being 'nothing but a hound dog'.

Kid Hangover walks in and pats me on the back, then asks if I have been attended to. I put on my best midnite party manners and howl, 'Waddya mean attended to? You crazy? Shake a leg boy, an give me half a dozen beers. I'm thirsty!' I pay him thirty-six bob of hard-earned pennies. As it is I don't need all those beers but there are janes around and a guy's got to make an impression.

In fact, I don't need beer at all – sissy stuff – and I could do with some hooch. But I know that midnite party hooch is always 'doctored' with methylated spirits calculated to knock the hair off your chest, after which the boys can get at your pockets undisturbed, to say nothing of the five-day-long hangover.

I can see that I've made an impression all right, 'cause no sooner have I opened the first bottle – without spilling a drop thank you – when I'm being surrounded by a batch of gum-chewing cherries all breathing down my neck and telling me that if there were more guys like me life wouldn't be the touch-and-go affair it is.

The girls howl for some more, and I oblige. This time we switch over to vodka.

In the wee small hours of the morning I find myself under one of the benches. Needless to say my boodle is all gone – whole week's pay. All I have between me and starvation is my hangover. That vodka must have been over-doctored. I brush myself and criss-cross home.

Three weeks later Kid Hangover corners me at a bus stop and tells me that he went and lost all his money at the races and it's about time he paid some more maintenance for his bambinos. Can't I loan him five quid?

This, I tell myself, is moral blackmail, since he knows I have money on account it's pay-day. I give him three begrudgingly, and remind him that I'm not his father.

Now here I am twiddling my thumbs and wondering when Kid Hangover is going to throw another midnite party – which I won't attend – so's he can pay me back the three quid I loaned him so's I can pay Aunt Peggy for the 'straights' I got on tick the month before.

(May 1958)

43

The above is by the 'Kid', also known as the black Damon Runyon and read from the Reef to remote villages in Ghana and Sierra Leone. Of the hard-core drinking trinity – Henry Nxumalo, Can Themba, Casey Motsisi – he lasted the longest, up to September 1977.

'Call me Moses,' he said to Obed Musi when Musi joined *Drum* as tea-boy and messenger in late 1955. Later when he became copy-boy the Kid said, 'OK, you can call me Casey now like everybody else around here.'

Karabo Moses Casey Motsisi – the Kid – got his nickname from 'Black Stan' Motjuwadi, who had grown up with Motsisi in Western and later worked with him on Bailey publications. Motjuwadi had the longest and fullest memory of those years, everybody said. He died with it just two weeks before our interview. But he's written about the Kid here and there.

'We called each other Kid Brother, I still don't know what the hell for. I knew Kid Brother before we both worked for *Drum*. We attended school together at Madibane High and sold sweets in the train for pocket money. After matric we were together at Normal College in Pretoria where we co-edited the school magazine.

'Casey had a style all of his own. Run-of-the-mill investigative reporting was too mundane for Kid Brother. He could look on benignly at the rat-race, petty jealousies and hatreds, and, detachedly, take the mickey out of us all. I am sure the bastard is in heaven. Nobody will ever fit into Kid Brother's size-one shoes.'

In the archive drawers there are lots of photographs of

Motsisi. Some, the more serious portraits, show a fresh-faced young man with a hint of humour playing about his mouth and his eyes. Then there's Motsisi looking distinctly worried at his first wedding, squashed in between bride and bridesmaid. Perhaps he sensed that his marriage to Grace Nkosi would not last long. She left him, taking all his earthly goods. 'My disgrace,' he used to lament. And then there are the humorous ones: Motsisi clowning with a strongman; Motsisi pulling faces under a top hat; Motsisi twirling an umbrella while he poses in top hat and tails.

Casey Motsisi was one of Can Themba's protégés. Themba had been his English teacher at high school. Themba rescued him from Normal College where he was supposedly studying, with little enthusiasm, and editing the college magazine, with too much enthusiasm, at least in the eyes of the principal. He expelled Motsisi because he wouldn't reveal the author of a 'naughty' article. It was, after all, against his journalistic ethics.

Motsisi responded to his expulsion with a five-page letter. It began: 'The worst thing that ever happened to me was being admitted to the Normal. It is anything but normal. The best thing that ever happened to me was to be dismissed by you.'

That at least is one version of how Casey Motsisi, being on the loose, went looking for a job. There's another version, and both are Motsisi's. As for the truth? Does it really matter? – the stories tell it all anyway.

The second version has it that Motsisi sent Themba a short story for publication in a 'racy and earthy magazine' called *Africa* – an unsuccessful Bailey magazine that lasted for about a year under Themba's editorship. Instead of sending payment, Themba sent a telegram suggesting that Motsisi start work on the magazine pronto, to use the Kid's word. Being in the middle of exams was no hindrance. He dropped everything and took the next train out.

Whereas Themba had once taught him Shakespeare's sonnets, he now started giving him a lesson in township life. Motsisi followed this Devil-may-care, witty, urbane man like a shadow from shebeen to shebeen. He says at first he tried to wean Themba off the booze, but as he had a taste for 'European liquor' himself he probably didn't put his all into it. In fact he may have done quite the opposite.

For instance, every Monday Motsisi would turn up for work with one odd, brown, broken shoe. After about an hour he would complain to Themba that it was troubling him and how about taking it across to Makhanda, the shoemaker, for quick repairs? Themba never wasted too much time in saying yes, and the two would disappear to the 'shoemaker'. A few hours later back they'd come with Motsisi now wearing matching blue shoes. The game had to be played all the way through.

Jim Bailey recalls that Motsisi was actually signed up in a Sophiatown shebeen where they'd gone to interview him. His story goes: 'We were interviewing tiny little Casey when a young coloured came in and sat down and started telling a story of how at the age of twenty he'd already murdered three people. It was all tremendously impressive, until tiny little Casey asked him two or three questions in his tiny little voice and pricked the bubble and the chap collapsed. So we signed Casey up.'

Motsisi's sense of humour soon produced a column in *Drum* called *Bug-Talk*. It was his form of satire. The fans loved it.

44

JO'BURG JAILBUGS

It was just a few minutes after dusk and the two bugs sat silently in a nook of the prison cell No. 13 in Section D of the Fort. Their eyes were bloodshot. (Bloodshot eyes are as much a part of a well-sucking bug as a paunch is of a wealthy rural Zulu.) The First Bug sighed and turned to the other. The Second Bug sighed too, for lack of something to say. Silence. The minutes fattened into hours.

'I can't understand human beings,' the First Bug barked, and looked into the wrinkled face of the Second Bug. The Second Bug nodded its ageless head in a manner which said, 'You're telling me.'

'Whenever they talk of the old days they refer to them as the "Good Old Days",' the First Bug continued.

'But to us bugs,' the Second Bug fell in with the conversation, 'the old days were lean days. Jolly lean, I say. Couldn't find enough prisoners to bug. We were practically forced to practise birth control, so lean were the old days.'

The First Bug coughed a little and spat out blood. No matter, it thought to itself, I'll refill tonight. 'I remember the seven lean years way back in 1887 – this prison was not built yet, only trees where it now stands. There were only two prisoners. I mean black prisoners, you know. I love black prisoners. They're so full of blood and so harmless. White prisoners scratch a lot. Insomnia, I guess. But as I was saying, there were these two prisoners here and a whole swarm of us to bug them. We bugged them dry, man, dry, and all most of us got was just a droplet. Then we decided to crawl over to the cells of the white prisoners.'

The Second Bug was shocked. 'Did you actually take such a risk? Why, you might have been squashed! The things hunger can drive a bug to!'

'We crawled over, all right. Lost a bucketful of bugs because of the disinfectants they use in the white cells, but some of us managed to get back just before dawn. I lay sick for a week.'

'When human beings talk of the old days as the Good Old Days they complain now that "Times are Bad",' said the Second Bug. 'To us bugs these are Good Young Days. More black prisoners coming in to be bugged by the pick-up-load every day. Permit raids, beer raids, pass raids, pickpockets, payroll snatchers, foreign natives, immorality, night specials, slogan writers, political agitators – why they all come in to be bugged ever so regularly. These, indeed, are the Good Young Days.'

'Shush,' cautioned the First Bug. 'Here come the boys from their hard labouring. And they look comfortably tired for us. The minute their heads touch the cement floor they'll fall asleep and we can go for our fill. Shall we make it a small drink or a blow-up?'

'Let's make it a blow-up, I'm thirsty tonight.'

'The way you like drinking, blood will be your undoing one night,' the First Bug teased. 'Say, there's a new one tonight. That fat one over there. Do you see him?'

'I know about him,' the other bug said importantly. 'He's a reporter. The ghost squad roped him in with two other men while they were drinking gin in a shebeen in Malay Camp – you know the one just opposite Marshall Square Police Station? We must bug him solid tonight because his editor might come for him tomorrow. You know what editors are.'

'Poor boy, we'll bug him so good he'll learn to leave the white man's liquor alone and develop along his own lines.'

(November 1957)

45

Casey Motsisi used to boast: 'I don't go out for my columns, my columns come to me.' And in large part they did, mostly because he was sitting in a shebeen at the time. He was known as the 'Shakespeare of the shebeens', and could be heard leaving the office proclaiming, 'No nooze is good nooze. But no booze is sad nooze indeed,' as he went out to take up his bardship. Shebeen life made up most of his *On the Beat* column:

It's rather lonesome in this shebeen in Fordsburg, which is run by a Syrian woman, and even the three bottles of beer I'm gulping and belching through don't prove good enough company. I begin to long for the sparkling atmosphere of Aunt Peggy's joint. But I can't very well go to Aunt Peggy's on account of some little money matters.

The only activity in the room is supplied by two small puppies busy trying to outsmart each other on the floor. I'm debating with myself whether the dogs should be pickled and turned into a rare Chinese delicacy when in walk two boys and two gals.

This foursome order six beers and a quart of 'madolo', which is the name by which the bright sparks call wine. Seeing as I still got two bottles left I take myself and the two bottles away from the table I've been drinking at, and ask these folk if I can join them. One of the girls turns her verbal ignition on, clears her throat and declares that she wouldn't mind if I did, but I don't like the greedy way she's eyeing my two bottles.

I join them. One of the guys, he's as tall as the North Pole, picks up something from the floor and dumps it on the table. I see it's a tuppence-farthing, nineteen-odd-odd model box camera that would give some of the shutterbugs at the office fits.

I'm just about to ask him where he picked up this monstrous anachronism when he stretches out his hand and says, 'By the way pardner, let me introduction you.' He tells me the names of the girls and I stand up, bow somewhat and say, 'Pleasedtomeetyou.' He points at his bearded pal, and what he says nearly makes me bring up all the beer I've been storing in my paunch. 'This is Casey Motsisi and I'm Peter Magubane of *Drum*.'

Somehow I manage to control myself long enough to shake these guys' hands. I tell them that I'm Kid Tapait. The beers come finally, and we begin to settle down to some hard work. But for the bull these guys are shoving down the ears of the two gals, I would be really enjoying this boozing session.

But since these guys are liberal with their drinks, I stop myself from telling the two poor gals that I think somebody's taking them for a ride. Mum's the word, I keep reminding myself every time I slug their drinks. At last, one of the gals manages to sling in a few words edgewise. She wants to know from Kid Camera when their pictures are going to be published. Kid Camera says something about 'in the next issue'.

The beers are thinning down and I make a slight hint to the fact that I see more empty bottles than healthy ones, when Kid Beard, alias Casey Motsisi, hollers for another half a dozen.

The stock arrives just when another guy walks in. Oh my God, it's Blubbermouth. I pray to my ancestors that he don't call me by my name. But my ancestors must have had the day off, on account they don't answer my prayer. He slides next to me and greets me: 'Hi, Casey boy. How 'bout a drink?' I can see Kid Beard look funny at my pal Blubbermouth, who proceeds to ask me where Peter Magubane is. Naturally, I point at Kid Camera, on account he introduced himself as such earlier. The two boys begin to look worried. The two gals begin to look furious. They want to know from Blubbermouth what the set-up is. He tells!

Next thing the gals, each with a high-heeled shoe in hand, are knocking the living devil out of the two guys, who make a break for it.

My pal and I and the two heel-swinging experts settle down once more to do justicee to the six bottles of beer. And boy, there's nothing as good as a beer with a gal cooing maudlin mush into your ears – especially when the beer is on the house . . .

(April 1959)

Except for a short period in the mid-'70s when he took a position on *The World*, a Soweto newspaper, Casey Motsisi spent his entire working life writing for *Drum*. He was back on the magazine when he died in 1977.

Sophiatown

46

In February 1956 *Drum* ran a photograph across the top of a left-hand page which showed three men sitting on the pavement playing dice. A peaceful everyday scene, but it's not the essence of the picture. That message is writ large above their heads: WE WONT MOVE. The letters bleed paint.

This is Sophiatown. It is doomed. By government decree the inhabitants are to be moved out and the area flattened for white housing. WHAT WILL HAPPEN IN THE WESTERN AREAS? asks the headline:

> The first sixty families in Sophiatown, Johannesburg, have been given orders to leave their houses, and have been offered accommodation in the new location of Meadowlands. 'You are hereby required in terms of the Native Resettlement Act 1954 to vacate the premises in which you reside . . .' The first date given is 12 February.
>
> These are the first of fifty-eight thousand people who are scheduled to be moved from the Western Areas of Johannesburg to new locations further out of town.
>
> Three days after the first notices were sent to residents the African National Congress issued a statement: 'The African people have rejected the removal scheme as a brutal and wicked plot to rob the African people of freehold rights and to resettle them in specified areas in tribal groups . . .
>
> 'If the Nationalists implement the removal scheme,' continued the statement, 'an extremely dangerous and explosive situation will arise.'

Meanwhile meetings have been held in all parts of the Western Areas to decide on future action. Walls have been painted with the slogans 'WE WON'T MOVE' and 'HANDS OFF NEWCLARE'.

What will happen? *Drum* interviewed Elias Moretsele, Transvaal president of the African National Congress, a Johannesburg businessman and Western Areas resident strongly opposed to the removal.

'Feelings are running high,' said Moretsele: 'most of the people simply want to sit down and refuse to leave. Property owners in Sophiatown are against being deprived of land and buildings that have cost them so much time, money and energy. Many tenants, too, realise that in Meadowlands they will be under severe restrictions. People simply don't want to be herded into camps like locations: it's against man's dignity.

'Congress, as you know, believes in non-violence and will discourage violence as much as is within its power. Let those who want to provoke do so; we have progressive forces on our side.

'There can be no talk of defiance in this matter.'

In the mean time some landowners in the Western Areas have already sold their properties to the government, and some tenants and landlords have already moved to Dube Village, where a thirty-year lease is available.

The government maintains that there is little genuine opposition to the scheme, and that accommodation at Meadowlands will be a great improvement on the overcrowded houses of Sophiatown and Vrededorp.

Undoubtedly the Western Areas scheme is an important and significant development, and the world is watching anxiously to see what will happen.

(February 1955)

47

Don Mattera: In Sophiatown nobody looked at the colour of your skin. It was who you were that counted. This is why I say that in another time Sophiatown will be reborn. Not the Sophiatown of the slum, but the Sophiatown of the idea, the ethic.

Esme Matshikiza: I knew Sophiatown very well. Although we didn't live there, all my relatives did. When it was established it was five miles from Johannesburg – a suitable distance away from the white town for natives to live. But by the time I knew it Johannesburg had crept a lot closer. The community was a mixture of professional and working-class people. You could have a traffic inspector on one side and a librarian or a dustman on the other: wealthy property owners living cheek by jowl with street sweepers, shebeen queens and gangsters. I was never threatened in Sophiatown, nor was Todd, nor Can, nor Bloke. I never felt threatened. No doubt there were no-go areas but I don't know anybody who was killed there. Obviously people were killed there, but they were also killed in Hillbrow or Alexandra township.

Anthony Sampson: I used to prefer spending my evenings in Sophiatown than in the white suburbs because it was such a fascinating place with a mixture of personalities in the shebeens, from well-educated people like Can Themba to the gangsters, businessmen or politicians just dropping in for a drink. It was wildly romantic and tremendously entertaining compared with the formality of the white world. Sophiatown was a meeting place for so many.

230

Nadine Gordimer: Sophiatown has been romanticised tremendously. It was a slum. But look at the slums we have
now: look at the squatters of Alexandra and Soweto. Look
at the vast rural dumping grounds of 'resettlement' areas
such as Botshabelo. Among them there isn't a sense of
community, a sense of fun and survival. Hogarthian though
it may have been, it was there in Sophiatown. But then
people were truly urban because they lived close to town,
they lived in the town, it was within walking distance.
Today there is a yuppie element in the townships. They go
to nightclubs and discos but there isn't the kind of fun that
people enjoyed at the House of Truth.

Trevor Huddleston: Sophiatown was a remarkable and
vitally vigorous community. It's extraordinary how many
gifted people came out of the place. The artist Sekoto, for
instance, not to mention the *Drum* writers or the musicians.

But you must also realise that there were about two
murders a week in that area. However I never felt threatened, and I used to go out a lot at night. I can even
remember breaking up a knife fight.

We were the only whites living in Sophiatown except for
a small group of Roman Catholics down the road. Our work
had been started by some high-class Englishwomen who set
themselves up to do social work from a religious foundation.
They built a house called the 'House of Peacemaking' from
which they ran their mission, and out of that grew the
beginnings of the real Anglican presence in Sophiatown.

When I went to Sophiatown the Anglican community had
been there ten years and we were accepted as part of the
scene. They had built what was then the biggest primary
school in South Africa, and they built the church and a clinic
and the first swimming pool for blacks at the back of the
priory. All this was done with financial help from the white
community, but despite all this there was no white protest
against the removal of Sophiatown, except from people like
the Institute of Race Relations.

Sylvester Stein: I spent a lot of time there. That Harlem-type of life went on despite the bulldozers, but they weren't terribly noticeable at that time in the mid-'50s. In my last weeks I decided to do a 'down and out in London and Paris-style' article. I blacked up and Can arranged for me to live with someone in Sophiatown. I went to stay with a man as a visiting Arab. The story was of no interest as it turned out, because I knew Sophiatown from the inside anyway. I didn't learn any more being black. I wasn't harassed by the police: it was a non-story. The worst thing that happened to me was that my make-up ran and I had to redo it and made it up a darker colour than I had been. The chap I was staying with thought I'd been suntanned.

Jean Hart: I come from Whitechapel, London, and even though I'd been to university I was still very working-class. I was ill at ease in middle-class houses and surroundings, so when I got to South Africa I was drawn into a middle-class style of life and a set of values that I was unacquainted with. I thought these people were incredibly rich. And coming from a place like Whitechapel it was most disconcerting to go into houses where people had servants and huge gardens and ate on patios beside swimming pools . . . so I felt very alone. In Sophiatown, which was after all a working-class black area, I felt at home. That may sound very romantic and very stupid but I remember the weekends I spent in Sophiatown. I would just relax. Even though it was a culture so utterly different from mine, Ma-Bloke was like someone I knew. I didn't know the actual detail of how she went about her life, but I knew why. Her making liquor and doing a bit round the back. Her admiration of Bloke and yet her irritation of him. Her pride, her self-reliance, her vicious, cutting tongue. All of it was exactly the same as what I'd come from. I felt absolutely at home. Absolutely at home with people who eat the way they ate. Who farted the way they farted. Apart from the music and the exotic excitement, it really honestly felt like home.

All the same, I couldn't walk around in Sophiatown by myself, even though I was well known. There were places – shebeens, streets – where I couldn't go because of the *tsotsi* gangs. It was only through Ma-Bloke that I began to realise how dangerous the place was for the people who lived there. She was a real Mother Courage-figure. She was shrewd and she had her fingers in all sorts of pies. For instance she had to pay protection to the *tsotsis* and the Afrikaans police. She was the safety net around Bloke and around all of us in many ways. Unless you were very sharp and very ruthless and very resilient you couldn't survive there. The fact that it was a warm and entertaining place was only maintained by people who lived on the edge all the time.

Of Jean Hart's antics in Sophiatown, *Drum* wrote: 'Dig that crazy white couple living it up in Sophiatown. Pshiooo! Was there a scramble when word went around Sophiatown that a white guy and his wife were singing and jiving opposite Kan Son's corner. Hey, it's an ad-stunt, man, said the crowd that sprung up. But no man, it was an English artist couple, Malcolm and Jean Hart, who'd learned how to sing and dance African jazz – and go, man! They were trying out their talent on the corner while spending a weekend with black friends in Sophiatown. Perfect, said the crowd, when they heard Jean singing "Ngihamba Ngedwa Laph Egoli" like she'd been born in Sof'town. That night they went on to a nightspot where Jean shook her hips in the African *kwela* with the Sophiatown socialite, Fatty Nkoana.'

By the end of the '50s Sophiatown looked like a bomb-site. *Drum* did a final photographic feature that showed people being evicted from their homes, their possessions strewn over the street. One photograph taken at night is of a man asleep on flattened sheets of cardboard. He is lying on the stoep of a condemned house, the windows broken, the doors off their hinges. In another a woman and her friends carry away her furniture while demolishers hammer down the walls of her home in the background. For some the parting was impossible. By day they wandered among the heaps of rubble, by night they sheltered wherever houses, or parts of houses, still stood. A fourth photograph shows a family of three in the nave of the Lutheran church. The woman lies on the floor covered by a thick blanket; the teenage boy and his father sit dejected, staring across the floor. About them are a few suitcases, pots, basins, card-board boxes – their belongings. They had been found among the ruins by some priests and given sanctuary in the church. But the picture that wrenches at the heart, as it was meant to, shows a young girl close up, crying, one hand patheti-cally rubbing at her eyes. Behind her, out of focus, are heaps of smashed concrete, bricks, walls partly demolished, door-ways to nothing, the graphic pattern of destruction.

LAST DAYS OF SOPHIATOWN was the feature's headline. And beneath it in bold type: *Big machines and men with picks are beating down the last walls of Sof'town. Take a last look and say goodbye.*

By 1960 Sophiatown was a memory. The same streets with the same names were still there but the new houses were occupied by whites. The suburb was now called Triomf (Triumph).

A Serious Man

48

'I just hated getting up in the morning and saying to myself, I've got to go to that fucking *Drum* office. I didn't like it at all, or myself either.'

The words are Es'kia Mphahlele's, the one who wasn't seduced by *Drum*, the only one of those talented guys who made it as a writer, a critic and an academic of international note. But then he never really was one of the '*Drum* boys'.

Like Can Themba, Mphahlele was a schoolteacher, but he had fallen foul of the government and been discharged without reasons and forbidden to teach anywhere in the country, a dismissal he was unable to contest in court because black teachers didn't have those sorts of rights.

He got a job teaching Afrikaans and Mathematics at St Peter's, but because he wasn't recognised by the Department of Education he had to be paid out of school funds – £18 a month. It wasn't enough but Father Trevor Huddleston, then superintendent of the school, couldn't afford to pay more. He offered to double the salary in Mphahlele's second year, but the school didn't last that long. In parliament the Bantu Education Act went through and Huddleston closed down the school rather than pander to the new and vastly inferior system of education being instituted.

Faced with the hungry prospect of being on the streets again, Mphahlele opted for journalism at *Golden City Post* – a Sunday paper for blacks which Bailey, flushed with *Drum*'s success, started in 1955 under the editorship of Cecil Eprile. As he's already said, the writer and teacher was totally unsuited for journalism and he loathed it even more than he would loathe working on *Drum*. But in those days the lure of a position on *Drum* was very much a matter of the greener grass on the other side of the fence. So when Sampson said Come over, he went.

'Despite my frustrations,' Mphahlele says now, 'working on *Drum* did give me a window on to another world which I would otherwise not have known about and it was a good thing, that brief exposure. But at the same time I hated it.

'However, I tried to be happy editing the short stories, and yes, I did enjoy it, even though I was told to concentrate on the sex and crime stories. I also did some political reporting on the side. For example, I covered the Treason Trial and other events as well, also the Sophiatown removals. I must admit there was no interference in how I wrote those stories.'

Arthur Maimane says Mphahlele always had the *gravitas* of a much older person. Unquestionably he was more serious than the rest of them in every way, especially politically. To him being born black was a political event and everything flowed from there. He was no killjoy – he would go dancing at the Ritz, but he wasn't given to Can-Casey-Henry's nihilistic drinking bouts. He would rather be at his fiction, or putting in more work on his Master's thesis.

'So much of the time Can and the others were playing the fool and having a really good time and in a sense they were,' he says. 'We were in a kind of sheltered employment; even though we were paid lousy salaries we were sheltered in a way other professionals were not and there were not that many options either: you were a teacher or you were a journalist or you were a clerk and there wasn't much else.'

Given that, imagine how this serious, intelligent man felt when hauled in to clown with beauty queens and cover girls as the *Drum* ethos demanded. How did he do it?

'I desensitised myself on *Drum*. I decided I wasn't going to worry about it as long as I knew where I stood myself. They were silly pictures, but of course they were great fun for *Drum*.'

236

Ah yes, one must never forget that, if nothing else, *Drum* was great fun.

For those indignities Mphahlele took his revenge in a novel called *The Wanderers*, where the real characters and situations appear very thinly disguised, as in this scene:

'I've had to play politics with these government chaps,' says Don one day to me and Cecil.

'How do you do it?' I ask.

A smile cuts his mouth open, the sides of the mouth pull down and he says:

'Hang fire with the exposures and simply coast along.'

'J-j-just what I-I-I'm doing in the *P-p-post*.'

The devil! I think.

'Politics are taking precedence in the minds of our readers,' Steve says.

Cecil takes out his tin of tablets, throws one into his mouth and chews. I keep wondering why he always grimaces when he chews his tablet. His face always looks like a baby's, and the grimace accentuates the impression.

Cecil's paper is a weekly tabloid, *Bongo*'s a monthly and we must come out with big follow-ups on the news.

'That's p-p-prof-f-found, Steve!'

'Hardly,' Don remarks. 'I just want us to lay off for a while instead – thrust into township social life and give some shrewd political speculation. Who's in, who's out in underground African political organisations, any up-and-coming young leaders – things like that.'

Cecil's body twitches as it always does, as if he were being bitten by a flea underneath.

'We-we-we have n-n-no p-p-problem on that s-s-score, Don.'

'I appreciate that,' Don says, 'that we must bear in mind our two rivals are thriving on light stuff, on the social life of the blacks.'

'I thought we were operating on another level anyhow,' I say. 'We've never looked at ourselves as a government paper.'

'Hell no!'

'We-we-we g-get s-s-several letters f-f-from readers c-c-com-m-m-menting on our s-s-social and m-m-music pages s-s-so they m-must b-b-be f-f-finding greater p-pl-p-pleasure out of them.'

'And let's cut out the short story. I can't think many people read it anyway.'

That last remark, of course, from Don.

The characters, in order of appearance are: Jim Bailey as Don, Cecil Eprile as Cecil Epstein, Mphahlele as the narrator, Sylvester Stein as Steve Cartwright. *Bongo* is *Drum*; the *Post* is *Golden City Post*.

The extract says a lot about Bailey's hand in the magazine, about his editors, about editorial policy, and finally about something which really annoyed Mphahlele and destroyed his already tenuous faith in journalism: the axing of the fiction section.

'That's where you can see what a very unsavoury influence on the magazine Bailey had. He was the man who abolished the fiction section. He instructed Stein to explain to me that fiction wasn't what sold the paper; it was the stories about real life. So that was it: it stopped dead. Yet it was such a small section of the magazine, one single story a month, and we had quite a substantial readership for the fiction. After that I became even more disillusioned with journalism. I decided I'd better just pack it in. But I couldn't really, so I continued as a sub and wrote political stories.'

To Bailey the decision was simple. 'Quite honestly, I didn't think the stories, certainly most of them, were all that good. I thought we could put the space to better use. The fiction wasn't selling *Drum*, it wasn't being read.'

Yet fiction had been flooding in to the magazine ever since the first short-story competition, in such quantities that a fiction editor had been considered necessary and Mphahlele had been hired for the job. Less than two years later, Bailey wrote it off.

But when Mphahlele joined he felt he was in the middle of a literary renaissance. 'People had been waiting for a journal to publish their work and now here it was. What they had to offer was lively, vibrant, with a style of its own and an English of its own. I don't think you could call it a *Drum* school of writing, because we were quite an eclectic group of people writing fiction at the time. Each one had his own individual style and yet it was a very vibrant style which has never been repeated.'

With the demise of the fiction pages in 1957, Mphahlele decided it was time to quit *Drum*. He did more than that – he left the country, becoming the first of the *Drum* writers to go into exile. After two decades of a nomadic existence in Africa and America he returned home because he missed the smell of woodsmoke at dawn.

49

LESANE [part of a series by Es'kia Mphahlele]

Fanyan felt awkward and clumsy being in Form 1 at the age of eighteen. 'Hey, you goat!' the Arithmetic master said. 'You, there, don't be such a clumsy owl!' shouted the English mistress. 'No, no, no, we don't construct a triangle like that. Where were you born?' the Mathematics master said. Fanyan felt a wild storm rage inside him, especially when the girls of his class said, 'Shame!' and clicked their tongues with pity. They made him feel as if he were soft.

He knew he couldn't do high-school work fast enough. His schooling had been retarded in the country, where there was so much hoeing and harvesting to do in between school terms. They hadn't told him at home why they had suddenly changed their decision to let him work. In order that his conscience should sit easy Lesane ordered Fanyan to stay at school for about a year. 'It will add to his country education. I went to country school myself. Did me no good.'

'*Wai*, Elisha, you used to write to me when you were courting,' said his wife.

'Yes, yes, but nothing more.'

Fanyan's going to school was part of the little reorganisation in the Lesane home. Ma-Lesane started to do white people's washing. The eldest boy of the three brats, a nine-year-old boy, was already in school. The youngest was sent to the Anglican nursery school two streets down. Fanyan had to carry the washing to the suburbs after school, the mother fetched it on Mondays.

He had just delivered washing at a suburban house one afternoon when somebody called him from the other side of the road. It was a policeman. Fanyan stopped. He sensed that the policeman wanted him to cross over to him.

'Where's your pass?' the constable said sharply.

The lad searched all his pockets. Then it suddenly flashed into his head that he had left it at home. He gaped at the constable. He tried to plead. Just then the pick-up van swerved maliciously round the corner and came up to them like a dog that had been sniffing for something and suddenly located it.

'Bung him in!' said the driver, a white policeman.

'Please, please, my pass is at home. Please, please, we can go and fetch it.'

The constables laughed heartily. 'Bung him in! Throw him in!' one shouted. Fanyan was thrown in.

Inside there was a crowd of others. It took time for his eyes to adjust themselves to the dark. When he could see the faces he couldn't recognise any one. He was in a fright. He wanted to jump out, but there was a strong gauze-wire barrier at the entrance.

The night in the cells was enough to give Fanyan a foretaste of the wrath of the law in all its frowning terror. A man from another batch was taken to the charge office at the end of the passage. He came out puffed, with purple eyes. Ripping laughter. Prayerful stuttering lips. Agonising thuds. Gasping, knee-buckling fright. Cheeky, passive snorting. He saw and heard them all within those greasy walls that looked like the Devil's own spitting ground.

The policeman who stood next to Fanyan's batch and kept prodding one here and another there in the ribs smiled when he saw how terrified the youngster was. Poor fellow, how green he is still, the policeman was thinking.

Out in the country Fanyan had actually stood five

yards away from a mounted policeman. He remembered how frightened he had been of the law that stood erect on four large hoofs and great lumps of animal muscle and stirrups and shining spurs. But he also remembered that it was not nearly as terrifying as the law on four wheels: the law that darted from one place to another with lightning effect on screeching tyres, the law that stretched out a large paw and caught you by the scruff of the neck, the law that often gave a long weird whining but sharp sound with a siren.

The next day Lesane paid ten shillings to have his son released. The police would not even look at the pass the old man brought. The fine, he said, was for failing to take out a pass when asked to.

A week later Fanyan was at Seleke's. There was something mysteriously charming about Seleke, Fanyan thought, even in the light of a candle, and she often showed a sisterly affection for him. He got used to calling on her. Seleke and her cousin had moved over from Nadia Street. 'Good for business,' as Seleke explained it. Like all other shebeen queens she was believed to have powerful contacts with the police. Fanyan reflected that perhaps it was just that kind of boldness Seleke had which he lacked that charmed him.

Her cousin, known simply as 'Seleke's cousin' – nobody cared to find out his real name – drank as much as ever. 'He simply can't help himself, poor chap,' said old Mbata with the usual shock-absorbing piety. 'Kiss your elbow if he doesn't wet his blankets at night,' Ma-Sibiya said. Lesane pointed to the skies and said, 'A cow will give birth to a pig if that cousin of Seleke's doesn't end up in a mental hospital.'

Seleke's cousin had ceased trying to help himself. He became more and more stubborn against criticism. He didn't work in town. He just did odd jobs at home for his keep, like digging holes for his cousin's beer, running errands and keeping their two rooms clean. He had long stopped trying to keep clean himself. His trousers were always either too small or too big for him. Often one of the constables who drank at Seleke's gave him articles from old police uniforms. 'The uncle with the government trousers,' boys would say.

'You think I'm drunk, eh?' he said to Fanyan, who sat opposite him in the front room. He turned to lower the volume of the radiogram music at the corner. 'Right, I'm drunk – hic. But I can speak English better than any of them – hic. The bloody cheap swanks! Why the – hic – hell can't they leave me alone? I live my own – hic – life, not theirs.'

Fanyan later understood that 'they' were the people who were supposed to be talking of Seleke's cousin as an incorrigible drunk – just a useless 'hole digger'. There was a tribe of such men in Newclare back yards who were prepared to drift from one house to another as long as the people were prepared to keep them while they dug holes for beer and kept watch against the police. When people labelled a man 'hole digger' they had given him up. And then they looked at one another smugly, with the obvious satisfaction that they had found a solution to an intricate puzzle.

Seleke came in from the back room. She gave her cousin a leg of chicken and one to Fanyan. 'You're going to be a great man one day,' her cousin said, pointing at Fanyan with the leg of chicken. He had no top front teeth, and his tongue kept flicking out between the two fang-like canines. He tore the meat with one fang, and, with a sinew hanging down mischievously as far as the chin, Seleke's cousin went over to Fanyan and leaned against him.

'Oh leave the boy alone. Never!' Seleke said. Even when she was not disputing anything she said 'Never!' Fanyan noticed that she was a little drunk. 'Don't mind him, Fanyan.'

One of the things Seleke's cousin had stopped trying

to do was to argue with her. He removed himself timidly, but not before he issued the final warning to Fanyan: 'You'll be a great man one day.'

'Scared of the police, aren't you?' she said to Fanyan. He nodded.

'Never! You'll get used to it, don't worry. Just hold your heart in two hands. A police badge used to make my toes sweat. It's like looking at King George's medal now.' Then she told of a frightening experience she had with the police when she was a girl. She got up to demonstrate with her arms that were shaped like a constable's baton. She had a heavy bust, and when she leaned over the table to support herself while laughing, Fanyan observed the division of her breasts. They parted where they united. At once bashfully, delicately and boldly. As she laughed the breasts seemed about to spill over the bodice of her frock, and Fanyan suppressed an instinctive urge to hold out his hands to prevent them from falling.

'Never!' she said without provocation.

'What gives you such a strong heart with the police coming in and out of your rooms?' Fanyan wanted to know. He marvelled at this thirty-five-year-old round bundle of vitality that had a streak of ruthlessness as well.

'When you want to live, then you've got to have a tough heart. Never!'

'How did you begin?'

'Like most of us in the townships. School, no money, school, no money, out, factory, out, no money, marriage, out, lie, cheat, bribe, live. Nothing more. Never!'

Fanyan made to go. 'Heavens! Do something good for me, Fanyan. Do. You know Shigumbu, four houses down? Of course you do. Run down there and tell him to give you a small packet. Bring it here. Do. Almost forgot. Never!'

Fanyan left. A few minutes later he was knocking at

a room in a back yard four houses down. Back yards, he observed, had their own peculiar life, with a continuous buzzing noise. Shigumbu opened the door. He was the dried-up bachelor from Nyasaland. After three years of city life he had decided that Johannesburg was 'rittel bit better than Nyasaland, bludder', quite aware that he was comparing a city with a country.

'From Seleke, are you not?' Fanyan nodded. Shigumbu looked groggy. He put a paper-wrapped packet into a glass jar, and gave it to Fanyan. He went out the room like a cat. 'Give her this.' The set of false teeth he had gave him an evil snarling appearance when they touched the empty gums of the lower jaw.

Fanyan got out into the street. He was going to swerve in towards the row of houses when he saw a policeman standing not far from Seleke's room. His heart seemed to fall on a concrete base in the pit of his stomach. He made a visible movement to change his course and walked back into the street.

'Hey! Come here!' the policeman said, going towards Fanyan. The lad bolted, and the policeman followed. He passed his home and made for the cross-street. He jumped on to the stoep of Lai Tong's shop. Another policeman turned the corner from the opposite direction. Fanyan stopped. Fear choked him and seemed to spin him round like a top.

The policeman who saw him first wrenched the jar from his hand and took out the packet. He unwrapped it, put his nose to it and nodded several times. Dagga, as he thought.

'Whose is this?' the constable asked, as if he were bored.

'My sister's – Seleke's,' Fanyan managed to whisper.

'U-huh. Where's your home?' The lad pointed down the street.

'Come. We go there first.' He felt the policeman's

grip tighten round his wrist. 'Thank you brother,' the constable addressed his colleague.

Immediately the two entered the front room, Lesane stood up. Then Diketso and then Ma-Lesane stood up, her hands dovetailed together and lifted up to the chin.

'That boy is not my son! He's not my son, do you hear me?' As if he had spent the last atom of his energy saying those words, Lesane collapsed, unconscious.

Ma-Mafate turned her washtub round to face Ma-Ntoi.

'Didn't I tell you?' said Ma-Mafate, adjusting the petticoat string which kept slipping down the shoulders.

'What?' enquired Ma-Ntoi.

'That woman Seleke. A hundred Sodoms and Gomorrahs put together in the woman's rooms.'

'I still don't understand, she wasn't arrested.'

'See what I mean?'

'What?'

'She's in love with the policeman who caught that Lesane boy.'

'Oh no.'

'What was he doing in front of her rooms?'

'Now I see.'

'My cousin in Nadia Street tells me these things. He knows all about her and the police.' She had tried so often to keep the petticoat string in place and simply left it to hang.

'But are we to say every woman loves a policeman if he does not arrest her?'

'What else?'

'She can buy him over to keep his mouth shut?'

'But I hear they were two policemen?'

'Buy both. She's got the money.' But Ma-Ntoi knew that this sort of defence would merely whet her friend's appetite for more talk and speculation.

'My cousin says it must have been her lover standing in front of her place.'

'No one has so far told us he saw the policeman. Only Lesane's family saw him.'

'They wouldn't talk about it in any case, surely. Somebody else must have seen the policeman.'

Ma-Ntoi shrugged her shoulders.

'Else how did we get the news that Fanyan was caught by a policeman and that dagga was found in the jar he had and that he said it was Seleke's?'

Ma-Ntoi looked around as if to locate the source of the rumour. She didn't know, but these things travelled mysteriously, she said.

'Here's Old Mbata. We'll ask him,' Ma-Mafate whispered. They waited.

'Greetings, old father!' Ma-Mafate called out to Old Mbata.

'Greetings, mothers.'

'Come over; let's hear something.' Old Mbata stepped over to the women.

'Give us a bite on the tip of the ear. We hear there's a bit of trouble in Lesane's house.'

'No trouble, woman. But Lesane's not well. You know he has had bad kidneys for a long time.'

Being cautious, eh? they both thought.

'This thing that happened last night?'

'Oh that? Nothing much. Lesane's lad is dead scared of the police. He had a bottle of herbs and the young fool dug his toes into the ground when he saw a policeman. Well, they caught up with him. But they found it was only herbs. Seleke's. One of these days that boy's going to scream in front of a policeman like a goat about to give birth.'

He shuffled off, thinking to himself, The babbling female creatures!

'The sly old man!' Ma-Ntoi said. 'He thinks we were born yesterday.'

247

As the news travelled the story of Fanyan and the police changed in plot as often as in the style of telling it. Some were sure it was nothing more than herbs. 'That boy's going to be the death of his father,' others said. Shigumbu, the dried-up old bachelor, made sure that, in Rosa Street at least, the story should revolve round herbs.

'I bought the herbs at Mai Mai myself, bludder. For a cough. Well if people want to think it's dagga let them, my bludder. Look at the moon and say it's a woman's breast, you can fly up and kiss it if you want it, bludder. I can't help it if the moon is not a breast, can I now? I didn't make the moon what it is. Solly, bludder.' He felt secure. Nobody could retrieve that dagga from the drain.

To Seleke, Shigumbu said: 'How could you send a rabbit-hearted fellow like that, sister?'

'Don't get excited, man,' said Seleke.

'Just think if the fellow wasn't the type whose tongue you can cut off with £20 – whew! I can't think of eighteen months in gaol, no fine, sister.'

Lesane took the better of an hour to come round. The sight of a son of his in the hands of the police was too much for him. Seleke came over the same night and then in the morning and got him to cool down. But the picture of a policeman and his son! He knew he couldn't easily forget it.

'I'm sorry it came to this, old father,' Seleke had said. 'Don't be hard on the lad. If only he doesn't lose his head when he sees a constable.'

'Why should he get used to seeing a policeman – to be the Devil's messenger?'

'No, old father, because he'll see many more.'

'Look here, woman –' Lesane couldn't finish the sentence. He knew how true it was and felt the pain of it. He dismissed Seleke.

'Next week you must go out and look for work.' That

was an instruction to Fanyan. 'No more school for you.' Fanyan was not displeased. He was only a little annoyed that it had to be announced with such tight-jawed gravity, as if it were important. But he soon realised how important it was – in more ways than one.

(January 1957)

A Farm Called Harmonie

50

In March 1955 Henry Nxumalo did another of his farm specials. This time in a district called Rustenburg, where farmer Johan Snyman, his son and his foreman Jantjie Thlome had been sentenced to eighteen months, six months and a three-month suspended sentence respectively for beating a labourer to death with a hosepipe. The court heard how they had whipped Elias Mpikwa until they were so tired they couldn't lift their arms. Mr Drum went to see what things were like with the elder Snyman still in gaol.

Says Anthony Sampson thinking back: 'Henry wasn't too worried about doing the Bethal story or the prison story and neither was I really. What was of concern, at least to me if not to him, was when he did the Snyman story. There he could have died, but he never showed any fear or concern for himself. He always downplayed things and of course he had a marvellous line in understatement. I think he had natural courage but there may have been some sense of despair behind it. He must have had some bitterness, but it very rarely emerged.'

'I used to keep a hand on all big stories so that I could at the very least keep the reporter safe,' says Jim Bailey. 'But I don't know if there was really very much we could have done had the Snyman story gone wrong.'

'Apart from the court hearing,' recalls Jurgen Schadeberg, 'a white man in the district had also given us a lot of information about how Snyman was ill-treating his labourers. I forget his name now, but he had put together a file of abuse cases. This man must have got hold of us somehow and Henry and I went out to his place near Koster to interview him. It was very strange: he was encased in an iron lung and we had to talk to the image of his face reflected in a mirror.'

Snyman's farm, ironically, was called Harmonie. Mr Drum approached it, barefoot, unshaven, carrying a small bundle of possessions over his right shoulder:

I went up the drive and knocked on the door of the farmhouse. A one-eyed old man called Jan opened the door and asked what I wanted. Talking in Afrikaans, I said I wanted work. Jan told me to wait for the boss.

A strong young white man came to the door dressed in khaki shorts, looking like a rugby player. He asked for my pass and I showed it to him. After he had interviewed me carefully he said he would hire me at £4 a month, which he would raise to £5 the next month. He said he would have me registered at the pass office next day. He asked if I was married. I said Yes, and he said he had a house for us, and we could get a monthly ration of mielie meal.

I was told to dig in the garden. Soon a van pulled in with labourers from the mielie lands. A tall, tough black man with several teeth missing came out from the driver's seat. I heard him called Jantjie and I felt sick in my stomach as I realised that this was Jantjie Thlome.

Jantjie eyed me suspiciously as we folded tarpaulins from the van. He asked me where I came from, and I said from Magaliesburg. He asked me if I had brought blankets with me, and I said No. He made a grim face and went away.

I was given supper with the other labourers in a shanty opposite the compound. It was dark and I couldn't see what the men were eating. One man told me I should have brought my own dish and spoon. I had to wait until he had finished to borrow his utensils.

The food was half-cooked porridge and skimmed milk: every meal was the same. There was about half a cupful of brown sugar for eighteen of us spread on some sackcloth when we started, but it was finished by the time I started eating.

I got talking with the other labourers: they talked about Johan Snyman, whom they called 'Ushabulal' umuntu' (One who has killed a man). After supper most of the labourers went away on bicycles. They said they were going to see their girls or gamble. One, Mnguni, who was called 'Slow Coach', stayed behind with me. He showed me the compound, with small pot windows and iron bars like a gaol. I recognised it as the same place where we had offloaded manure earlier in the day.

I asked Slow Coach where the light was and he said there wasn't a light. I asked him about blankets and he said there weren't any.

'You sleep on sacks here, and cover yourself with sacks,' he said. 'Go next door to the store room and get some. But be careful – there's a ghost there. That was where Mpikwa was killed. One night Picannin, who cooks our food, was coming back to the compound from the village. He saw Mpikwa's ghost sitting on the box in the shanty where we have our food. He dropped everything and ran back.'

I sat down in the pitch-darkness on the stone floor of the compound. Then I summoned up courage, and ran to the store room next door. I picked up any sacks I could feel and dashed back. I couldn't fall asleep. I lay awake, fully clothed, all night. Three of the labourers who had gone to the village came back, one by one. As far as I could tell, they slept in their clothes too. I kept on thinking I could hear the ghost of Mpikwa: there was a dog barking and rats were at work.

At about 5 a.m. I heard a voice from next door saying: 'Ishayile (Time), "New One"!' I got up and found all seventeen men, including Jantjie, standing round a pot of coffee. Someone passed me a small jam-tin, and I scooped up some coffee and drank it. Then Jantjie shouted 'Haak!' and started the tractor engine. We jumped on the trailer and drove to the mielie lands about a mile off.

We weeded between the mielie plants with hoes, each taking a row. I was left behind and Jantjie scolded me. Later the white man drove up to the lands in a big car. Jantjie told him that I wasn't working fast enough.

The white man shouted to me angrily: 'Jantjie is the boss-boy here. If he tells you to work faster you must do so. Work now, let's see . . .'

He scolded me again and then left.

When he had gone one of the other labourers said: 'Thank God for that, New One. He picked on him and forgot to kick us around. He didn't want to frighten the New One.'

Later I found out that I was the first labourer to join the Snymans' farm since Mpikwa was killed. All convict labour had been withdrawn from Harmonie and the Snymans were finding it difficult to get labour.

Meals were all the same – hard porridge and sour milk for breakfast and lunch. By the time we knocked off in the evening at seven, my hands were swollen, my feet were sore and my back was stiff and painful. I went back to the compound after supper, to another sleepless night in my clothes on sacks and bare cement.

I got quite friendly with the other labourers. They talked a lot, mostly about women. They told absurd lies about Johannesburg, which they had never been to. I had to pretend I had never been there either.

I gathered that most of the labourers at Harmonie had arrived without passes. They knew that if they ran away they would be caught by the police. But they didn't seem unhappy. They joked and talked a lot; but they weren't willing to talk about Mpikwa when I asked them.

I noticed in the store room at Harmonie a noticeboard tied between two petrol drums. It said: J. H. SNYMAN,

HARMONIE. I asked one of the labourers why it wasn't on the gate. He said it was taken down during the case.

The next day was just the same. I was tired and miserable. I didn't know how I would survive another day.

The fourth day was harder still. We were pulling up mielie plants which were too close to each other and we had to use our hands instead of hoes. It was baking hot, but I managed to keep pace with the others. In the afternoon it started raining. I was half-way through my row and Jantjie said I had to finish the row before taking shelter under the trailer. By that time I was soaked through to the skin.

When we knocked off at seven that evening I told Jantjie that I wanted to tell the boss that the work was too hard for me and I couldn't go on. Jantjie laughed and joked about it to the others. They all said I was looking for trouble.

'On this farm you don't just quit when you want to,' said Jantjie. 'You wait till the boss wants you to go. But it's not my farm. You'd better speak to the boss.'

So when I got back to the compound I went to see the boss. I went up to him and said I couldn't do the job. He said I was lazy. After some talk he called Jantjie. He told him to chase me at work next day and report to him. He then dismissed Jantjie and told me to stay.

I stayed with the boss, shaking in my boots. He asked me for my pass and I gave it to him. Until then I still wasn't registered as his employee. He tore it up into little pieces and threw them away on the lawn.

'Now you haven't got a pass,' he said. 'You can't leave without my permission. I can have you arrested and imprisoned. If you don't want to work fast like the others, I'll hand you over to the police and have you charged with refusing to work.'

So I promised to do my best next day.

I thought he had finished and I started walking away.

But he beckoned to me to follow him and I thought he was going to show me another job. But he led me to the bathroom in the outhouse and shut the door behind him. Then he repeated what he had told me outside. He said he treated his workers well and paid them well, and they were quite happy to stay on his farm. He didn't know what had got inside me.

He told me that if Jantjie complained about my work tomorrow he would beat me up and then have me arrested. He clapped me on the left cheek with his open right hand and told me to face the wall. Then he kicked me between the legs three times with his hard boot. I shuddered with the pain.

Then he told me that he wouldn't stand any nonsense from me on his farm. He asked me if I would work hard on the farm next day.

'Yes baas,' I said.

He told me to face him and stand to attention when I talked to him. He clapped me on the face again and said in Afrikaans: 'Hard work, rubbish.' Then he told me to go.

I joined the other workers at supper in the back of the yard. They all asked me what had happened and I told them.

One of them said: 'We told you so. You're lucky old Snyman is in prison. If he'd been here you would have been beaten up and undressed and given sacks to wear so that you couldn't run away.'

I decided to abscond that night but I didn't say a word to anyone. No one suspected that I would try and get away without a pass.

I waited for my room-mates to either leave for the village or fall asleep. I felt certain that the white man would check up if I was in that night so I slipped away as soon as I could. I didn't want to attract any attention so I left all my less important possessions in the compound and walked out barefoot with my jacket over my shoulder. I walked out of the Snyman gate with my heart thumping. I reached the main road and every time I saw the light of a car approaching I hid in the grass. Any farmer who saw a black man dressed as I was might be suspicious and stop me.

Then a car looked as if it was slowing down and its lights flashed directly on to me. I tried to run away from the road but the front of my trousers got caught in barbed wire and I was caught with my feet in the air. I waited helplessly and heaved a sigh as the good motorist drove right past. I lit a cigarette to celebrate and trudged on, on my sore bare feet.

At last I reached Koster station and went to the house of a friend of mine. He put me up for the night while I rested my exhausted body. The next morning he sent someone out to see if the village was safe. He came back to report that the police were looking at passes everywhere. I laid low until just before my train to Johannesburg was due to leave. Then I was driven to the station. Even there they were searching for passes, but I managed to get on the train without trouble, and away to Johannesburg and safety.

At the end of his account Henry Nxumalo pleaded: 'Mr Drum realises that many farmers are conscientious and considerate to their labourers and that the Harmonie prosecution is a terrible exception. But there are still many other farms like Harmonie. Unless workers are given freedom to complain or leave, and until convicts cease being sent to farms without supervision, there will always be cases of labourers being seriously ill-treated.

'Not only farmers but African foremen and labourers take part in these brutal assaults. Mr Drum knows from his own personal and painful experience that these things continue to go on. He appeals to the authorities to take steps to end this dreadful barbarism, which has done such untold harm to race relations.'

(March 1955)

Into That Kaffir World

51

The 'rather cold Englishman', as Anthony Sampson describes himself, who 'always felt a bit detached', finally sold the motor bike that was often to be seen in the streets of Sophiatown, resigned from the magazine that he'd helped make a part of the '50s, and sailed slowly back to England up the east coast, writing a book that was so vividly to capture his time on *Drum*. No matter how impossibly remote South Africa seemed each day to Sampson, behind him the country of paradox continued.

It was the middle of the decade: the hopes, the romanticism, the optimism were still rolling despite forced removals, bulldozers in Sophiatown, or the apartheid Acts passing rapidly through parliament: Bantu Education, Group Areas, Population Registration, Immorality.

Drum got a new editor, but to his credit nothing changed. The magazine continued to look as chaotic as the life it reflected: its pages were still filled with enterprising journalism, exciting photographs and vivid writing. Circulation was still going up.

The editor was Sylvester Stein, a young journalist on Johannesburg's morning paper, the *Rand Daily Mail*, who was already in a senior position as a leader writer. When people heard he'd taken the job at *Drum* they said he was crazy.

'I was advised by all my contacts and friends that I'd be mad going into the kaffir world, as they called it. Here was a man with a good position on a respected newspaper throwing away his future prospects to join a creepy magazine. That was the way people thought then, even liberals, who were numbered among my associates. You didn't go and work with natives. On the other hand I thought it would be interesting and I could see a future there as well.

'So it wasn't that difficult a step to take. But while I was a successful journalist and writer, I had no knowledge of magazines at all and at the time I'd never even read *Drum*.

'I remember one of the things that made life difficult for me was the start of *Golden City Post*. It really was awful, the worst form of tabloid imaginable, and all the *Drum* staff were seconded directly to it. Nobody cared a damn about the magazine during that period because they were so excited about this first ever black newspaper. I used to have to fight to get people to do stories for *Drum*.'

Stein suspects that Jim Bailey never really liked him, or was at least diffident towards him. It's also possible that he never really liked Jim Bailey, although you wouldn't get him to admit that. Certainly their relationship wasn't an easy one and it ended badly. But for all that, Bailey is not unappreciative.

'Sylvester had an outstanding nose for news. His first major feature emphasised that there were rules to the Olympic Games which disqualified national teams that had been selected not on merit but on race. It was only after this *Drum* article that the black sports bodies in South Africa woke up to their opportunities and started putting pressure on government. And then, of course, there was international pressure and eventually South Africa was disqualified from the Games. Obviously *Drum* staffers didn't want to see South Africa disqualified, but we sought equal opportunities for all players.'

Stein, however, was not due to spend long on *Drum*, in fact a little under two years. The reasons probably had more to do with his own restlessness than anything else, but during his period he clashed with Bailey on a matter of editorial integrity.

'As I remember it, I had given notice, not because of *Drum*, although I was often about to resign on a point of principle, although we managed to overcome these differences . . . No, on this occasion I had given notice because I wanted to live in England to see if I could apply the knowledge I'd gained to *Picture Post*. I gave Bailey six months' notice and we negotiated a further year during which he would send me to west Africa to put that edition on its feet and then he would ship me on to England.

'In my last two or three weeks I had a fortnight's holiday to work on my second novel. When I came back I discovered that – in my absence Can was acting editor – the cover, a picture of a white tennis player kissing a black tennis player, had been dropped by Bailey. He had simply decided he couldn't run it and he ordered Can to change it. I decided that wasn't the right thing to do. The upshot was that I resigned with rather a hollow feeling and never took up the post in west Africa. But I felt that editors couldn't be told what to put on to their covers. Also, of course, I had different aims to Bailey; he was the publisher and possibly I was a more reckless character.'

Bailey sees the incident this way: 'You must understand how precarious our position really was, politically. We couldn't run a photograph of a white–black boxing match, unless we cut out one half. Despite the optimism, the atmosphere of those days was very delicate.

'To have run the picture Sylvester wanted was playing a card before its time. My principle was that if you wanted to rile the authorities then it was best to do it if there was something socially important to be achieved by it. To do it for its own sake was silly. You had a very limited store of goodwill and you didn't want to spend it on trivial issues. It was awfully easy for an editor in those days to get his paper stopped by the government and become a ten-day hero in the liberal world. But I had to pick up the bits afterwards and find jobs for the reporters when we were closed down. Maybe that photograph wouldn't have resulted in a close-down, but that attitude would have.'

Stein left in 1957, and for nine months the paper was without an editor.

52

But all that was in the future. Now, in the early months of 1955, there were major issues like the iniquities of the colour bar to expose. And Sylvester Stein went for them consistently, certainly with a greater intent than had been shown before in the magazine. First came the Olympic story, then a look at how white boxers were secretly sparring with blacks:

SOUTH AFRICA'S COLOUR BAR

A special *Drum* enquiry shows that South Africa has no right to ban non-whites from Olympic teams. And now sporting bodies with no colour bar will try to 'break the Olympic ring' by applying for membership to the world Olympic committee.

The non-white athletes of South Africa want to join in the great world march to the next Olympic Games. Slowly non-white associations and individual athletes have begun to realise in recent years that they are also entitled to take part in international sport and they are starting to do something about it now! In fact, right at the moment an important letter is being prepared by the South African Amateur Boxing Federation that may have tremendous repercussions on South Africa's entry to world games meetings – and may at last force the breaking of the sports colour bar, which is quite unconstitutional!

Next month in Paris the International Olympic Games Committee meets – and there are many non-whites of other countries that belong to the Olympic association.

What will the committee say when it receives this letter pointing out that South Africa debars four-fifths of her population from contending in the Games? No one knows the answer to that yet. But everyone does realise that the sending of the letter and the other new moves will make big changes soon.

. . . Since the inception of the modern Olympic Games in 1896, no non-white South African has been selected to represent South Africa in any event. The question naturally arises as to whether the Games are for the white races or not?

The fact that the Olympic Games are open to all persons regardless of colour means that non-whites can take part. It means, in effect, that the South African Olympic Games Association should not retain a colour-bar clause in its constitution, and if it does it should not be entitled to retain recognition from the international Olympic body. South Africa, as such, might not then be allowed to take part in the Games.

. . . It is evident, therefore, that the South African Olympic Games Association is unconstitutionally and illegally practising a colour bar contrary to the charter of the Olympic Games. *Drum* interviewed a prominent official of the South African Olympic Games Association to find out whether non-whites from the Union could take part in the Olympic Games.

The official pointed out that there is nothing actually in the constitution that prevents non-whites from participation but admitted that, because of the social and political traditions of the country, no cognizance is taken of non-whites when it comes to selection for participation in the Olympics.

He went further, to point out that there has always been fear, in the higher circles of the South African Olympic Games Association, that once the legality of South Africa's participation is raised at the international meeting South Africa may be banned from taking part in the Games unless she gives her non-whites the opportunity of taking part.

Nobody would like to see South Africa banned from the Games because of her colour policy. What all true sportsmen would like to see is that the opportunity of entering the Games should be opened to non-whites. Given that opportunity, South Africa should be able to produce a very strong team that would be a force to be reckoned with.

. . . Will white South Africa stick to its rigid colour bar in sport and stand the risk of being barred from international competition and the Olympic Games, or will they allow non-whites to strengthen their teams in the same way as do the Negroes in the United States?

(May 1955)

The answer to that question finally came eight years later when, in 1963, South Africa was debarred from entering the Olympic Games. She has yet to qualify for re-entry. That it took so long for the International Olympic Committee to make their decision probably says as much about inherent racialism in the West at the time as it does about their concern with South Africa's apartheid policies.

A few months after the Olympic story *Drum* turned its attention to black boxers sparring with whites. Today such sessions are taken for granted; then they smacked of exploitation because a black man couldn't step into the ring with a white man to fight for a South African title.

The headline said WORLD CHAMPIONS FIGHT WITH BLACK SPAR MATES:

. . . How they've kept it silent! Through all these years since the war South Africa's great black boxers have been the spar mates for world champions and would-be world champions in training sessions – yet the facts have hardly ever been allowed to slip out.

Once, in 1952, when champion Vic Toweel was

floored by an African bantamweight, a trickle of information appeared in the press. But otherwise the sporting articles have simply referred to 'sparring partners'. Unless they were white, there was no mention of who they were or what they were. It was all very anonymous and modest.

It reminded one of those official mining-tragedy announcements: 'A European miner, Mr J. J. Smith, was injured in a fall of rock yesterday. Nine natives were killed.' No names, just unknown 'sparring partners'.

But Toweel had been knocked down that day three years ago in the presence of international boxing figures – Jack Solomons and his assistant, Sammy Burns. There was no question of keeping it quiet. After a day or two the facts leaked out into the papers. To most members of the public it was the first information that South Africa's top whites used non-whites to pep up their training. And what's more, they insisted on using them because they were the best to be obtained.

Press pictures of these sparring sessions were prohibited. The spar mates used to slink quietly in and out of the gymnasium so that there was no publicity. Yes, the whole thing has been kept as complete and shadowy a secret as possible.

. . . The sparring bouts are enjoyed by fighters on both sides of the colour line. Speaking to a number of white boxers, I learned that many of them are keen to have non-white helpers because they are given a tougher time than with white helpers. One even went to the extent of saying that white helpers cannot 'take it'. A hard punch generally chases them away from further sparring sessions. Why, even a trickle of blood will make some of them say goodbye to any further rounds. Not so the non-white fighter. The harder the sparring, the better for him.

The non-white boxers also enjoy the sessions. They

feel that sparring with white boxers helps them to learn new tricks of the trade. But more than that, the money they receive from helping white boxers is an added incentive.

Some malicious friend of mine had suggested that it is the money that accounts for the non-white boxer's staying power, since he is paid according to the number of rounds he lasts. Well, that's as may be.

Generally, professional boxing in this country is not as active as in England, America, or other overseas countries. But because of the economic conditions, the white boxer can afford to pay his sparring partners. So when non-whites help their white counterparts they are paid for doing so. The pay is not uniform. The top-line boxers pay their non-white sparring partners anything up to 10s. a round. And even then they hand-pick the partners who are to be paid ten shillings.

. . . Some of the lesser fighters in the boxing world pay very little, and others do not pay them. In the latter case both sides agree to help each other whenever one has an engagement.

But not all non-white managers are keen to have their boys sparring with white fighters. Their reason is that some white fighters make their helpers wear sixteen-ounce training gloves while they themselves wear lighter ones. They say this turns their boys into punch-bags.

Some non-white managers refuse to allow their fighters to help whites because certain white boxers take advantage of the weight factor. For instance, a welterweight may spar with a non-white featherweight. There is nothing wrong in a featherweight sparring with a welterweight, provided the purpose of the spar is to sharpen the heavier man's speed and not to turn the session into a slugging affair.

I have had the opportunity of seeing many mixed sparring sessions. And I endorse the view that there are white fighters who are rather unfair on the weight question. Last year I saw one of the present white national champions sparring with an African many pounds lighter and going all out for him.

. . . Meanwhile, don't let's keep it a secret that our non-white fighters spar with the leading whites. Let's bawl it out aloud to the whole world.

(September 1955)

From Drum 1

53

BE-BOP GOES BOXING!

Our boxing writer, J. A. Maimane, was unable to cover the title fight. So we sent music writer Todd Matshikiza, a real jazzman, to his first boxing match. And got our funniest boxing story yet.

I went to a boxing match for the first time in my life on Wednesday 1 June. Two welterweights, Fondi Mavuso and Simon Mbata, were to fight for the South African Welterweight Championship title. That means nothing to me. Flyweights, middleweights, welterweights and heavyweights. Let alone bantamweights. What's the difference? They're all out to kill each other off in support of the main bout.

The first bloody fight was between Sidney Lekwape and John Monokoane. Bantamweights. A lazy, unbalanced fight in which the two boxers were obviously not matched properly.

I wasn't impressed with boxing after that fight. 'Legalised murder', as someone once put it. And there were lawyers witnessing the match! I said to myself when I saw them, Shucks! These fellows Nelson Mandela and Oliver Tambo are actually enjoying this cruel sport.

But the silliest fight of the evening was between two tired men who plodded through six tired rounds of boring boxing. They were Raymond Mkonza and Billy Wilkens in the welterweight division. Nelson Mandela sat through that fight with his finger on his cheek. John

Mokuena, the boxing manager, looked away at the more interesting faces of the spectators. Everybody was bored. Rex Tatane's interest flagged and he's one of the keenest boxing fans known in the medical profession.

This fight was so slow that I like to think of it as the 'walking fight', in which you walk towards your opponent, deliver a sad blow, and walk away.

Richard Morobe fought Kid Sponono in the flyweight division.

That was a promising fight between two battle-scarred little men who seemed every inch determined to defend their scars against further injury.

The main fight of the evening, between Fondi Mavuso and Simon Mbata, was full of tense moments for me emotionally.

I admired the beautiful body of Fondi Mavuso and wondered why he should want to have it mutilated and scarred through a stupid boxing game. His body looks like a masterpiece in bronze, weighing 146 lb. They call him the 'Iron Man', and he truly looked as though he was made of iron. His opponent and challenger, Simon Mbata, looked nervous. He looked too small to me to face the 'Iron Man'. I saw and watched him sitting amongst the audience before the fight and he was looking nervously this way and that. My heart went out to him out of sympathy. In the first round, Fondi was hitting him left and right and taking no chances to lose his title. Hitting left and right, I said. At the end of the round, Simon stooped quietly to pick up the rubber gum-shield which had been knocked clean out of his mouth by Fondi. And Simon looked as though nothing had happened to him.

Round 9 was full of torture. Fondi was fighting like a drunk because he had failed to floor Simon. That's where he would have saved his title, if he had been able to floor him.

Round 11 saw Fondi fighting like a tiger let loose. A

man of iron and blood and strength and fight and non-stop motion forever forwards.

But Simon was taking it. Suddenly his small body seemed to grow bigger. He was cool and he was using every split-second opportunity to land a blow on the champion's jaw. Slick. Just like that.

Simon Mbata. A gentleman of a fighter who never forgets to clean his nose on his glove each time Fondi lands a blow.

On my honour, I would never take such punishment as Simon took from Fondi. Not so much from Fondi's blows, but from his endless stamina. Nothing stops him. It was quite clear that the points throughout the fight had gone to Simon. And now Fondi was all out for a knock-out, the only thing that would save the title.

But when the fight ended at a quarter to twelve, and J. R. Rathebe announced Simon Mbata as the new holder of the welterweight title, it was not without excitement – even from the little chicken-heart that I am.

(July 1955)

54

BOXING GOES TO THE DANCE

To make up for Todd Matshikiza's BE-BOP GOES BOXING *last month, J. Arthur Maimane, our boxing editor, does this month's dancing article – and proves Todd isn't the only jazzman.*

I am not a very good dancer. In fact, as my wife tells me, I can't dance at all. Even at school, whenever there was a dance, I would grab a lady – preferably my wife, who wasn't my wife then – and walk up and down the hall till the end of the record.

And then too, I don't have an 'ear for music' as they tell me; that's why I don't know the difference between a foxtrot, quickstep, rumba, tango or any of the many other dances they have. Don't ask me why they have so many, whereas in boxing there's only two kinds: a boxer and a fighter – generally.

But, unfortunately, I know the difference between jive and mambo. And thus I can attend a dance with some confidence, as I know that at some time or other they'll play hot jazz, and I can cut a rug.

So when the editor said: 'Go to the "Daft Friday" dance and bring me a story,' I wasn't very keen, but I thought, There will be jive, and, anyway, as it is a daft dance, it might be more interesting than the usual 'formal dress only' affairs that bore everybody from the door keeper to the band leader.

The daft dance turned out to be not so bad for some rounds. Like the first jive number; or the fights, which are something that I could understand and appreciate, especially as the dance was held in the same hall (the Bantu Men's Social Centre) where I go twice a month on un-daft Friday nights to watch the palookas go at it – with gloves. I'm still puzzled, though, how people can fight before an audience without gloves and without boxers' licences.

Though I appreciated some straight rights to the jaw that could have, with careful training, raised the man to maybe a good fighter, I wasn't very pleased with the fighting on the whole, as it was the wrong time and promotion; and because they always seemed to be fighting near my wife.

According to the experts, in the long intervals between the fights and the jiving, I was being treated to good ballroom dancing by good dancers. Like this guy Mr Banda; or the other one Mr Gordon. These fellows had grace, the lithe grace and footwork that could have made them smart fancy-dans in the ring – after shedding about forty pounds' weight.

But my anonymous hero was the short, hefty guy who reminded me of 'Two Ton' Tony Galento, and had even better and faster footwork than the erstwhile heavyweight contender. This guy stomped the jive. Not just one number like I did before my knees started buckling, but everyone of them. Fast too. And he didn't get tired. Now that guy! he had the right leg stamina, and would have made quite a guy in the ring: if only, like Galento, he wasn't so short that he'd never win the heavyweight title from Willie Kongane.

The tickets and posters for the dance said NON-STOP DANCING FROM 8 P.M. TO 2 A.M. Well, the dancing didn't really start until well after time, which would have got everybody into trouble with Mr H. C. Liebenberg, big-jowled secretary of the Transvaal Boxing Board of Control: there'd have been a lot of purses cut, all right!

And then still, the dancing wasn't so very non-stop

you'd notice it. There were long periods when the band just sat talking and drinking tea and everybody else stood around the hall talking, arguing, or threatening each other.

I don't blame Peter Rezant, leader of the Merry Blackbirds, or Sonny Groenewald (same of Sonny's Revellers) for those no-non-stop-dancing periods. Especially Rezant. His arms must have been tired from all the shaking he did of two calabashes (anyway they looked like them to me) with stones in them during the South American numbers. Man, he shook those things so fast, so long and so indefatigably that if only he'd been moving his arms straight ahead, he'd have had a classic left or right jab.

Then we would have had a mustachioed and always smiling welterweight contender, Kid Music, Kid Rezant or Battling Tango – anyway, something as silly as the names a lot of the boxers have these days.

After midnight, I was getting bored. The fights hadn't stopped yet. And I was past appreciating even the straight rights, as who wouldn't when you haven't got a clear view from a ring-side seat? I'm not used to such things. But my colleague Todd Matshikiza, who was busy taking notes for *Nite Life* and *Social Swing*, is used to them, and easily stepped in to help stop the fights without even removing his expensive cigar.

Because I was bored, I began doing something rather impolite – they told me: smoking while walking up and down the hall on tired feet with a woman in my arms and a cigarette between my lips. So I resorted to doing this only when dancing with my wife, who understood that because I was so bored I had to smoke to keep from falling asleep on my feet.

As I said before, the dance wasn't all bad. For one, there were pretty women who had me craning my neck: like pint-sized Alice Smith, who I would have liked to dance with because she's shorter than me, and also because she's a friend of mine and is beautiful.

But I guess the people who'll like the dance best – even though they weren't present – are the kids who'll go down to Durban for a holiday on the money raised, which must have been plenty. And so we come to the end of the last round in the main supporting bout.

(August 1955)

55

SPORT IS DARNED CRAZY, SIR!

Casey Motsisi Esq. takes a look at sport and gives his considered judgement.

The professors call it recreation. The simple man in the street calls it clean, wholesome fun. But I prefer to call it what it really is – stark, incurable madness. Yes, that's what it is, this thing called sport.

Sometimes it's just a big, sad laugh. But it is always as crazy as a bedbug.

Take boxing – 'the art of fistiana' for e.g. Some people say it's nothing less than 'legalised murder'. I don't know about the legal part of it, but believe you me it is murder. In fact it's suicide!

Look at it this way. Two guys who probably don't know each other from Adam step into a 'ring' – and a square ring at that – and start sniffing, shuffling, sweating, slugging and generally beating the life out of each other. At the end of it all they are a sorry twosome of blood, thick banana-like lips and puffed-up eyes. And then they have the nerve to say that they have been having fun, they have been enjoying themselves. Of course, others will make an excuse for this unparalleled madness by maintaining that they box only for the money in it. To these I can only say, 'Whattaway to make a living.' It's not worth it, man. For all you know you might die – and many have actually kicked the bucket – whilst you are trying to make your living.

If that is the meaning of recreation, then I might just

as well go and play hop, step and jump on the crater of an active volcano when my leave comes round.

But there is an unpopular set of pugs without plug.

(Personally I think they are astute.) They wait for the gong to sound and then, instead of pouncing at each other like they are supposed to do, they start hugging each other like infatuated schoolkids, or do a waltzing act that would make Fred Astaire at his best look like a clumsy elephant, amidst hysterical protestations and unsavoury catcalls from the too, too bloodthirsty audience – some of them ladies.

Then there is the other silliness called soccer. Wow, now that's a scream. (In this game, like in all others, I always make sure that my position is 'left-right-out'.)

It takes twenty-two crazy clowns to make it all the crazier. That is if we don't count the psychopathic study called a referee – the man whose sworn duty it is to make sure that there is method in their madness.

He blows his whistle and, gangway! they're off, and the stampede is on. Somebody get the kiddies out of the way! Fancy chasing and kicking a poor innocent ball for ninety minutes solid. Why, sometimes they even give it a few jolts with their wooden heads into the bargain. Ouch! But the craziest of the clowns are the goalies. From the minute the whistle blows they will start jumping and hopping from pillar to post like a kangaroo which has had its pocket picked.

The trouble with this kind of madness is that it is contagious. You should see the affected crowd yelling their heads off. 'Daaapa, dapaaa. Mi-i-ghty Joe You-u-u-ng!' And for all you know 'Mighty Joe Young' might turn out to be a scrawny snip of a man. Anyway, that's how it is in this game. The names usually belie the characters. When someone is called 'Chicago Express' you can bet your life that a lame snail can outrun the guy anytime. 'Masked Marvel' has nothing in the form of a disguise except perhaps the smudge of dirt covering

27. *Amalaitas* fighting while police with sjamboks look on

28. Major Att Spengler (*front left*) and security police taking notes at a Congress of the People rally

29. Robert Resha, Patrick Molaoa and Nelson Mandela arriving for yet another session of the mammoth Treason Trial

30. Can Themba being hustled out of a Seventh Day Adventist church during an investigation to see if blacks would be allowed into white churches

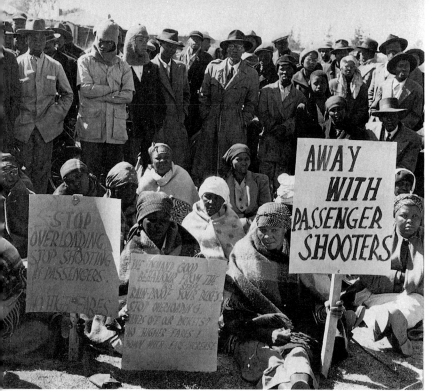

31. Commuters protesting against raised fares and lawlessness on the buses during the Evaton bus boycott

32. In 1955 twenty thousand women marched to the Union Buildings, Pretoria, in protest at legislation designed to include women in the pass laws

33. Lewis Nkosi

34. Nat Nakasa

35. The high-kicking *famo*, a sex dance much admired by the Russians

36. Witch-doctors

37. *From left*: Peter Magubane, Jurgen Schadeberg and Bob Gosani

his face. Be advised, folks. Never go and witness a soccer match unless you want to end up in a madhouse. I tell you, just watching that fantasy is enough to drive anyone mad!

Then there is golf, the goofiest game going. Tennis and ping-pong are punchy, wrestling is whacky, and so on to the point of insanity.

But brother, motor racing takes the cake – or should I say the whole delicatessen? Imagine a decent, God-fearing and devoted family man getting into a coffin on wheels which he smugly calls a car and scit-scat-scoots down the 'Death Track' for no reason at all except that he wants to break records and make a name for himself. More often than not, he ends up by breaking his own neck – and in record time at that.

Preposterous? Absurd? Perverse? Brother, they call it sport. Recreation. Or haven't you heard? All work and no play makes Casey a clot. (And believe me I'd much rather be a safe nitwit than grapple with the high cost of intelligence.)

Lucky for me I don't have to make a name for myself on the death track or the square 'ring' or any other place. I am *somebody* already. You see, my mother was intelligent enough to give me a name when I was born. Bless her ageing heart!

Yes, it's a mad world and getting crazier by the second. I don't know when people are going to realise that the only sensible sport in the whole wide world is – bullfighting. At least you can eat the bull after killing it (that is if it doesn't kill you first). Ah, meat! What could be more sporting? Yum! Yum! Yum!

(October 1955)

56

THE PRETORIA BARE-FIST FIGHTS! by Moses Casey Motsisi

Every Sunday afternoon at about four-thirty a horde of rowdy *'amalaitas'* (bare-fist fighters) advance slowly to the little township of Bantule, Pretoria, from various directions, to the accompaniment of mouth-organs.

Some of the *amalaitas*, most of them domestic servants, come from as far as seven miles. They come down in groups of between thirty and fifty, and each group has a leader. The leaders of the various groups jump and prance about, shouting praises about the strength of their groups, while making all manner of pugnacious gestures as they approach Bantule. The groups do not seem to belong to any particular faction and the ages of the members range from between fifteen and forty.

Even as they sing and prance their way to Bantule, a string of cars from Pretoria and the Reef and a constant flow of other people on bicycles and foot also make their way hurriedly to the same 'secret' place. For not far from the local church, symbol of love and the brotherhood of man, and a stone's throw away from the football grounds, stands the arena to which these people flock to watch the *amalaita* fights.

This arena, which is about eighty yards long by forty yards wide, was built in 1945 by the Pretoria City Council and costs about £100 a year to maintain. Before the arena was built, the *amalaitas* used to fight in open spaces under the supervision of mounted police.

The arena was built as an experiment to give domestic servants who roamed the streets and robbed and assaulted over the weekends an outlet for their 'superfluous energies' and 'animal spirits', and was considered a success in its original form.

But by 1948 the fights had assumed such a medieval ruthlessness that a visiting American correspondent who witnessed one fight said it was one of the most barbaric scenes to be seen in the world. He also confessed that he 'couldn't take it'. He was forced to leave before the end of the fight. And this from a hard-boiled bullfight fan!

A few weeks later the *New York Times*, an American daily, carried a report which made headline news about Pretoria's brutal Sunday spectacle – the *amalaita* fights. The American public was startled by the report of how *amalaitas* clashed in savage contests while Europeans stood by and gloated.

The Union government information department at once ordered a full enquiry into the details of the story, which was described as 'another grave distortion of South African conditions'.

The South African press also carried reports of these fights. But soon after that, restrictions clamped down on the press. As far as the greater South African public was concerned the fights had stopped. But that was not the case. Ever since the hue and cry of 1948, the fights have continued under the greatest secrecy. Pressmen were refused entry into the arena, and the Pretoria City Council erected big noticeboards around the neighbourhood of the arena warning the public not to watch the fights.

(They read: EUROPEAN AND NON-EUROPEAN SPECTATORS ARE KINDLY, BUT URGENTLY, REQUESTED NOT TO ATTEND THE *AMALAITA* FIGHTS.)

When I went to Pretoria to report on the fights with photographer Bob Gosani, a white policeman stopped me at the entrance and asked what I wanted. He kept looking at our camera as if it were some secret Russian weapon. I told him I was a reporter and was interested in taking a few pictures of the fight. Without a word, he bundled me out of the entrance and told me never to set foot anywhere near the arena on pain of arrest.

But our photographic wizard, Bob Gosani, got the pictures!

A few minutes before the fights begin, the *amalaita* troops converge and sit near the arena for last-minute instructions from their leaders and supporters. Meanwhile two huge, cage-like police vans ('*kwela kwela*') arrive at about 5 p.m., and the police, both white and black, file out of the vans and chase the *amalaitas* into the arena with sjamboks and batons. Some of the *amalaitas* scale the low walls of the arena in the confusion. The troops then form a human bullring. The eastern side of the arena is set aside for 'Europeans Only', mostly women and children.

The presence of Europeans at these fights at once imparts a suggestion of the Roman amphitheatre to the scene, and the *amalaitas* themselves fight as slave gladiators of old.

A white officer blows his whistle. The *amalaitas* jump into the ring and start prancing and shouting to warm up for the fight. One *amalaita* worked himself into such a state of hysteria that he was soon foaming at the mouth, posturing and making strenuous acrobatics – turning cartwheels and banging his head on the hard earth floor. About twenty to thirty *amalaitas* fight at once. They hurl strong words and make pugnacious gestures at each other as a sign of challenge.

When they clash, the *amalaitas* attack each other like tigers and all to the delight of the people who watch them.

Blood flows freely as lips are split, head wounds inflicted and noses cracked. 'The show becomes an orgy of shouting, fighting and blood-spilling, in which Europeans and non-European audiences join as fully as do the actual participants. European encouragement is often as vociferous as that of the various bands,' reported the *Sunday Express*, years ago before reporters were kept away.

The barbarous battle soon reaches its peak. Clouds of dust trail across the place as men fall and rise to fight again. They wade into each other like beasts of prey. Now and again a few *amalaitas*, temporarily dazed by the non-stop pummelling, wander around the arena in a sort of stupor. But they always come back and pick up a fight with anyone they fancy.

One *amalaita* who entered the ring without removing his bangles of plastic and wire brass soon had a few opponents bleeding through their noses and lips. He was obviously the 'champion', and would at times stand in the centre of the arena and bellow like an enraged bull while his supporters poured handfuls of fine sand over his sweat-streaked body.

There are no apparent rules of fighting that the *amalaitas* observed, except that now and again one would be whipped by the police if he hit someone who was still on the ground. But apart from this it is no holds barred. The *amalaitas* simply bash away at each other. They butt with the head, trip, kick in the groin with upraised knee and do all manner of harm.

At the end of the fight the officer in charge again blows his whistle and the *amalaitas* desert the arena in less than thirty seconds, the police driving them out with sjamboks, batons and canes. After the mad rush the Europeans file leisurely out of the arena. Only a few *amalaitas* remain, to clean the dusty boots of the police.

The *amalaita* fight is over! But how many of these *amalaitas* are able to return to work the following morning? Some are punch-drunk, some swollen-eyed, some injured. Surely there must be a healthier way in which these people could spend the Sabbath day profitably!

(November 1955)

Mozart and Champagne at Sunset Boulevard

57

Among the staff members who joined during Sylvester Stein's time were three men whose names have passed into the legend. First to arrive was William Modisane, then Lewis Nkosi, and finally Nat Nakasa.

Modisane's name had appeared in the magazine as far back as 1952 with the publication of some of his fiction, and he was a runner-up in the short-story competition won by Can Themba in 1953. He took the third prize of £6 with this entry:

THE RESPECTABLE PICKPOCKET!

'Oh! My purse, my purse. Stop that boy . . . He's got my purse. My money!' the woman screams. 'Help! Stop that boy!'

I tear down President Street, Johannesburg. Snippy, Joey and Steve are hot on my trail. Maybe these boys are trying to set a new world speed record by overtaking me . . . only they won't live to see the day. Standing about ten yards away is a pot-bellied man with his hands stretched out. I aim my head at his stomach and charge at him like an angry rhinoceros and sink my head into his stomach. I get up and continue my hurried journey while the chivalrous gentleman reels in agony

At Rissik Street a man with phenomenal shoulders hits me on the mouth and I land flat on my sitters. Some white ladies with sympathy shining in their eyes gather round us and I tactically scream like mad.

'Why you hit me, boss?' I shout. 'I done nothing . . . I'm good boy, honest I am, boss.'

He shoots out his mountainous chest and beams broadly. Perhaps he expects the ladies to smother him with kisses . . . Or present him with the Victoria Cross for distinguished valour. It's a pity that these ladies don't seem to recognise heroism when they see it. 'Gallant Knight' is so busy showing off his Charles Atlas torso that he even forgets to keep an eye on me.

I run my hands through my crispy hair and knock my hat off. Gallant Knight loosens his hold and I bend to pick it up. I mould a fist and aim at his stomach. It's got to have every ounce of my 145 lb behind it, otherwise Gallant Knight will reduce me to something lower than his heels. I sink it beautifully. He recoils and gives out a yell that can be heard in Alaska.

I dash through the crowd and run to the Sophiatown terminus. When I get home I hide the money in the tea-can and wash the blood off my face. My three not-so-bright friends walk in practically bewildered.

'How did you get away?' Snippy says, his eyes almost popping out. 'I sure thought you were a goner.'

'All this wouldn't have happened,' I snap, 'if Joey hadn't been damned clumsy. How many times do I have to tell you to distract her attention before trying to close the handbag?'

'I'm sorry,' Joey says. 'I couldn't help it. I was nervous.'

'You were nervous?' I say. 'Take a look at my mouth . . . and that's not all. That ape took the money too.'

'You mean he took all the money?' Steve says. 'All the . . .'

'. . . Yes.'

'How am I going to take my girl out?' he says. 'I'm broke.'

'You're breaking my heart. I thought I warned you about Tandi . . . she'll get you to the dog house yet.'

'I don't see you trying to keep away from her.'

'That's because I'm smart . . . I can handle my women, and my money.'

'I don't believe you, Alan,' Snippy says, 'about the money, I mean.'

'Why take the money and let you go?'

'They didn't let me go . . . and for another thing, I don't like people accusing me of dishonesty. I come from a respectable family. Are you insinuating that my parents raise thieves?' I make my face serious and all. 'If you don't believe me, go on, search . . . search the house.'

'That won't be necessary.'

'Hey Steve,' I say. 'If you really need the money, I might be able to get you some . . . see me tonight.' After giving me a lot of bull about thanking me and all, I ask them to leave. They walk out and I start counting the money. If more people went about with £19, this job would really be worthwhile.

With about £16 in my pocket, I feel big. Why not go to Club Casino and give the other fellows a swell time? I dress in a way that becomes a man with money. When I get there a Chinese girl smiles coquettishly and asks what I'll have. I order a dozen beers and a brandy. I spot Tandi, who beams at me.

'Hello, you big handsome boy,' she says.

'Hello yourself, you bundle of joy. Go on, sit down . . . no, not there, come closer . . . there, that's better.'

'I hate to do this to you,' Tandi says to me. 'You'll have to drink alone. What happens when we become too drunk to move away from here?'

'We could go to my room, if it's OK with you?' I say.

'Under one condition: you don't get cute after you've had one too many.'

'What do you mean, cute? I'm a respectable young man.'

'Don't get sore,' she pleads; 'a girl has to protect herself.'

She cuddles closer and smiles in a way that interferes with my blood pressure. When we get home I play my Frank Sinatra records and adjust my paraffin lamp to give a dim light.

'What more could you ask for?' I say. 'Dim lights and soft music . . . and to put the finishing touch, you have me.'

'You think a lot of yourself, don't you?'

'Let's just say I know my limitations.'

'. . . I think there's someone at the door.'

A man hands me the drinks and I tip him. Tandi has removed her coat and is changing the record. The melody of 'I Fall in Love with You Every Day' and a few glasses of beer makes her a little too sentimental. She throws her arms around my neck and starts kissing me like I'm distantly related to Clark Gable. I pretend to be indifferent. She hangs on savagely and kisses me as if her life depends on it.

'Who's getting cute now?' I tease.

'Oh, you're a beast,' she says through her teeth. 'You have no feelings. You're just a piece of . . .'

'Only a piece? I thought you said I was a big . . .'

'Here, have another,' she says.

My head starts spinning. She grabs me and we start cutting a mean jitterbug. Tandi gets heavier and swings me all the more, until . . .

My mouth is dry. I shudder when I see the bottles of brandy on the floor. Something is wrong, I don't remember buying a dozen brandies. I run through my pockets . . . the money is gone.

Losing all that money brings new complications. I have to go to town.

I'm walking in Eloff Street when a white man says:

'Will you accompany me to the police station?'

'Why?'

'You stole money from a certain missus yesterday.'

If I resist I'll only be showing guilt and, knowing that

nobody will believe his story, I agree. The white sergeant says that nobody has filed a complaint, but he locks me up just in case.

On the fourth day I appear before the magistrate, who calls the patriot to take the stand.

'Will you tell the court what happened in Eloff Street on Monday?'

'I saw this native deliberately bump against a certain lady, and after a while she screamed that this native . . . I mean the accused, had stolen her money. Immediately after she screamed, the accused and three other natives ran down President Street.'

'Do you personally know the accused?' the magistrate says.

'No, your honour.'

'Then how do you know he's the one?'

'I just recognised him.'

'Is there anything particular about him. Something conspicuous?'

'No, your honour, he just looks like one of them.'

'I see,' the magistrate says. 'That will be all. Alan Osmond Martins, take the stand.'

I should feel worried by his stern face, but I'm not moved. The face is just a bluff and I know it.

'Can you explain why this man recognised you as one of the thieves?'

'As for the motive your honour, I wouldn't say. But this much I can: all natives look alike. I was a spectator of that shameful incident, but unlike him, I was curious. I wanted to know if those crooks would get caught.'

'I don't suppose you could recognise them if you saw them again?'

'It's like I said: all natives look alike.'

'Why do you refer to them as natives, aren't you one yourself?'

'No, sir. I'm a coloured.'

'If you're a coloured then I'm an Eskimo.'

I almost tell him I wouldn't be surprised, but then I know which side my bread is buttered. He indicates to the prosecutor that he has no more questions to ask, and the prosecutor gets up to earn his pay.

'How was it that you were there at that particular time?'

'Fate has a way of playing tricks on people.'

'You leave fate out of this,' he says.

'Since the theft of the money,' the magistrate suddenly says, 'has not been reported, and no definite proof has been brought against you, the court cannot hold you. But there is yet another case against you. Your prints show that you are not Alan Osmond Martins, you're not even a coloured. You're a native. Your name is Ezra Gumgade. You have two records of house-breaking and six for pickpocketing.'

'Your honour,' I say, unperturbed, 'my name couldn't be Ezra, why, that sounds like the name of a Siamese cat! Those prints could be wrong. I'm a coloured and I have a certificate to prove it. My parents are law-abiding people and I was brought up to respect the law. It would kill them to learn that I've been mistaken for a common criminal.'

'I think you're the most artistic liar I know and, believe me, I've met them all. You're not charged with masquerading under a false name. The court finds you guilty of vagrancy and I sentence you to six months.'

The farm I'm sent to is not exactly what might be called a health resort. We start work in the wee hours of the morning in the fields with our legs deep in water till sundown.

On Sundays we are allowed to bask in the sun and have recollections of home. Me, I reserve my thoughts for Tandi. Every night she walks up and down for me in a command performance, swaying those hips. I believe she could force Venus to a good second place in a hip-swaying contest.

285

I've learned all I want to know about this place. It's about twenty miles from Johannesburg and roll-call is on Mondays. That means I would have a twenty-four-hour start before the farmer would discover my absence and start raising Cain instead of chickens. Sunday has to be the day I bust out of the dump.

I loll around until the farmer and his family go off to church and after the second bell I make my bid for freedom. A sense of dire disappointment surrounds my escape . . . this is all too simple. There are no search-lights trying to locate me, no determined police faces with Sten guns, not even dogs sniffing about. I would have liked to be dodging bullets . . .

It's about nine o'clock when I get to Sophiatown, and I am possessed by a burning desire to touch something soft. I go to Tandi's home. She is wearing a tight-fitting frock which shows her curves to advantage. She virtually throws herself at my feet and says:

'Alan, where have you been? I've missed you so. Don't you like me any more?'

'Listen, baby,' I say. 'For the last two weeks I thought of nothing else. Every time I sat down to rest you would appear, swaying those seductive hips.'

'So you do like me a little, huh?'

'Yes . . . but only a little.'

'I may be a bad sort, a drunkard and a siren, but I love you. Please give me a chance to prove myself worthy of you?'

'Look, I don't like sentimental people . . . sentiment is a sign of weakness. I love you too, but we don't have to be stupid about it.'

'Is that your way of saying you don't love me?'

'It's my way of trying to do you a good turn.'

'All I know is that I love you; nothing else matters. I'm no angel but I love you and I want to make amends. The last time I was with you I stole your money, and now I'm returning it.'

'I'm sorry, but I didn't lose any money.'

She stole it because she needed it; why then offer it back to me? Is it any wonder that I hate honesty?

'I'll keep it for you,' she says. 'One of these days you will need it and when you do, come right over.'

Insanity is a contagious disease and listening to this woman spreading the contagion is too much for me. I take my hat and clear out.

I learn that Snippy, Joey and Steve are in gaol and that they are going to court tomorrow. Being my friends I naturally have to go to court.

The easily irritable prosecutor is having the time of his life drilling my friends. That they were caught with the stolen articles makes their case a hopeless one. They are sentenced to six months with compulsory labour and four strokes apiece. The prosecutor casts a proud glance over the people and suddenly his eyes widen like he's seen a ghost.

'What are you doing here?' he says to me. 'You were sentenced . . . what are you doing here? How did you get out?'

'The witch-doctor got me out.'

It's about lunch-time and the court is adjourned to two o'clock. The next case is of a pickpocket and I decide to come back. I'm at the same seat when the prosecutor looks at me and grins. I must be looking rather fetching today. My irresistible charms have got the prosecutor eating out of the palm of my hand. I really must change my blend of personality . . . I can't stand this mass enchantment.

A big fat policeman comes in and the prosecutor points me out to him. I look round; even the exit is decorated with a police badge. This outsized man writes finis to my interest in the case.

By four o'clock I'm back at the Fort, only this time I'm in solitary and pulling weights tied to my feet. If I had accepted Tandi's love I would be safe in her arms . . .

(January 1954)

58

William Modisane, Bloke Modisane as he was called, is a fascinating character. In him can be seen all the tensions and conflicts of those years. He is a walking embodiment of all the contradictions, all the paradoxes, all the ironies, all the hurt of being a 'situation' on *Drum*. A 'situation' was street slang for the educated guys, the snobs. It was derived from the *Situations Vacant* columns in the classified sections of the white newspapers. The implication being that only educated people could apply for the white-collar jobs advertised there. None of the *Drum* staffers liked the label because it classed them as a cut above everyone else, in other words not one of the people, which may have been another reason they spent so much time in the shebeens.

Before he joined *Drum*, Modisane worked at Vanguard's Bookshop in Johannesburg. This was the city's little intellectual haven for all Communists, Marxists, anarchists and socialists, and attracted not only Modisane but Todd Matshikiza before him. Modisane got to the magazine via *Golden City Post*, which he joined as a reporter. In the mean time he was also writing entertainment columns for *Drum*. He finally moved to the magazine's masthead when Sylvester Stein became editor.

'We called Bloke "Black Jesus",' says Obed Musi. 'The name came about because Bloke would pontificate whenever he could. He was social editor, doing showbiz, jazz, etc. And yet in his house there wasn't a single jazz record. Tchaikovsky, Mozart, yes, but no jazz.

'And once again Bloke, like Can, spoke and thought in English. In his house Bloke would serve tea with sugar cubes. He was the most pretentious of people I've ever met. He'd get champagne from a white liquor runner and serve it in his room, always quoting some fancy name on the label. But who cared in those days? His wife Fiki died recently, not thinking well of Bloke at all. He treated her very badly.

'Bloke wasn't a Christian, at least that's what he told us. He tried to give the impression that he was an atheist. I suppose there was something intellectual about being an atheist. And yet to maintain this façade meant living a rather superficial life: bow-ties, lumps of sugar.'

'Bloke was probably the most debonair of them all,' recalls Anthony Sampson. 'He had tremendous charm and was extremely funny to talk to. His room in Sophiatown was immaculate and he had this love of serving champagne. I once had champagne with him at "Sunset Boulevard". Bloke was a playboy, he certainly wasn't a political animal. Of course he wrote very well, as you can see in his autobiography, but he never did justice to himself there because he was a much more eccentric character than the one he portrayed.'

'Oh yes,' says Jim Bailey, 'I got on very happily with Bloke. He was a good journalist, but I don't think he was one of the best.

'One of my last meetings with him was in New York: we had lunch together. He had been sent to the southern states to look at the race position there by the London *Observer*. "Jim," he said to me, "it's worse than anything in South Africa." He said, "You know in South Africa we're in the majority and sometime everything's going to come our way, but they're in the minority and you can look in their faces and see they've got no hope."

'But I think the last time I saw Bloke was in London. He took us to a very grand club where he was an honorary member and got us free drinks. It was a most snobbish club, well in the tradition of the Sophiatown Bloke who had called his room Sunset Boulevard.'

Yes, here in the middle of Sophiatown, off a stinking back yard, was a tiny shack called Sunset Boulevard. Inside, an elegant room with bookshelves resounded with classical music, usually Mozart, and the popping of French champagne corks. Uncharitably, Modisane can be seen as a playboy, an extremely elegant playboy with a penchant for young white girls.

'I think,' says Philip Stein, a friend and colleague dating back to his Vanguard's days, 'that in some perverse way he saw his conquests of white girls as political victories. I tried to dissuade him from these rather ruthless love affairs, if only because in those days sex across the colour bar was a criminal offence, but he wouldn't listen to me.'

'It was difficult to assess the attitude of a person like Bloke,' says Es'kia Mphahlele. 'He had this openness, this urge to be friends to everyone, white and black. Also he was a kind of dandy who would love to be surrounded by white girls. I don't know if it was out of a desire to revenge himself that he slept with white women; to me he just looked like the kind of person who loved to see himself in that situation without necessarily feeling that he wanted to take revenge.'

'Bloke was always trying to be middle-class in his mannerisms and his behaviour,' says Jurgen Schadeberg. 'So in his little room in Sophiatown, yes, he would serve champagne and play Beethoven or whatever. It was all very nice but it was somewhat pretentious. Also you wouldn't go there and spend a whole evening drinking champagne. It would just be one glass.'

'For me,' says Nadine Gordimer, 'Bloke epitomises the waste of those years. What a good writer he was, what a nice man. The last time I saw Bloke was in Germany about three years ago, shortly before his death. It was so extraordinary, because there he was with a German wife writing for German radio – such an indication of the waste and the loss. In his writings he shows bitterness. It's there in *Blame Me On History*, a very good book, an exceptional book. But then, especially when writing such a personal book, all that is deepest in the writer is going to come out. There he is free in a way which he isn't in his personal relationships. I must say I didn't sense any bitterness while I was with him.'

At the age of thirteen, Modisane was called home from school to see his father slowly, agonisingly dying in the dust of their back yard. He had been battered into a deformed mash by a man with a brick.

'She [a neighbour] informed me, between sobs and sniffles, that the battered and grotesquely ballooned nightmare, hardly recognisable as a human being, was my father; the swollen mass of broken flesh and blood, which was his face, had no definition; there were no eyes nor mouth, nor nose, only a motionless ball, and the only sign of life was the heaving chest.'

This description comes out of his autobiography *Blame Me On History*. Part of the dedication is to 'the memory of my father Joseph who was killed by the Sophiatown which they bulldozed into the dust'. It's no wonder Modisane didn't want to see Henry Nxumalo's stabbed corpse.

In the early '60s Modisane got out, and went to England to write his book. Suddenly here was a bitter, tortured man, eaten up by a cancerous hate for whites.

'Among [the] liberals,' he wrote, 'are included personal friends I respect in their private capacity as individuals, but in the public image they are white, they live in white privilege; they have not rejected the fruits of being white; they live in "Europeans Only" suburbs, they eat in "Europeans Only" restaurants, go to "Europeans Only" cinemas, theatres, bars, art galleries and other public places. I have yet to listen to a white South African objecting to and rejecting the privileged condition of his lot; some have complained about my poverty, the slum conditions, but never about their inflated opulence.

'I am instead insulted with multi-racial tea parties where we wear our different racial masks and become synthetically polite to each other in a kind of masquerade where Africans are being educated into acceptance of their inferior position . . . I [have] sipped my tea with an observance of the social graces of the upper classes . . . but the elegance of the occasions, their propensity for opulence, seldom failed to emphasise the poverty and the squalor of my life. Every time I returned from these things, Sophiatown became all the more depressing.'

His book was published in England in 1963, and three years later was banned in South Africa along with everything he'd written when the government banned him under the Suppression of Communism Act. The banning order was finally lifted in 1986, the year Modisane died in Dortmund, West Germany. Like Can Themba, an exile unto death.

'As you know,' says Mphahlele, 'Bloke wrote that book outside the country. I think he was regretful of the kind of life he'd led, the kind of life where he would entertain himself with classical music and have parties in his room with black and white so he could display his aesthetic taste and the high life in Sophiatown, which was a joke. After he left he became influenced by the PAC and remorseful about what he'd done and hence the bitterness with which he writes.'

But perhaps the comments offering the most insight come from Jean Hart:

'I think he very seldom showed the real Bloke. That urbane, funny, warm, open character I don't think was the real Bloke. The real Bloke was the one who was resentful, bitter.

'Bloke was lying most of the time in his friendships with people. I think he really hated white people. I think he really fundamentally hated them. I think Can kept the real, objective complexities in front of him, as a kind of barrier, because that was one way of being honest with himself. Bloke on the other hand suppressed it and tried to pretend that friendship and the day-to-day easy dealing with all of his friends was reality.

'Of course when he went home at night he resented the

fact that we lived in a flat in Yeoville and we could patronise him. For instance, when people went home from a party they had to have a signed letter from a white saying that they had been kept late at work. Otherwise, if they were stopped at a road block before they got into the township, they'd be detained. We had to write those letters before they left. And writing those letters at the end of a party was an act of patronage: it symbolised that we had power and they didn't. You can't build friendships on that kind of inequality. Can knew that and would say so outright. He would say, You and I can never be real lovers, you and I can never be real friends, because our power-base is unequal. Bloke would avoid it and say, We love one another, there's nothing society can do to us. Then he would go away and curl up in bed and be enraged by the fact that I, a white woman, had to sign a chit for him to get home. He lied to himself a lot about what the situation was.

'I think when he came to London he played black. He would sit round with a lot of whites talking about African customs. I would sit and think, Bloke, what are you saying! Because all that stuff about tribal customs was as much a part of his life as it was of mine. He played jigger-bo in an environment – he came here in the '6os, remember – that was so predisposed to having an exotic love affair with South Africa out of guilt and interest that he just played everything they wanted him to be. And I couldn't cope with it. Neither I nor Malcolm, who was very close to Bloke, could really cope with it. One can always speculate about this but Can chose not to get out of southern Africa I think because he knew what it would do to him.

'Bloke had no defences and I think he ate himself up with resentment and hatred privately and I think that's why he never wrote more or produced more. He'd been lying to himself for so long. I think writers have a dialogue with themselves, which is true: if you don't have that then what comes out doesn't have the true sound. He wrote what he thought the whites wanted at the time, even *Blame Me On*

History is a kind of you-want-me-to-be-an-angry-black-man response. He had, though, started writing it in South Africa.

'Can was a professional journalist. Bloke personalised everything to make it a battle with his own psyche. He was a great womaniser, absolutely unbelievable. With Bloke those relationships were actually the building blocks of his own frail personality. He would have someone at the bottom of the garden at one point in the party, someone else in the shed, then he'd go upstairs and have somebody else in the bathroom.

'I spent all my time refusing Bloke. Then he'd be vicious and would do the you-don't-want-me-because-you're-a-racist number. I think there might have been retribution in his conquest of white women. But white women also represent power, so the more that you have of them the more you absorb that power into yourself. They also, of course, represent repression, so the more that you defile them the more you are fighting the battle and winning. But both sides exist. He was very proud of his conquests. And was endlessly telling me about how he could come fifteen times a night. He loved to talk about his sexual prowess.

'There was another level too: Bloke also needed reassurance and was never able to find it in any kind of friendship, not even with men. So he looked for it in women. Only when I had the affair with Can did he back off and finally stop pestering me. Then we actually became quite good friends. He became really quite warm.

'But I think you must realise that Bloke would have been a weak man in any society. He was mother-ridden for a start. Ma-Bloke dealt with his love affairs, with his illegitmate children. He shouldn't have called his book *Blame Me On History* – an overblown title if ever there was one – but "Blame Me On Ma-Bloke". So it's dangerous to see Bloke as symptomatic of what was happening in South Africa.'

But Bloke Modisane is not symptomatic, he's symbolic. And there's a further point: in all the *Drum* photographs of Modisane, except for that one at Nxumalo's funeral, he's always smiling.

59

EDUCATION SHEBEENS by Bloke Modisane

Education shebeens! Yes, that's what they are calling the Cultural Clubs set up by the ANC to train the eight thousand African children who cannot or will not attend Bantu Education schools. Education shebeens – where the children can furtively get some of the 'strong drink' of knowledge.

Playing Sip and Fly with knowledge! Because the law says no private schools may be conducted without registration by the Native Affairs Department. Because if the Cultural Clubs could be proved to be private schools they would be forcibly stopped for selling illicit education.

In Brakpan, Benoni, Germiston, Natalspruit, Alexandra Township and Moroka the children are crowded into shacks, leaking halls, dilapidated cinemas and even the open veld. Not as snug as some liquor shebeens! Most of the children are the rebel scholars who boycotted Bantu Education months ago.

The African National Congress said No thanks to Bantu Education, and the parents of the children said they would not let their kids receive inferior education . . . 'rather let them roam the streets'.

But the ANC is not keen to see the children in the streets and, as an answer to Bantu Education, started the Cultural Clubs.

People from various political organisations – educationists, church denominations, private individuals of different opinions – have joined to form the National Education Movement.

The function of this movement is to draw up 'lecture' programmes of activities aimed at giving the 'rebel' children a wide range of general knowledge, to organise number and word games, and to raise funds. The NEM also plans to set up branches in European areas, to encourage sections to adopt these clubs and organise fund-raising programmes, and to supply the adopted clubs with equipment.

Scraps of carpentry tools for equipment for boys and rags for sewing kits for the girls are supplied, and each is left to his own creativeness. At present they are progressing 'along their own lines' and soon it is hoped the proper instructors will be available to them.

. . . At these clubs it is illegal to give the children direct tuition, such as teaching them to read and write – even writing the letters A-B-C. The penalty for giving the children direct school is a £50 fine or six months, and just recently three people from Germiston were arrested for running a 'school shebeen', but were acquitted because it was not proved that they were doing actual teaching. This threat of arrest looms over all the leaders in these Cultural Clubs, and the police are constantly going round to find just one instance of direct teaching.

But the National Education Movement is determined that no such situation will become evident. It is presently busy drawing up careful lectures and instructions for leaders, and a kind of syllabus for the parents to follow in their home instruction. The idea behind the starting of the clubs is to mould the children into true citizens in the true concept of democracy.

Mr Robert Resha, ANC president of the Transvaal, said in an interview: 'The need for Cultural Clubs has long been in demand; we would have started them even if there was no Bantu Education. Although the children cannot be taught to read and write, there is a lot to be learned in the clubs which cannot be found in Bantu Education schools.'

A few weeks back about thirty police stormed to Nabadula Hall in Benoni, blocking all entrances and surrounding the entire building. It was a raid. The 370 children trembled at the show of rifles and Sten guns and batons, but Mrs Muriel Mkwanazi, the leader who had been leading them in song, calmed their fears and got them singing again. The Benoni Cultural Club was being visited by the police to check whether the children were being taught illegally.

A man in the police detachment got on the stage, ordering the leader to stop the children from singing. When the children would not be quiet, the man picked up a broomstick and menaced them with it. After hitting a few over the head and body, the tots panicked and hid under the stage and beneath the benches. They were asked to give their names and addresses.

The leader, Mr Matime, was arrested because his pass showed that he was unemployed. When it was the turn for the children to give their names and addresses, Beauty Moroane ordered them not to comply with the wishes of the police, leading them in Congress slogan songs and doing the Afrika sign. The children also made the sign.

The smaller children were frightened by the police and started screaming and running about in confusion. Beauty Moroane on the one hand was urging the children to calm down and sing, and the police on the other were chasing them round the hall. Beauty was then bundled into the van.

The older children, eighteen of them, volunteered to go to gaol with Mr Matime and Beauty Moroane. The police shoved all into the van. When the police left Nabadula Hall, the rest of the children marched to the police station shouting Congress slogans and doing the Afrika sign.

Andries Meketsi, who led the march to the station, was arrested and later charged with public disturbance. In the late afternoon lawyer Leo Lovell MP came round to the station, and later £2 bail was paid for each of the arrested children, and £10 for Andries. On the morning of Friday, Andries's case was held *in camera*, and he was sentenced to six cuts. Lawyer Lovell, who appeared for Andries, has lodged an appeal.

(November 1955)

60

xmas and me! by William 'Bloke' Modisane

To me one Christmas is so much like the last that I am unable to see why people make such a fuss over it. In my Sophiatown, Christmas insinuates itself on and from 16 December. I become rattled by the constant crack of fireworks. I jump and rush out to see if anybody I know has not been shot. Women scream every night.

I have enough worries of my own. I begin to worry about what the children at home are going to wear; a new suit for each of the two boys, a dress for the little girl. Shoes, socks, hats, shirts and maybe toys (if I can get them on the sly). A new dress and shoes for Mother. I would have to borrow more money to buy my girl a present . . . something expensive. There must be a chicken or a turkey (most assuredly a turkey) and perhaps a bottle or two of brandy.

Christmas Eve, which is also pay-day, I come home laden with gifts but before I reach home I meet a group of people in comic dress singing jazz or pop songs they have made up for the season. Women's bodies bulge disturbingly in men's attire, and men with painted faces and lips, wearing short dresses, walk with an awkward sway. I follow them aimlessly, lured by their song and frolic. I follow them along dirty twisting streets and through smelling back yards, walking into pools of stagnant water. But because I have lived all my life surrounded by this filth, I don't mind it much. I find myself miles from home and *tappet* [rush] back to find friends waiting for me.

'Happy Christmas!' they shout, shaking my hand. I'm expected to offer drinks, but past 'dry' Christmases have taught me my lesson. I ask them to make me a drink and five minutes later they find some excuse to drift out. I feel mean, but I can't afford to give everybody a drink. Then the girls walk in. They are lovely, they are happy and distracting, as only African girls can be. I find myself putting a bottle on the table. Jazz trumpets blare in the background as we drink and dance round and round in the room until I collapse.

Then it is Christmas morning. My head is heavy, my tongue is bitter and my body is numb. The little girls in the streets are attractive in their bright yellow, blue and red dresses; and the boys in their new suits, white shirts and ties play a game in which they jump over the gutters. One would miss his footing and fall into the dirty water.

The streets become swarmed with merrymakers carrying drinks, because nobody gets arrested at Christmas. Girls wearing trousers shout 'Happy!', and if I know a few (which I usually do), I ask for 'Christmas box' and get kissed. Cars speed wildly along the narrow streets, forcing us into the gutters. The stench from the gutter is laughed off as a woman pulls her foot out of the filth, and shakes off the mud by stamping her foot on the ground. Sometimes she swears at the driver. Somewhere along the way we find a little girl's body on the side of the gutter. She was unlucky.

We meet other groups, exchange drinks and greetings, then break up or join forces. We go up one street and witness a fight. Four hoodlums are stabbing one man. He tries to break away from them and run for it, but they stay with him, their blades sinking into his body until he falls. One of the four 'heroes' kicks the fallen man in the face, and they walk off brandishing their blades and threatening to stab anybody who gets in their way. The sight of a man dying always fills me with horror. I get our group to walk off.

Somewhere on our way a woman screams and complains that a certain man wants to drag her away by force. We turn round to face the man and find ourselves confronted by a hostile gang of armed thugs. The girls scream and rush in all directions. Some of us get stabbed. Then I walk home. Dejected.

Ambulances stream past with frightful regularity. The groups become fewer, the wails of women long and frequent, and I shut my door and feel sorry for the race of man and for being part of it.

The greatest killer in the locations is the season of Christmas, and the one day I dread to look at the newspapers is the day after Christmas.

But in my mind I know there should be a Christmas away from the crowded streets, the smelling gutters and the killing animals, which cannot be happy without causing misery. It will be full of good cheer. Perhaps I am a dreamer. If so, then I never want to wake and find myself with the Christmases I know.

(December 1955)

Makhalipile

61

I WILL PRAY FOR AFRICA by Trevor Huddleston

In the twelve years he has been in South Africa, Father Trevor Huddleston CR has become the greatest figure of controversy here. On both sides of the political fence people have formed violent views about what he says on the race problem. Now that he may leave his 'Beloved Country' to go to England, he gives a special message to the South African people. Many will agree, many disagree – but there is no doubt that his words will cause tremendous interest everywhere.

'So much to do, so little done . . .'

It is said Cecil Rhodes used those words on his deathbed. I believe that anyone working in South Africa, though he might live twice as long as Rhodes (who was only in his early forties when he died), would always have to say the same thing. And certainly, on the eve of my departure from this 'Beloved Country', it is that thought which is uppermost in my mind. So much to do! So much to do! And seeing that, it is an agony almost beyond endurance to have to leave it all. It is not that I feel for a moment that there are no others who can lay their hands to the task. It is simply that I long with all my heart to be allowed to continue my small share of it. Which is, I suppose, a form of pride.

Leaving aside the purely personal issues, which in any case are unimportant, I would like to try and assess the situation in South Africa as I have seen it develop in the past twelve years. I would like also to try and give some idea of what I believe should be our objective for the next decade or so. And I use the word 'our' deliberately. For, when people say, 'I hear you are going home,' I feel like saying, 'Not at all, England is no longer my home and never will be again. I am an African.' Is it so fantastic, I wonder? I find it quite impossible today to stand aside and watch, for I know myself to be identified with the struggle of the African people. And one of the hardest things for me is to have to face the long, bleak years when in fact I shall be 'outside'. (I seem to have returned to the personal angle again, forgive me!)

When I first came to South Africa in 1943, the end of World War Two was in sight. A new dawn was breaking. It would be . . . surely it would be . . . a dawn of freedom, and above all of freedom from tyranny.

But we were wrong. Hopelessly wrong. For men are stupid and arrogant. I had, of course, been warned what to expect in South Africa, for my community had worked here for over forty years. We were always conscious of the struggle, even in the quiet monastic seclusion of Mirfield. It was, and always will be, one of the chief objects of our prayer. But, of course, I had to learn from experience what it really meant. I had to make contact with my people, my parishioners, at every level of their life. Those six years at Sophiatown were for me flooded with a new light, a light moreover which cast deep shadows. There, for the first time, I witnessed, and began to feel in my own inmost heart, the full horrors of racialism.

It was, and remains to me, the time of an awakening to this dreadful truth. Racialism in any form is an attack not only upon the nature of Man, but upon the nature of God Himself. It is a blasphemy. For it says, in effect, that man created in the image and likeness of God can be an object of contempt, of derision and of hatred . . . because of his race.

I saw, at first hand, the pass laws in action. I knew,

from my own experience, the attitude of the police. I watched the apathy which could allow thousands of African children to die from hunger, politely called malnutrition.

The fantastic paradox of South Africa began to emerge and to become evident to me in its sharpest and most clearly defined shape. In Sophiatown one saw the full implication of a Western industrialised society: one was living with and ministering to people who were totally integrated into that society . . . and yet who were told (and treated accordingly) that they had no place in it. The injustice of a social order which could claim the blood and sweat and tears of a man for its wealth, but which could reject his company and his dignity because he was black . . . this was borne in upon me by every hour of every day.

The African Children's Feeding Scheme; the Newclare Squatters; the Western Areas Removal; the Bantu Education Act; the long string of protests; the daily queue of people coming to the mission and later the Priory with their problems; the Europeans whose consciences were troubled because they had to live with this injustice. All these things and so many more taught me the meaning of South Africa's tragedy. I only pray I may never forget the lesson; but I was only just beginning to practise what I had learned. And now there is no time left, so it seems. I can only believe that somehow God has a plan and a purpose for me elsewhere, and that in due time He will make it known.

So little done! So much to do!

What are the tasks of the future? If I had my time over again what would I do with it? How would I begin? I should like to reduce all these questions, or the answers to them, to a great simplicity.

As Alan Paton has recently said, 'What South Africa most needs is a new nationalism.' Perhaps a strange and question-provoking statement. But underlying it a profound truth.

For what is called 'Nationalism' today is nothing more or less than naked racialism based on prejudice, on fear and the evil determination to maintain a 'supremacy'. And there is the ever present danger of African nationalism, embittered, hating and hateful, rising in opposition to this concept. Whereas the nationalism we most need and must work for, must even suffer and die for . . . is that true nationalism which recognises that the state exists for man, not man for the state.

The basic evil in South Africa is contempt for man, a refusal to recognise the dignity of the person.

All my energy, as all my prayer, would be directed to the ending of this evil. And, looking back over twelve years, I think that has been the one guiding principle of my life and work here – however ineffective, however unfinished it has all been. But there is a condition of success . . . a condition without which none of our hopes can be realised. It is unity.

I shall pray with all the strength I have that the African people, Congress and non-Congress, Christian and non-Christian, urban and rural, may soon unite to smash the evil of this racial pride, not by force but by the good of an ideal which demands sacrifice and courage and labour. For all this I am certain: there is no place in the modern world for South Africa as she is today. Tomorrow is yours. And tomorrow is soon. God bless you all and thank you for allowing me to be and to remain an African.

(December 1955)

62

Before Father Trevor Huddleston left in January 1956, Sophiatown threw a farewell concert that he was to remember all his life. Dolly Rathebe sang. Tandie Klaasens sang. And with St Peter's choir, Todd Matshikiza at the piano played the chorale he had composed for Huddleston. It was called 'Makhalipile' (The Dauntless One).

In his tiny kitchen at St James's, Piccadilly, Huddleston played a recording on a small 'ghetto blaster' while we waited for the kettle to boil.

Makhalipile, please pass this way.
Makhalipile, please come and save us,
Your children are hungry!

When it finished he said: 'I have vowed never to go home until apartheid is abolished. And I am an old man now.'

Home? I queried.

'Home,' he replied.

Brothers in Christ

63

The highlight of Sylvester Stein's editorship is a two-part investigation focusing, firstly, on black churches which had broken away from the established white churches, and then on whether blacks and whites were brothers in Christ. They appeared in February and March 1956 to mark the magazine's fifth anniversary – the last time that *Drum* was to celebrate with a courageous piece of journalism. The first piece, written by Bloke Modisane, told the story of how colour prejudice in the traditional Christian denominations had forced half a million black Christians to form their own sects. Needless to say these sects were soon labelled un-Christian and anti-white. *Drum* then went out to see if the white Christian was willing to pray side by side with his black 'brother'.

BROTHERS IN CHRIST, the story was headlined:

> I visited several churches, English and Afrikaans, in and around Johannesburg. I went to Irene, a Dutch Reformed Church, in Quartz Street, Johannesburg.
>
> I walked through a side door into the body of the church and sat down. The service had started. There was no comment, though after the service, as I walked out, there was some whispering.
>
> My next visit took me to the Central Methodist Church in Kruis Street. A church official with a smile on his face asked me to go to the gallery as, he said, the hall downstairs was full. But there were many empty seats. The following Sunday I went to the Nederduits Gereformeerde of Hervormde Kerk (DRC) in Bez Valley.

Youths who were sitting in a pew motioned for me not to sit next to them. I moved their Bibles aside and sat down, then they edged away until a good three feet separated us. Somebody in the pew behind me patted me on the back and said, 'This is a white church, you can't be in here. You must go.' I turned round to face him, then he and his friend yanked me to my feet and led me out of the church. Outside their Christian calm returned to them, and they explained to me that I should go to 'my own church'.

The Presbyterian Church in Noord Street allowed me in, yet the one in Orange Grove refused me admittance. They explained that the hall was rented from some boys' club whose policy did not allow non-whites into the hall. They also said something about the laws of the country.

At the Kensington DRC Gemeente, an aged church official was just about to close the doors when he saw me. He bellowed in Afrikaans: *'Wat soek jy?'* (What do you want?)

'I've come to church,' I said.

He shoved me violently, shouting for me to get away. I walked away dejected. A few yards away was the Baptist Church, and as I walked that way I began to think that people didn't want me to share their church. As I walked through the Baptist door I was tensed, waiting for that tap on the shoulder . . . but instead I was given a hymnbook and welcomed into the church. I sat through the service.

At the Fairview Gemeente of the Assemblies of God the welcome party at the door invited me in but offered me a seat at the back. Everybody was polite and very Christian; they wanted to know where I came from. This up-and-down treatment wasn't doing my nerves much good. The previous day at the Claim Street Seventh Day Adventist Church I had been stopped at the church door and told I could not go in. Then another church official thought that perhaps I could be placed somewhere at the back, but the other was definitely against it. So I turned away. A week or two later I went again and was asked to sit at the back. Later I was asked to leave. 'We object to your presence,' said a large white man.

On yet another Sunday I went to the DRC Church, Langlaagte, Johannesburg, in the company of a photographer. I walked up the pathway to the door of the church, where I was stopped by a young European usher. I explained to him that I wanted to attend the service.

'But this is a church for whites only. Why don't you go to one of your own churches?' the usher said. He hesitated for a while, then he took me round the side of the church, and made me wait outside while he consulted with someone inside. After a while he returned and said, 'I'm sorry, but the baas says that you cannot come into this church.' Just as I reached the gate on my way out I heard someone hurrying after me. It was the deacon, he was calling me. 'What is it you want, my boy?' the deacon asked.

'I wanted to worship in this church. But they say I cannot.'

'All right, my boy, follow me.' The deacon took me inside and led me to an isolated pew. The service began. I saw the deacon walk up to whisper something to the predicant, and immediately after the doors were locked. I made up my mind to behave correctly. It just so happened that it was *Nagmaal* [Communion] and my fancy was caught by the ritual. When the collection saucers came round I prepared to give my little coin, but the official passed me. As they sang the last hymn, I rose quietly and tiptoed out. Just as I was walking down the stairs I noticed three plain-clothes men coming towards me. I hesitated. Calling me by name, one of the three men told me to follow him into a car.

Inside the car a thick-set man said: 'What are you people trying to do?' I kept quiet. 'You are from *Drum*, are you not?' I remained quiet. 'I'm Major Spengler, Special Branch.' I was impressed. 'Are you a member of the ANC?'

'No.'

'Any other organisation?'

'No. Only *Drum*.'

Another white man joined us in the car. He was asked to identify me. He scrutinised my face then shook his head. Then an old lady from the outcoming congregation was saying: 'Where is he? Where is he? I've got to see him.' She bent down to look into the car. She looked at me and said: *'Jou Satan!'* [You Satan!] Major Spengler instructed a police officer to take me in the car and drop me in town, 'otherwise the boys will flay him'. At the corner of Commissioner and West Streets, African policemen were called to identify me. They ended by arguing with me about my surname, said it wasn't genuine. Then they released me.

Next day the Special Branch quizzed the editor, asked him if he believed in apartheid! All this police action just because a non-white wanted to go to church.

On another Saturday I again went to the Seventh Day Adventist Church. I walked through the people waiting outside the church, hoping to find somebody I could ask to allow me in. At the head of the stairs in the doorway of the church I was suddenly yanked off my feet and rushed down the steps. A big, hefty man, without even stopping to ask me to leave the church, twisted my arm behind my back and together with two others they bundled me over a waiting car. It was the 'bum's rush'. When we got to the car my huge escort pressed me sharply into it. My head struck the side of the car and started bleeding slowly. The editor, who had been watching from the street, came up to protest at my arrest by these church-goers. He was grabbed, too, and bundled into the car. The car drove off, churchmen crowded next to me. Meanwhile, our photographer made a dash for it. The last time I saw him he was taking the corner with members of the congregation chasing hot behind his heels.

I was driven to Marshall Square, where I was formally charged with trespass at the insistence of the deacon. There was no charge to bring up against the editor, who was released. I was 'cooled off' for an hour and then released on a bail of £5, and later went to court.

But they couldn't find any charge to pin against me either, and the case was later withdrawn.

On another Sunday I went to St George's Anglican Church in Parktown. It was a beautiful church built in a lovely garden, and it had all the signs of being for 'posh' people. I walked up the garden path to the door and walked in. I selected my seat. Nobody paid any attention to me; no one stared. There seemed to be nothing unusual about me being there. I still had another church to go to, so I left in about fifteen minutes. On my way out a priest asked me why I was leaving. He advised me to hurry back before all the seats were taken.

Almost every Anglican church in Johannesburg would allow me to attend. One priest said there was a special 5 a.m. (!) mass for non-whites and it would be best not to attend a 'white' mass. Another said he wouldn't allow 'experimentation'. But one priest said, 'Why not come over for tea afterwards?' Thirteen Catholic churches gave me the OK. Priests said: 'Yes . . . sure . . . certainly . . . you don't have to ask . . . doors open to all.'

I hurried on to the Methodist Church, Orange Grove, walked briskly to the door. Somebody met me at the door and offered me a hymnbook. I selected my seat and sat down. I was paging through the book when a man walked over threateningly from the front pew to me – then he said, 'Glad to have you with us!' There was a big, Christian, brotherly smile on his face, and the grip of his handshake was firm and sincere. They were trying to make something of people being 'brothers in Christ'. Their battle was a difficult one, but at least they had one thing on their side . . . the promise that man was fundamentally good.

For by one Spirit are we all baptised into one body, whether we be bond or free; and have been all made to drink into one Spirit – Corinthians 12:13.

(March 1956)

64

Oddly – but then this was so often the case with investigative reporting on *Drum* – the story is dry, almost emotionless, the prose flat, the drama casually dismissed. But then behind it lies another story.

Although Bloke Modisane was flattered at being asked to handle the investigation, because it was like stepping into Henry Nxumalo's 'Mr Drum' shoes, he couldn't pull it off. The cynicism of the story on the breakaway sects he blames on Sylvester Stein, and yet his own attitude is ambivalent, swinging from detached repugnance to an almost sordid wallowing in the ritual showmanship of the clergy and their followers. In his autobiography he wrote:

'I attended several church meetings, faith-healing ceremonies and baptismals, and found myself in a world I never dreamed existed; the ritual was exciting and colourful, and there was a kind of showmanship and joyousness behind the pulpit which made this Christianity commercial; I was to find myself admitting that if Christianity was anything like this – a joyous noise unto the Lord – then I could allow myself to be reconverted.'

But what is to be made of the next sentences: 'The sermons were animated and invariably attended by histrionics, the congregation sang happy songs to a rhythmic chant of hand-clapping, and as the spirit moved them they went into epileptic fits, into howling shrieks which would have seemed more appropriate in a sanatorium for the bewildered; they stood in athletic trances or collapsed in the aisles possessed with fainting spells. The excitement generated from the pulpit probably intended the reaction in the aisles'?

This is Modisane confused, his romantic yearnings and his cynicism doing battle.

Gathering material about the breakaway churches was easy: everywhere he went the reverends were only too willing to talk or to allow Bob Gosani to take photographs. But bending his knees in white churches was something altogether different.

'Be careful,' warns Stein. 'Don't be provocative.'

So Modisane isn't.

He visits fifteen churches. At some he's politely taken outside and given directions to a church for his people. At others he has his hand shaken. When he's welcomed he stays for the whole service out of sheer gratitude, which has Jurgen Schadeberg and Stein pacing back and forth in annoyance outside.

'Obviously we could do only so many churches each Sunday morning,' says Schadeberg. 'If we'd done things Bloke's way it would have taken us three months to do the story. Being such a nice guy, he didn't want to leave if people accepted him. As it happened, the first couple of churches we went to were English churches which actually welcomed him and he sat down and a couple of people went over and shook his hand. In the mean time Stein would be outside in the car and would soon realise nothing was happening and start hooting for us to come out again. I would get up and walk out but Bloke couldn't leave.'

Modisane hated the job and, although he never mentions an argument in his autobiography, Schadeberg says there was one and Can Themba took over.

'Bloke was scared about doing this one,' says Stein. 'He was a dear friend, but he was not really a hard-news man and he didn't relish the thought that he'd be slightly manhandled. Can on the other hand could cope with going into churches and being bashed around and frog-marched out.'

'Bloke was not a very good investigative journalist at all,' says Schadeberg. 'He was too nice and decent and maybe too timid for that sort of job, whereas Can and Henry were pretty tough – they couldn't care less.'

The tactics at each church were simple. Schadeberg, being white, went in with a hidden camera while a photographer, Bob Gosani or Peter Magubane, waited outside in case there was any action.

'Initially I got myself a big Bible and cut it out and put the camera in but that didn't work,' explains Schadeberg. 'I then concealed a little Leica in my waistcoat with the wide-angle lens sticking through a hole where the pocket should have been. All I had to do was push my jacket aside, shoot and then let the jacket fall closed again. I took pictures as I walked in or out of the churches.'

The trouble started when Themba invaded the Christian tranquillity of that Dutch Reformed Church in Langlaagte, an Afrikaner stronghold. Themba's story was published; this is Schadeberg's: 'I don't know how they'd worked it out, but they knew who we were right from the beginning. When I realised nothing was going to happen I got up to leave. But the doors were locked and one of the deacons said to me, "Why don't you go and sit with your friend?" They had suspected us although we went into the church separately. They obviously recognised us as being different. When we got outside there were police with Sten guns all over the place and Major Spengler was sitting with Stein and arguing. They thought it was a political demonstration, a Defiance Campaign effort.'

The incident found its way into Johannesburg's English and Afrikaans dailies, stealing a lot of *Drum*'s initiative, which may account for the cold tone of the story in the magazine. Certainly by the time it appeared it was old news. Nevertheless, the following weekend they decided to visit a Seventh Day Adventist church in the centre of town.

It's a Saturday morning, the streets are loud with traffic and pedestrians, revving engines, hooters and the cries of hawkers. A car with Sylvester Stein, Can Themba and

Jurgen Schadeberg stops a few blocks down from the church.

'Good luck,' says Stein, leaning round into the back.

Themba grimaces as they all get out. They separate and Themba walks slowly towards the church, whistling, his hands in his pockets. Schadeberg's about ten paces behind him. Stein keeps up with them on the other side of the street, only crossing to their side when Themba turns into the church.

Themba pauses, takes his hands out of his pockets and goes up the steps away from the hot, crowded pavements into the quiet interior. And that's where they grab him: two heavies come out of the dark recesses either side of the door, twist his arm up behind his back, spin him round and plunge back down the steps. At the curb there's a car, its door open, some big men inside. Themba goes in, striking his head against the metal in a shower of blood, crumpling on to the seat.

Schadeberg's there now, slightly to one side, his jacket pulled back, the fish-eye taking wide, distorted pictures of the violent churchmen, of Themba's pain and surprise.

'There's another one,' shouts a tough, grabbing Stein by the collar, pushing him towards the car.

It's a lynching party, thinks Stein, bent double, tumbling against Themba in the car.

Then they spot Schadeberg.

'Catch the kaffir lover.'

Schadeberg runs. Down the street into the shoppers and traffic, behind buses, in front of trucks, his short legs pumping hard, his hand clutching the camera under his waistcoat. He can hear the young men behind him shouting, cursing, and faces in front turn towards him then slide away before anyone can act. He's breathing hard, gasping, and the men are catching up.

At the next corner he turns into a quieter street and then quickly dodges into a building. He takes the stairs two at a time. First flight. Second flight, his legs aching, the taste of blood at the back of his mouth.

But it's OK, he knows where he's going. He crashes through a door on the fourth floor, already winding the film from his camera, thrusting it into a surprised man's hand.

'Keep it safe. Don't let anyone get it.'

In the dark-room he hides under the developing-basins, his legs trembling, his chest rasping so hard he wonders if he's ever going to breathe properly again. He can hear the young men with their Bibles cursing and calling in the stairwell. But they don't search thoroughly and soon leave.

As for Themba and Stein: 'Although the heavies looked set for some rough business,' says Stein, 'once they'd driven us out of town I really don't think they knew what to do with us. So they drove us around for a while and then dropped us off in the middle of nowhere. I think we probably walked back and caught buses and taxis.'

None of this is in accord with Themba's account, where he's taken off to Marshall Square and charged with trespass. Modisane says the Seventh Day Adventist church was visited twice and backs up Themba's story about the police station. But then when he was writing his autobiography he may have had *Drum* as a source to jog his memory. Either way, Stein and Schadeberg stick to the middle-of-nowhere account, and really the truth hardly matters because the story works however you tell it.

A Sense of Inevitability

65

WILL OUR WOMEN CARRY PASSES?
RASH OF RIOTS
THE BOYCOTT THAT HAS BECOME A WAR
TREASON TRIAL ARRESTS
BIG NOISY TRIAL
A COUNTRY MARCHING INTO TROUBLE
STAY-AT-HOME WEAPON
TREASON TRIAL — ROUND ONE

Those are just some of the headlines between January 1956 and July 1957 which mark a gathering political unrest and an increasing tendency in *Drum* to run more political features. The photographs show women thronging the steps of Durban City Hall in protest at the pass laws; a band of men armed with sticks, pangas and axes during the bus boycott at Evaton township; a clash between police and demonstrators on the bus boycott's 'Black Monday': fists, stones, sticks, batons, guns which leave two dead; the Treason Trial defendants being led into court at the start of a long futile court case; and during the stay-at-home campaign, crowds with banners: DOWN WITH APARTHEID, STOP BANNING!, STOP DEPORTING, FREEDOM IN OUR LIFETIME, WE STAND BY OUR LEADERS, VERWOERD MUST GO, WE WANT £1 A DAY.

There is a sense of inevitability here, a quickening, an urgency . . . This is how *Drum* responded:

> . . . Women arrested for vagrancy; women arrested for night specials [prostitutes]; women watched by Influx Control! 'Letters of privilege', identity cards, location

permits! Is there a new pattern somewhere? Is South Africa about to bring in passes for African women?

That's the very big question of the new year. That's the question that has set the country tick-tocking over faster than ever. Deputations and demonstrations in Durban; delegations in Pretoria; decisions by the African National Congress in Johannesburg to consider defiance of the pass laws . . .

. . . But the slightest suggestion of 'passes' for African women is a tender spot with most Africans. The women were quick to protest. 'We will never carry passes under any conditions,' said Lillian Ngoyi, president of the ANC's Women's League. 'We know what these passes are doing to our males. We have seen them bundled into vans and sent to farm labour camps. Passes will place us at the mercy of the police . . .'

(January 1956)

. . . Within the space of three months, the Union has been rocked by a series of disturbances. By 10 May there had been no less than seven and all of them involved violence. It was almost as if a rash of riots had suddenly broken out on the face of the country . . . and it looked ugly. A common tendency was the quickness with which the people and the police took to violence. Ours has become a trigger-happy country – reminding you of those cowboy films where the whole town struts through the streets, thumbs tucked in gun-belts and a villainous look in the eye. But this will not do. We cannot live in a society where almost everybody is jumpy and rarin' to go to arms. Here then is the story of the riots that have occurred in various places. We hope it is not just the story thus far . . .

On a day in February a party of policemen, black and white, went to an African reserve near Bergville in Natal. They were on one of their usual dagga raids. On the hillside a group of tribesmen were working. By the end of the day a white policeman had been knocked down with a knobkerrie. Another was also struck down. A constable ran to a dark cave where he waited till dark before he made his way back to Bergville. Three African constables were struck down, too. The tribesmen were weeding a maize field belonging to one of them and, as is the custom, traditional beer was plentiful. Suddenly someone had come running with the report: 'They are here – the police have come to the reserve!' What happened thereafter was confused.

. . . Thabong (Place of Joy) in the Free State: Staff Sergeant Matsa, of the municipal police, told *Drum*: 'We arrested a few women for being in possession of beer. At ten o'clock, when the beer hall normally opens, we saw a group of women gathered round the beer hall. A few minutes after the hall was opened the crowd outside had grown to nearly two thousand people. And suddenly a riot broke out. Eighteen of us – including eight Europeans – were trapped in the hall. We started fighting our way out. A car pulled up and the crowd's attention was diverted.'

Staff Sergeant Matsa sustained head injuries during the clash. Many other people were injured, including Mr Ngake, a member of the Advisory Board, whose car was mobbed by the crowd on his way from church. Nobody discussed the issues involved carefully. Again people just jumped to rioting.

Over to the Cape. The scene is Mendi Street, New Brighton, Port Elizabeth. There has been a ban on gatherings of more than ten Africans in the area of Port Elizabeth. So people who wanted to get together organised processions of marchers like religious revival groups. It was during one of them that the flare-up took place. As the procession passed along, suddenly the air was broken by a number of ominous reports from a gun. Men, women and children ran. Some fell to the ground injured. Another man fell down never to rise again. He was shot in the chest. His name was John Nangoza Jebe, an African National Congress volunteer. More than thirty thousand people attended his burial. Volunteers carried the coffin, which was draped in the colours of the ANC, on their shoulders all along the route to the cemetery. The clash had occurred when a van carrying ten African constables and a European sergeant was sent to investigate an alleged 'political meeting' that was being held in New Brighton.

Germiston, in the Transvaal. For the Transvaal, home of riots, was not to be outdone. About midnight on Sunday 8 April, part of Robert Strachan Hostel in Germiston Location was burned. Documents, shelving and furniture were burned out in two offices – the administrative office and a depot. A number of window-panes were damaged. The Fire Brigade units were called but they could not enter the premises at first. Tongues of flame licked the outside air from the two rooms. The police arrived armed with Sten guns. An order was given to the hostel men to surrender. Later the police opened fire. Before morning, four men were killed and eight injured. Three of these are still in hospital with bullet wounds.

And, of course, that controversial piece of God's earth, the Western Areas. On 12 April, when the men were still drinking down the dregs of their beer in the Western beer hall, the police encircled it on a poll-tax raid. Somebody inside peeped over the corrugated-iron fence and spotted them. 'A raid!' the word went round, and pandemonium broke loose. They stormed the entrance and some burst out of a hole in the wall.

Eight African men were treated for bullet wounds at the Coronation Hospital after a clash with the police on this occasion. Six policemen were injured. The rioting spread to the Main Road which runs through Martindale, where European trams and motor cars were stoned. Seven people were injured. One white boy has since lost an eye. Many of those injured, both white and black, had nothing at all to do with the original trouble, but simply got caught up in the stone-throwing and shooting.

. . . But here is one riot that has not specifically been against authority. It took place in Randfontein on Sunday afternoon, 15 April. Although it lasted only thirty minutes there was swift killing. Four died and fifteen were injured.

The riot was between location men and mine workers who had come to drink beer at the municipal canteen on the location. The supervisor of the beer hall told *Drum* that for quite a long time location men had felt sore about men from neighbouring mine compounds coming to drink at the location beer hall. This was a snob riot. That afternoon the men assembled outside the hall, and as soon as a few mine workers came out they attacked them with knives. The mine workers retaliated with bricks and sticks. All four who died came from the mines.

Perhaps the best illustration of how quick police and people are to take to violence is our latest riot, the 'Klerksdorp Affair'. The residents of Joubertina Location wanted to see the superintendent to complain about pass and beer raids. The superintendent thought they should see the Advisory Board first. He refused to attend a meeting called in the location.

Then followed a swift, unhappy train of events. At the meeting the municipal police told the people that they should disperse in five minutes' time. When the people failed to break up, a shot was fired, and the police charged. At some stage there was stoning, the police say. Frightened people ran all over. Many were hurt. Thus the score is seven riots in three months. The most disturbing thing about it all being the kind of mentality that believes everything is solved by violence. This business must stop!

(June 1956)

It didn't. By July, the Evaton bus boycott, which had started a year earlier in protest against a rise in fares, had turned into a war between boycotters and anti-boycotters led by the Russians – a gang which often took up the cause of the authorities. *Drum* sent Es'kia Mphahlele to report on the violence. 'The fifty thousand residents of Evaton live in mortal terror,' he wrote. 'They suspect one another. You meet the people and talk to them. They are very homely and no one looks sick or anaemic like the typical townsfolk. They show a fat sense of humour. But somewhere you sense a sickness in the air. Fear. When they see a bus enter the township, smiles curdle and muscles become tense. "*Azik-welwa!*" (Don't ride them!) someone shouts. The cry is relayed from street to street.'

Further down the article he comments: 'The entry of the "Russians" in the boycott affair has precipitated something that may one day touch off a spark that will throw Evaton into a blaze of faction war. There is clear evidence that they are against the boycott move, and the people never know if any of them are employed by the bus company to "protect" the buses. I ran into a nest of men dressed like "Russians" early one morning when our photographer stopped for a photo of an empty bus. The men threatened us with violence, wielding clubs and looking vicious, and sent us scuttling back to our car.'

Shortly after this piece appeared in July 1956, negotiations between the boycotters and the bus company brought the boycott to an end. It had been a long and bitter fight, but the people of Evaton won a return to the old fares, a hand in drawing up the timetable, and the appointment of black ticket inspectors.

Meanwhile the Nationalist government had been hard at work collecting evidence which they believed proved that a vast group – mostly comprising ANC members – was conspiring to commit treason. Eventually they felt their dossiers showed a plan to subvert law and order, so before dawn on 5 December 1956 the police arrested 156 people. It was a massive country-wide operation that had the victims bussed or flown to prison in Johannesburg. This enforced gathering caused ANC president Albert Luthuli to comment laconically, 'It was rather like a joint executive of the Congress . . . Distance, other occupations, lack of funds and police interference had made frequent meetings difficult . . . [Now] delegates from the remotest areas were never more than one cell away.' Ironically, people who during the Defiance Campaign had shown themselves to be dedicated to non-violence were now charged with treason. However, because their plight attracted international media coverage, a Defence and Aid Fund was organised, which immediately hired the best lawyers in southern Africa. Soon the accused were released on bail – an odd decision given the seriousness of the charge.

Drum wrote up the preparatory hearing under the headline BIG NOISY TRIAL:

> The Treason Trials started off like an action-packed cowboy film when 156 men and women came before the court in Johannesburg at a preparatory examination.
>
> The Treason Trial, now the talk of South Africa and the world at large, started with a bang-bang-bang. There was drama inside the Drill Hall, where the preparatory examination, into charges of high treason alleged against more than 150 persons from various organisations, was held before the chief magistrate of Bloemfontein. And there was drama outside in the streets of Johannesburg when the police clashed several times with the crowd. All because the Drill Hall could not accommodate all of the five thousand people outside. If it had, there might never have been any trouble.
>
> First, it was a booing that led to a baton charge that led to a stone-throwing that led to a gun-shooting. And side interludes of snatching press cameras and arresting photographers. Everybody was in a dirty mood, and as the police and the public were taunting each other, it

looked like a situation that could any moment turn dangerous. Meanwhile, inside, the prosecution was outlining its case against the accused and the fog was lifting slowly over what the accused men and women are alleged to have done.

Still, outside, the police were 'keeping order'. The mood of the public was electric and any moment threatened to spark off a nasty riot. From the threats and taunts hurled by many people it was clear that the drama outside the Drill Hall was packed with menace. For some reason the police could not abide a clicking camera. One of our cameramen, Peter Magubane, was manhandled and arrested no fewer than four times. Bob Gosani was roughed up once. Jurgen Schadeberg was arrested once, Can Themba was manhandled once. Even other photographers – the *Rand Daily Mail* photographer was manhandled, the *Transvaler* photographer was arrested and his camera damaged. People were suggesting that the police were scared of photographers who kept a clear, irrefutable record of everything the police were doing. But senior police officers kept explaining that it was all a mistake, some misunderstanding, and there was no intention to interfere with the press.

Inside things were sedate on the surface but deep down everybody knew in his heart that more than 150 men and women were defending perchance their lives. And Mr V. C. Berrange, for the defence, said the allegations made against them were a fantastic plot.

(February 1957)

Jurgen Schadeberg: I remember Peter Magubane being roughed up at that hearing. Obviously the police hated having their photographs taken by a black chap, that was just disgusting. They got him into a corner and roughed him. I saw red and took a dive and landed on top of the whole bunch, shouting, kicking them. So they arrested the two of us and took us to Marshall Square police station. They confiscated our cameras, made us take off our ties then put us in the cells. I had hardly sat down when a cop came back, called me by my first name and told me to follow him. Both Peter and I had our cameras and ties returned and off we went back to the Drill Hall. The police were totally astonished to see us back taking pictures of them again. What had happened was that someone from the German Press Agency had seen the incident and phoned the German embassy who had phoned the police and told them to release us. Which they did. Can you imagine that happening today?

With the country in such ferment, Can Themba and Todd Matshikiza wrote an analysis:

> . . . In the last few months the Treason Trial arrests and the great [Evaton] bus boycott have helped to hot up political tempers in South Africa until we have suddenly arrived at a dangerous point on the road, with even more dangerous corners ahead. It's a time of crisis and a time to have a look around properly.
>
> There are, as anyone can see, two forces pushing strongly at one another. There is the thrust of the up-and-coming African who wants to get his full shares in the life of the future, and there is the reaction of the ruling state, which wants to keep things just as they always have been. The Irresistible Force and the Immovable Object. Look at the Irresistible Force first: it seems clear that he is the force of the future; before many years he must surely get what he wants in Africa. Look at the Object, look at those in charge of the state; they don't show the slightest sign of handing over even a fraction of what they've got. Well, what happens when the Force and the Object meet? Trouble, big trouble – somewhere, sometime, there is bound to be an explosion.
>
> Thinking on these lines, nearly all the expert

observers and historians of South Africa have come to the same conclusion, as they pack their bags ready to get out in a hurry. As the most eminent of them, Professor De Kiewiet, said, 'The future of South Africa is so obscure and opaque that the wise man can do no other than contemplate it with fearfulness but with a determination not to lose hope.'

He wrote that before the new events of this year. Now the arrests and the boycott seem to have brought that troubled future even nearer, and today even ordinary people are beginning to feel some of that fearfulness. Even the settled businessman is wondering if trouble isn't visible around the corner; he's wondering if prospects are still so sound and settled.

We've got to probe deeper, look right into the minds of the patients lying there on the psychoanalyst's couch, to find the answers. Let's examine Mr Average Boycotter first as he lies there under examination. What's he dreaming? He's thinking of a warm, happy, comfortable future for himself and his kids, where he doesn't get bullied around for passes, where schools are open to all, where jobs are open to all, you can be sure. True, he's probably also thinking of a new pair of shoes to be obtained right away so that he can keep on walking his twenty miles a day, but underneath the immediate determination not to pay more than 4d. from Alexandra to town have grown the deeper, stronger thoughts about the future. Economics have become politics, as anti-boycott whites have said in alarm. (No one seems more disgusted at the idea of politics than the politicians themselves.)

A boycotter kept on walking because he felt it was one protest that he could make with complete success. He would 'show them'. He wasn't going to be won over with a compromise either. He wanted the 4d. back, as an immediate step, and he wanted a review of wages to follow. Not just promises.

And this was all tied up in his head with the treason arrests somehow – it helped him to be 'agin the government'.

All those things were stirring around in Mr Boycotter's mind; stirring very vigorously, too, for he is a determined fellow, it seems. This determination has made the man in the street – the man in Louis Botha Avenue – the leader of the militant new forces, and the existing political parties have had to break into a run to keep up with him. The man in the street was often ahead of his own elected committee even. That's perhaps the basic object-lesson of the crisis: the leadership and the militancy is in the hearts and minds of the people, not of any parties or 'agitators'. There's something boiling up right inside the people.

What about the other patient, the state? If there was ever anyone more determined and truculent than Mr Boycotter, it's this guy. Though he lives in the same country, shares the same flag and patriotism, you'd think he doesn't want to have anything to do with Mr Boycotter. He won't give in to his demands, he won't even listen to him put forward his demands. Instead of talk he gives him police treatment. Why? Because if you look in his mind you find that fear, worry, anxiety are filling it up. Here's a guy with complexes all right. What makes him worry is that he realises well enough that he will certainly have to change his tune in the future – but he's trying to keep the comfortable present lasting out as long as possible. He can't bear to think of change, but he can't bear either to think of the consequences of not allowing change, and so he turns his mind in on itself and lets it gnaw away at its worries. If anyone ever does draw his attention to the trouble and misery that's everywhere, he shudders and looks like the old miser who asked his servant to chase the beggar away from his door 'because he couldn't bear to see such suffering'.

You get two determined and truculent sets of people like that – what happens? What does happen when the Irresistible Force meets the Immovable Object? Ask the men who split the atom. This country has managed to get along in the past, certainly, helped by its riches. But it's not going to have a very long future if the atom gets split. It's time now for some new thinking. That guy has to decide to climb down from the pedestal he's put himself on, he's got to withdraw his little isolated army of occupation, and settle down among the people.

Isn't there a young crop of thinking ones growing up who know they have to live in this world and this South Africa of the future? If they don't start on a new approach, they will suffer more than anyone, they will be to blame for setting off the atom. Yes, young gentlemen, you are the ones who must have your heads examined now, quickly, so that you can hear from the analyst just what those complexes are, so that you can learn what your sense of guilt and your sense of fear may do to the country. You've got to throw away those old used-up ideas of the nineteenth century and start living in the modern world.

Isn't there anyone who will be wise now, before it's time to pick up the pieces?

It's sad to say it, but there seems to be no thinking-out of things or doing of anything at all sensible. Faced by the growing trouble all the state does is to use its force to press the lid down on the boiling pot harder than ever before. In this operation the security branch of the police is the strong arm of the state.

'Be careful now. Big Brother is watching you,' prophesied George Orwell in his book *1984*. It's 1957 in South Africa, but already the big-brotherly watchers are on the job. Non-white organisations – political, semi-political and non-political – are being carefully watched by the paternalistic authorities. There are special detectives, spies and secret agents everywhere.

At the meetings that you address, in the schools that you attend, even in the shebeens that you patronise, there is that dark, silent shadow who listens intently for that stray word, that unguarded comment that might brand you as 'subversive'.

The activities of this department come at different levels. There is the level of the security police, the so-called Special Branch of the police. They look after the internal security of the Union and counter the actions of whatever foreign agents there might be in the country. Then there are lone agents, who watch the work of politicians and report back to high-up officials. There are also a number of informers at various people's organisations and schools who report on the activities of fellow members. Here and there are men who have high and honourable positions in organisations like the African National Congress but are prepared to sell their information. Major A. T. Spengler, head of the Witwatersrand Security Police, can well afford to say, 'I've got an efficient Special Branch, you know . . .'

(April 1957)

Major Att Spengler stalks through *Drum*. There is a photograph of him, a large, thick-set man in an open-necked shirt at the site of a sabotaged electricity pylon. He is often pictured without a tie and on this occasion without the cigarette that's usually held lightly between his lips. In another one, taken at a Sophiatown meeting, he's arresting Yusuf Cachalia, joint secretary of the Indian Congress. There's a quizzical expression on his face, that cigarette, and he's wearing a checked cravat and a white Bogart-style mackintosh. Beside them Father Trevor Huddleston protests vehemently, but the major is unconcerned. Again in Sophiatown he is photographed at the arrest of Treason trialist Sampie Molope. There are trucks and vans and uniformed police with .303s. But Spengler looks relaxed, the cigarette in his mouth, the open-necked shirt, the cravat, the sporty jacket.

Jurgen Schadeberg: I never talked to Spengler. I only saw him around and photographed him. Somebody from the Indian Congress told us he had been interrogated in Spengler's office and he saw a small bust of Hitler on his desk. Sylvester Stein suggested I go and take a picture of it. I put on a brown suit and brown shoes. In those days the headquarters were in Grayson Building and there were other businesses in the other parts of the building. I took the lift to the fifth floor. I walked up and down the passage trying to look busy with a camera underneath my jacket. Then I saw Spengler coming out of an office. Once he'd turned a corner I dashed in and took the picture of the bust standing on the mantelpiece. It was a very small bust. We never used the picture. Spengler's explanation subsequently was that he'd taken it from someone and left it in his office.

Es'kia Mphahlele: I remember Spengler had a kind of wickedness about him, he was a very wicked man. He may have been a fool but if so it was of the Nazi type, a straight mind in blinkers. He did his job and did it thoroughly and concentrated all his energies on it. He was that kind of man.

Jim Bailey: Major Spengler looms large in the '50s as a figure of fun. While Att Spengler was running the security branch we used to meet him at Andy's printing works in Market Street for a drink after work. Out would come the bottles of brandy and in would come some of the political characters of the day – Mandela, Tambo, Dadoo and some journalists – and we would discuss the day's affairs in the most light-hearted manner. There was a reasonable relationship between the two sides; it was only when [General Hendrik] Van den Bergh came in and the Security Branch was made lethally efficient that it became totally disastrous. But in the '50s with Att Spengler it was almost a form of entertainment, which had its good sides.

Jurgen Schadeberg: There was an occasion when the Special Branch started taking photographs of us. So Stein or Bailey

sent Peter Magubane round to the Grayson Building with
instructions to photograph all the Special Branch cops walking out of the building. Eventually Spengler phoned up and
said, 'For Chrissake stop it.'

At that time there was a certain amount of gamesmanship.
Obviously there must have been brutal battering of criminals
but it hadn't become what it is today. I'm sure there were a
lot of heavies among them, but there were also a lot of
romantics, who had a sense of honour.

Esme Matshikiza: We were always able to identify Special
Branch people at meetings. In a way, in the days of Major
Spengler, there was not too unfriendly an atmosphere
between the security police and the politicians. I remember
walking behind Spengler in Johannesburg one day. He and
a colleague were so engrossed in a conversation that they
walked across an intersection against the traffic lights. A car
screeched to a stop right in front of them, and I remember
Spengler kicking the car quite hard before he walked round
behind it. It was very difficult to take him seriously at all.
He was a lamb compared to what is going on now. Sure, he
was a nasty guy, no question about it, but underneath he
was a joke. We all thought he was very funny.

Trevor Huddleston: We had no experience of BOSS [the
Bureau for State Security] or the Special Branch. We tended
to look on them as being dim-witted men who went around
in overcoats. You could identify them at any meeting quite
easily – at least the white ones – and they would respond in
a sullen silence. They were really a joke in the '50s, there
was no sense of them being torturers. Obviously they were
rough and beat people up, and the pass laws gave them
carte blanche to do what they wanted, and so they were hated
– but they were stupid, or seemed stupid. Of course, we
were probably wrong because some of them weren't so
stupid, I'm sure. But I never ever felt that they were sinister.
I mean I enjoyed the confrontations with the police. I

suppose it wasn't until they started bulldozing the Sophia-town houses and moving people out that we really began to see the beginning of the apartheid plan. And of course we were the first population removal. You know, the older I get the more radical I get, and looking back now I think I must have been a fool to think that things were going to get better.

Es'kia Mphahlele: Certainly nobody, except perhaps the politicians, anticipated the frightening security force which was to emerge in the '60s. There was even a type of camaraderie between the ANC leadership and the black police force, who were, after all, just there to do a job. Usually the police would warn the ANC if a raid was planned. So I don't think the ANC treated the police force as an enemy at all, in spite of the frustration they caused them all the time. Certainly nobody paid much attention to security police when they attended a meeting.

Walter Sisulu: The security police were inefficient but they were always there. They were in our conferences, but we could sometimes even chase them out of the conference. Then in the early '50s the raids began. Raids on our homes, raids on the offices. It became impossible to keep any proper records from that time on. You couldn't keep a diary, you couldn't keep minutes, and not having proper records was very frustrating. There was a lot of harassment, which made my job as secretary-general very difficult.

Despite the seeming inefficiency I think there was a fair amount of sophistication in the force of that time. I think Spengler was a fairly intelligent chap, but of a completely different calibre to those who were to come in the '60s.

Jean Hart: I was very much involved with the underground schools that were started up by the SACP after the Bantu Education Act was passed, and I can tell you now that the Special Branch was a great deal more knowing than we in our naïvety believed. These 'schools' were to counteract the

333

effects of Bantu Education. I instructed teachers in how to teach English. We had been told that the security branch were watching us but we thought we were being careful. Then our flat was raided at two in the morning. I remember the one cop was a very urbane, educated, polite man. He showed us a file that was full of photographs of every single visit we'd made to the school. They knew everything. They knew the different school cadres that I belonged to, the places I'd taught. They just knew, and they were very open about it. Their approach was, Silly little girl, kind of thing, isn't it about time you went home. You don't really know what you're doing, you're involved with dangerous stuff, you should leave it to us. It was all really quite civilised. And then they said, 'We think you should leave. We think you should leave within thirty-six hours.' There was no brandishing laws at us, nothing, just this quiet We want you out. We got thoroughly frightened. Ruth [First] and Joe [Slovo] suggested that it probably would be a good idea if we left because we were endangering others. So we sold up and started hitch-hiking out. We didn't make it within the thirty-six hours; it took us about two days to sell up but they didn't come back. We did have a phone call from the man who wore an immaculate suit. Once again he was very polite, just wanted to know how our arrangements were getting on. Could they give us some assistance? All this happened just after the Sharpeville massacre . . . that was when we met the face of the new security branch. I'd never met anyone like that before and it terrified me. They had confidence, conviction. It was then we realised something had happened in South Africa, and that something ugly and frightening was going on.

In the Last Years

66

The place: Johannesburg pass office. The date: sometime in 1957.

For the third time in as many weeks Sylvester Stein is ushered down a thin grey corridor to a grey room with its square of light looking on to the street. Outside the men queuing for passes shuffle and wait in hopeless patience. Inside, the man behind the large wooden desk says, 'We've considered this again, Mr Stein. We can't give this boy a pass. You must find a local native.'

'I don't think you understand,' replies Stein. 'We want him. He's the only one able to do the job.'

'Ag, come on Mr Stein, what's so special about him, this Nkosi, that any one of those boys outside can't do?'

Stein sighs inwardly, but controls his temper. The man continues:

'You know the trouble with you people is that you bring in all these foreign natives which just makes things worse here. How do you think we're supposed to control things if you do that? What we need is a bit of co-operation.'

'We want to employ this man, Mr —. He's a journalist, we're a magazine, we need journalists, experienced journalists to write for us.'

'So why can't you train one of the boys out there?'

'We do have cadets, Mr —. But this time we need a man with experience.'

'Ja, OK Mr Stein, I just don't know. You're asking a heck of a lot here.'

'What we were asking for,' says Stein, 'was a reporter

with active experience, the ability to speak and write English, and able to type. This official wasn't able to understand that. It was so idiotic. As if black journalists grew on trees. Nkosi was the only one in the whole country. We had to go through those channels again and again until eventually they gave Lewis permission to live and work in Johannesburg.'

Lewis Nkosi, then working on the *Ilanga Lase-Natal*, had responded to an advert for a tough young reporter, made an impression on Jim Bailey and been hired by Stein. But when Obed Musi went to meet him at the railway station there was this scrawny little guy.

'Tough! Him! Oh God!' laughs Musi. 'He used to carry a copy of James Baldwin's *Go Tell it on the Mountain* under his arm. He was never assigned to the courts or township stuff; he did the egghead stuff, the background stories.'

Despite all the persistence in hiring Nkosi as a reporter, he was initially stuck into the dark-room at *Drum*, a job he hated. It only lasted a month or two, then his name appears with the reporters on the masthead. But an Nkosi by-line is a scarce thing in those late-'50s *Drum*s. Although his name appears on the masthead he was working almost exclusively for *Golden City Post*, so his inclusion as a '*Drum* writer' is by default and also because it's a mantle he likes wearing.

'It soon became apparent that being a *Drum* man did not consist merely in fulfilling one's obligation to the paper professionally, but carried other extra responsibilities,' he wrote. 'For instance, even in one's personal life one was supposed to exhibit a unique intellectual style; usually urbane, ironic, morally tough and detached: one's dedication was to be to a pure form of realism which would eliminate the thinnest traces of self-pity, especially in reporting the uncertainties of urban African life in the face of rigorous apartheid laws, as well as in reporting the wanton gaiety, lust and bravery of this life. Above all, in *Drum* it was generally assumed that one couldn't deal professionally with urban African life unless one had descended to its very depths as well as climbed to its heights. A *Drum* man took sex and alcohol in his stride, or was supposed to, and stayed in the front line of danger so long as there was danger to be endured. Of course, the *Drum* style was more implicit than prescribed, but no less paramount in one's life for all that.'

For Nkosi, adopting the 'intellectual style' came naturally. With his jacket and tie, his smart shoes and books, he seems to have been the epitome of a 'situation', a man trying for a serious position which, ironically, *Drum* couldn't give him.

Nevertheless Nkosi took to *Drum* life with alacrity. 'A favourite shebeen for *Drum* writers was within a stone's throw of Marshall Square, Johannesburg's biggest police station. It was raided regularly, but though it was often too late to conceal glasses beneath sofas and settees before the police marched in, no one was ever arrested there in my presence. With the glasses clearly visible behind chairs it then became necessary for the raiding police squad to pretend it did not notice the glasses and for the drinkers to pretend they did not realise that the police were pretending not to notice the glasses. It was a role which both groups enjoyed immensely.

'The police would then take Aunt Suzie, the "shebeen queen", into the kitchen for a brief business chat after which they soon emerged surreptitiously stuffing their pockets with something – perhaps with money. On the other hand in Fordsburg one was always in danger of being interrupted by fierce Boer policemen in the middle of a drink. A "crier" shouted the warning of their rapid advance and there was then an awful stampede for various concealed exits. Once I was having a drink with Nat Nakasa . . . when the warning of the imminent arrival of the police was issued to customers. Loaded with books I had just borrowed from the Wits University library, I tore away through a back passage which, at the critical moment, proved too narrow for quick exit. My jacket got caught on a steel hook of the gate and I dangled there helplessly, waiting for the frightful fracas to abate.'

In 1961 Nkosi was awarded a Nieman Fellowship at Harvard University and left the country. Along with his other colleagues he was banned under the Suppression of Communism Act, so his work has only recently been released in South Africa. Among his titles is a play, *The Rhythm of Violence* (1964), about a group of white and black students who plan to blow up the Johannesburg City Hall during a right-wing political meeting. One of the main themes is the relationship between a black youth and a white Afrikaans-speaking girl. It was a theme he would return to in his acclaimed first novel, *Mating Birds* (1986).

'Clearly Nkosi had a hang-up about white girls and never could seem to make up his mind about whether he should be married to a white,' says Es'kia Mphahlele. 'It seems to have bothered him a lot.'

'Nat Nakasa brought Lewis Nkosi to this house,' remembers Nadine Gordimer. 'Lewis was such a funny, cocky young man. Immensely sophisticated at the age of eighteen, nineteen. And yet such a strange phenomenon. He sat around looking very bored and finally he said to me, "Any music in this place?" "Yes," I said, "there are the records." "This is not music," he said, "it's all classical."

'Lewis couldn't stand living in a township or Sophiatown. After he had been here a year or two he moved out and lived with a white girl in Parkview, a white suburb of mostly professional people. He lived there quite openly. He often said the way people treated you depended on the way you dressed and the way you looked them in the eye. He would come out of that house in the morning along with all the whites who knew he was not the "garden-boy", but he carried it off with his Jean-Paul Sartre under his arm.'

'He was a cynic by nature, a very good social drinker,' says Sylvester Stein. 'But I think he's had problems in his life, mostly to do with drink.'

'Lewis was a bit strange,' says Juby Mayet, a friend and

colleague. There is a photograph of them: Mayet probably in her late teens, hair in pigtails, bobby socks, talking to Nkosi who as always is smartly dressed and standing nonchalantly with his hands in his pockets. They're outside the Odin cinema in Sophiatown. Behind them is a poster advertising a wide-screen, technicolour western called *A Lawless Street*. It's one of Mayet's favourite photographs. 'If someone had said to me he had committed suicide I might well have believed it. Because he was a bit strange.'

'I think,' says Jean Hart, 'that he had the same attitude as Can and Todd: This far you come and no further. I think he wore glasses when he didn't need to. He was a bloody awful writer: he tried to write in a scholarly, literary style and he would use very long words. He would come round to our house and borrow the heaviest, thickest book. Lewis, who had no background to give him access to these books, would struggle through them and you knew he was reading page by page by page and he was actually reading it even though there was no context in which to place it. But he would read it and probably memorise a few phrases which he would throw out. For him it was like wearing a badge to be able to quote a bit of this or a bit of that. And he'd walk around with these books. When I was working on *Drum*, if I came near his desk he would very loudly have a discussion with me about the book he was reading so that everybody in the office knew that he was talking intellectual.'

Nkosi, like his great friend of those years, Nat Nakasa, was never of 'fixed abode'. He drifted round the townships and the white suburbs, sleeping wherever someone would offer him a bed. Today, Nkosi seems to be still as nomadic. Nobody really knows where he is. 'I thought he was teaching in Lusaka,' one will say. 'No, he married a Polish woman. He's living in Warsaw,' says another. 'Oh yes, Lewis. He drifts through here from time to time,' says Ben Okri, the Nigerian writer living in London. 'He'll suddenly pitch up on his way to or from the States. He's around quite often, but I haven't got a permanent address for him.' The latest rumours have him living in the south of France.

339

67

A few months after Lewis Nkosi, Nat Nakasa joined *Drum*. His story is not a happy one. It got to the stage where he was saying things like 'I can't laugh any more – and when I can't laugh I can't write.' Then one summer's evening, at the age of twenty-eight, he fell to his death from a New York skyscraper. People are still asking why, although it's a rhetorical question given the circumstances.

Everybody liked Nakasa tremendously. They say:

'He did some quite good stuff' – Jurgen Schadeberg.

'He was a sweet, soft, cuddly young chap' – Sylvester Stein.

'He was a likeable young man' – Es'kia Mphahlele.

'He was a good talker, but never a bore. He laughed a lot, but he was also a serious person' – Nadine Gordimer.

Juby Mayet says she knew him well:

'I thought he was a pretty stable character. I mean when I heard about his death I was shattered. I couldn't imagine Nat doing a thing like that. I heard one rumour that he may have been pushed. If he was here I might have said it was a political act, but he was too far away. But as for Nat committing suicide, that I can't believe. He drank, but not as much as the rest of us. I could drink Nat under the table anytime. Sure he drank but he didn't go overboard like Casey and Can and me.'

Nadine Gordimer knew Nakasa as a very young man, long before he started working on *Drum*. 'He was a very sensitive person, and the terrible thing is that nobody seemed to realise what was happening to him in New York. He was having a full-scale nervous breakdown and it was just ignored or regarded as an amusing eccentricity. His death was a tragedy. But whether it had to do with a family history of mental instability – his mother had been in a mental hospital virtually all his life – or whether it had to do with what the Americans call "culture shock", we will never know.'

Obed Musi blames Nakasa's way of life:

'Nat began his career as a street preacher, then moved to journalism. He was a good journalist, but he lived in this dream world, this white world. As did Themba and Modisane. This created immense problems for them. He was another one who spoke only English.

'If I remember correctly, there was a history of mental imbalance in his family. Certainly there was a trace of paranoia in him, especially when he was drinking. He would suddenly leap up and quote lines from Shakespeare. I think he was totally unbalanced. I'm sure it was his instability that led to his suicide. We had no hesitation in thinking that.'

Consider the poet Mongane Wally Serote's assessment of Nakasa which appeared in a literary magazine called *Contrast* in 1973:

'Nat is a very important milestone in the struggle of black South African writers. To those who had eyes to see and ears to hear, he significantly and clearly whispered a very important message – Black man, you are being lied to. And to whites, he put a mirror before them, and they saw a monkey jiving. Some whites marvelled at this black curio, and Nat went there buzzing. Other whites clenched their teeth, and waited for the right moment. How can he defy the white definition of black?'

Again: 'Nat tommed. He tommed while we were rat-racing for survival; he had the time and energy to say to us, "There must be humans on the other side of the fence; it is only we haven't learned how to talk." We replied, "Humans? Not enough." One may further ask, "Have your humans learned our language, Nat? You soon found their language, did you find humans?"

'If by going to Parktown, Lower Houghton, Hillbrow and all those places that are supposedly Hope amid disaster-bound South Africa, Nat wanted to create humans who would cross the fence to this side and walk the streets with kwashiorkor-battered, grey-bellied kids, going to buy *magwinya*, or humans who would come and walk with Oswald Mtshali at night and sing, "Nightfall, Nightfall, you are my mortal enemy," – poor Nat, you failed.'

Here's Es'kia Mphahlele on Nakasa's suicide:

'Nat lived with us in Orlando West shortly before we left the country. My wife tells me that he did look pretty mentally unstable but he was functioning. He was writing some very good stuff, excluding the *Rand Daily Mail* articles which were flabby, they didn't have any grit in them. But still he was functioning.

'In New York he stayed for a time with a friend of mine, Jack Thompson, who subsequently told me what happened the night Nakasa died. Although Nat didn't drink much, he had been drinking on the night he died. Jack tells me that Nat must have gone to the window, it was one of those low apartment windows, and probably thought he was going through to some other room. This is Jack's interpretation, but he also says that Nat was pretty much disturbed that day by the rejection of an article he'd done for *Time* magazine. They had sent him to do some reporting in the south and that rejection had been the first refusal he'd met. He was pretty much disturbed and talking about his loneliness and why was it he had to be living outside South Africa and going through this kind of thing and couldn't go back. Possibly the two things, the drink and the depression, combined to create that kind of situation.'

This kind of thing. That kind of situation. It was like this.

Nakasa was also hired from the *Ilanga Lase-Natal* and moved up to the Reef. It was Can Themba who met him at Johannesburg's Park Station.

'He came with his suitcase and tennis racquet – ye gods, a tennis racquet! We stared at him. The chaps on *Drum* at that time had fancied themselves to be poised for a dramatic, implacable kind of life. Journalism was still new to most of us and we saw it in the light of the heroics of Henry Nxumalo, decidedly not in the light of tennis, which we classed with draughts.'

Being a 'native bachelor', Nakasa should have gone to live in a hostel where he would have shared a dormitory with ten other men. At least that's what he was legally required to do. But Themba came to his rescue, although the accommodation sounds very rough and ready. Nakasa once described his stay with Themba to Jim Bailey.

'At the time Can was sleeping with Linda, his delicious piece of adultery, in a bed at one end of the room. Can woke up on the first morning, and sat up in bed. Nat asked Can for the time. The man in the next house said, Half-past seven. A few nights later Nat heard a scuffling in the bedroom and awoke to find a burglar had broken in and was searching through the pockets of Can's discarded trousers. Can woke up, sat up in bed, saw what was going on, lay down and went to sleep again.'

If he wasn't dossing down in Themba's room, there'd be a makeshift bed for him in a flat in Hillbrow or a house in Lower Houghton. If all else failed he would just sleep on his desk at the office.

Once, he and Lewis Nkosi advertised in *The Star* for a white woman to come and live with them in Sophiatown. How many they interviewed is not recorded, but Bailey says there was one 'sporting lass' whose name he has now forgotten. He describes her as 'good enough looking but very tall and thin – I could not banish the impression that she was originally constructed by being drawn through a hole, like a wire'.

Did she go and live with them? No, it was all a joke.

'Just a lark,' says Obed Musi. 'It could not have worked. The idea was to take the mickey out of whites. It wouldn't

343

have been safe for her to live in Sophiatown. It was a rough place.'

Nat Nakasa was more than just a journalist. Although he had no formal education beyond school, he had a great fondness and respect for words and literature. So much so that once, in a shebeen called the Classic, he bought the drinks and declared: 'I've got an idea, let's start a good artistic magazine for all of us: blacks, whites, coloureds, Indians.' And so with the help of Nadine Gordimer *The Classic* was born. It was to feature many of the '50s writers who no longer had a creative outlet in *Drum*, which was now running fiction only occasionally.

A year after Lewis Nkosi, Nakasa too was awarded a Nieman journalism fellowship. He applied for a passport, but that application carried all kinds of side issues apart from the monumental patience it called for while the authorities dallied.

'Nat had to consider from the start how the refusal of a passport would affect his life,' says Nadine Gordimer. 'He had to decide whether the place he had made for himself, astride the colour bar, merited electing to stay should the passport be refused; or whether he should, like others, accept exile as the price of a breath of the open world. It was not a decision to be dictated only by personal ambitions; part of his development was that he had come to the stage, now, when he had to weigh up the possible usefulness to his people of the position he had gained. It was not, of course, an overtly political position, and its value was not something that could easily be measured; there is no scale for the intangibles of the human spirit.'

At one stage he made up his mind that unless he had free access into and out of the country he was not going. Then his passport was refused and the exit permit offered. He could leave but he could never return. Nakasa made his choice quickly.

'Sometime next week,' he said, 'with my exit permit in

my bag, I shall cross the borders of the Republic and immediately part company with my South African citizenship. I shall be doing what some of my friends called "taking a grave step".'

68

After Sylvester Stein's departure from *Drum*, the magazine was temporarily edited by Can Themba, Jurgen Schadeberg and Humphrey Tyler, although Schadeberg claims Themba was absent or drunk for most of that time. However, the magazine didn't suffer for it, and continued in the messy, exuberant style that had become its trademark under Anthony Sampson. If anything, though, it was starting to repeat itself. The stories on drink, the stories on gangsters, had all been done before. Only the ever changing sports scene and the never ending series of pretty girls kept it alive.

Jim Bailey wasn't content to leave *Drum* in the hands of Themba, Schadeberg and Tyler, so he hired a 'big name'. In 1958 the new editor arrived. He tried to lay down a code of conduct for the reporters, and tried to instil some order into the daily news diary. He did bring white space to the previously crammed pages and a sense of graphic design to the layout of pictures and text. He sanitised. He cleansed. It was just what *Drum* didn't need. As Sylvester Stein says, '*Drum*'s whole strength was its wild bloodthirsty abandonment.'

The new editor was Tom Hopkinson.

Now Hopkinson was a man with a reputation. A respected novelist, a revered journalist, a man with years of experience on *Picture Post*. What's more he'd known about *Drum* for some time, so his appointment didn't exactly come out of the blue. If you look through the archives you'll find his pencilled remarks about the magazine's design failings on most issues going back to Anthony Sampson's days –

'People should look into the page', 'This bigger', 'That smaller', 'Headline badly positioned'.

'We'd sought his opinion on layout matters quite early on because that was one skill that none of us had,' explains Jim Bailey (although whether anyone took any notice is a moot point). 'So when Stein left I thought he'd be a good replacement.'

'Can't understand why,' says Jurgen Schadeberg. 'Can and I ran that magazine for nine months between editors without any problems, and Can was hardly there most of the time.

'Nor did I think Hopkinson's criticism of the magazine was all that useful. Certainly by the time he arrived everything was sliding down as far as the characters that worked on *Drum* were concerned. Can Themba was on his way out, he'd been drinking himself to death. Henry had been murdered. Bob Gosani was out, he had lost one of his lungs and was drinking himself to death and had become totally unreliable. Bloke was still there, and Arthur had for some time been working for *Golden City Post*. Lewis Nkosi had joined and Nakasa, but they were doing a lot of work for *Golden City Post*, they weren't just working for *Drum*. They were part-time.

'What Hopkinson wanted to do was another *Picture Post*. He had this British Labour Party idea of society which was totally unrealistic for South Africa. Although he'd known for nine or ten months that he was coming to South Africa, although he'd been seeing the magazine for years, when he arrived he didn't know anything about the ANC or PAC or anything about the political personalities. At our first conference he was totally clueless. I was very upset because I felt he'd had enough time to familiarise himself. And as he had criticised *Drum* he should have read it properly. But he hadn't and was very muddled. Also he wanted to inject the type of story that was not for Africa. He didn't understand South Africa. He was an ideal editor for photographers: he used pictures well and he had a good understanding of

347

layouts. But he made the magazine almost clinical. And of course that type of photography was very romantic, which he didn't realise. He thought it was realistic. But if you look at it now you can see it was romantic. But by that time *Drum* had lost it.'

To the accusation that the photography was romantic Hopkinson says, 'I don't know what it means as applied to photographs. *Drum* depended almost entirely on two cameramen, one white and one black. The African, Peter Magubane, won a leading photographic award in the first year I worked with him. Ian Berry, now an internationally renowned photographer, won the *Encyclopedia Britannica* Award in 1959 and 1960. No overseas cameraman had ever won this award in its history. These two great news photographers were doing a splendid job at an intensely difficult moment in history.'

Anyhow, in walked Hopkinson. A very different kettle of fish to the previous editors.

Says Jim Bailey: 'You must remember about Tom that he knew nothing about Africa and he had said to me when he came that he wasn't prepared to trawl around township shebeens like his predecessors. So he lived his white middle-class life but didn't actually know what was going on around him.'

All this Hopkinson admits. 'All I ever did before arriving in South Africa was to go through copies of *Drum* sent me by the editors. I knew very little about South African politics when my wife and I went out, apart from what every journalist would know.' He saw neither this nor his reluctance to join the shebeen life as a handicap in editing a black magazine. What he did see as a handicap was the apparent chaos in the newsroom. There was no editorial diary; reporters were working on stories but they all sounded rather vague. And then they'd disappear so often to the Classic, a shebeen tucked away behind a dry cleaner's, and come back drunk if they came back at all. Or get in late in the morning still boozed up from the night before. Rules had to be set.

'Look,' he said to them, 'if you want to get drunk during your time, that's fine, but what you do on the job is another matter. I want this to be a top-class magazine, and we can't have that if you don't stay sober. So we're going to have some regulations about drink. From now on, anyone who gets drunk during office hours or on the job will be sent home for one week without pay. A second offence earns a month at home without pay. Anyone who does it a third time is out. Fired. And there's no discrimination here. It applies to whites and blacks. If anything it's milder than you'll find on Fleet Street.'

'Those rules were made,' says Hopkinson, 'in response to their heavy drinking and particularly because it was such a critical moment in history. I couldn't afford to have drunk staff. Because Can Themba broke that rule I had to fire him. It would have been hypocritical to keep him on when drunkenness among the staff was the great enemy of good journalism.'

That the regulations didn't get them all fired is a miracle, but then Hopkinson wasn't all ogre. He would haul out of bed in the middle of the night to bail Casey Motsisi out of Marshall Street police station, or Themba out of the offices where he'd been locked in after a long drinking session. And he did try to ensure that their salaries were increased. But he'd be rebuffed with memos like this one from the financial director:

> In regard to your recommendations for staff salary increments I am obliged to reject those in favour of X and Y because as I told you the Proprietor has directed me to inform you that in his opinion these members of your staff are not necessary and should be retrenched.
>
> Since we discussed this position, it has again been raised by the Proprietor who reaffirms his view.
>
> Kindly inform me what action you intend to take on

the above as the salary costs for your paper are threatening to be grossly in excess of the amount budgeted.

Money was a sore point to both Bailey and Hopkinson. The proprietor thought his editor was spending as if he were on Fleet Street; the editor was just trying to pay what he thought was a worthy price. This haggling got to them both in the end and Hopkinson resigned in 1961.

Says Bailey today: 'I am sure that Tom correctly looked on himself as being far more frugal than he had ever been before, but nevertheless his newspaper costs ran higher than his newspaper income and they landed me in substantial losses. The situation was made a great deal worse by the fact that we had a very weak manager who in the last year, in order to conceal the losses, misrepresented the monthly trading figures. When the balance sheet giving the correct figures appeared I spoke to the manager who then spent some days in hospital. I had made Tom a director. I gave our directors, all in Tom's presence, the corrected balance sheet. I then found it advisable, partly because of our accumulated losses, to sell my beautiful home and move to Johannesburg. It was therefore not a little vexing to read, in Tom's account of his stay with us, that he had made the magazine pay.

'The parting of our ways was most certainly a loss to me, and one I shall always regret.'

These days Hopkinson is reticent about his disagreements with Bailey, on both editorial and financial matters. He still feels he was right to demand what he did for staff and contributors. He still feels he was spending as frugally as decency would allow. And he is adamant he was steering the magazine in the right direction despite Bailey's demands for more sex and sport. 'If you want any more reasons for my resignation,' he says, 'put the rest down to incompatibility and temperament.'

As Hopkinson has raised the matter of salaries it's worth taking a closer look at the amounts for which these journalists were, in some cases, risking their necks. The topic got them all fired up then – Casey Motsisi used to refer to their salaries as the 'monthly mockery' – and still does so today.

In his autobiography, Bloke Modisane recounts one of the more humorous occasions when this topic was broached with Cecil Eprile, editor of *Golden City Post*. It also reveals a rather obsequious Modisane.

'During and immediately following the 1957 bus boycott in Johannesburg, there was an activity of talk in the Chamber of Commerce; a discovery was made that Africans were in actual fact living on, or below the breadline; but there was also this talk about an enquiry, with a view to raising the level of native wages. The *Golden City Post* praised in an enthusiastic editorial the realistic stand of the Chamber of Commerce on native wages which that body was rightly examining. It was a brilliant editorial, at least Lewis [Nkosi] and I thought it was; we were hopeful that, inspired by the courageous vision of the Chamber of Commerce, brighter things would result in our own back yard, if the tone of the editorial was anything to judge by.

'Lewis winked at me as he shuffled, lanky and jogging, into the office of the editor, and although I shared his enthusiasm I was not keen to thus embarrass the editor by the countenance of our friendship. Lewis congratulated him on a brilliant and far-reaching editorial; touched and awkward with modesty, he thanked the young reporter, and, nodding at me, he reaffirmed his hopes that something of value would result from the influence of the Chamber of Commerce. The genuine sincerity with which he expressed this hope detracted from the quality of humour which we had seen into the incident. We were embarrassed and uncomfortable when the editor ambled out and summoned Lewis into the office. The tension was disturbing. He had come to realise the implication contained in Lewis Nkosi's enthusiasm.

'Lewis got a rise two weeks later.'

Obed Musi tells another humorous tale about asking for a

wage increase. 'It concerns a guy called Joe Gumede who is now working for the United Nations. He went into Bailey's office alone one day and said, "Look, give me an increase. If you don't I'll go outside and tell the guys you did." So Jim gave him an increase. At least that's the story.'

Es'kia Mphahlele: We were paid just miserably on *Drum*. I remember I was being paid £43 a month to start with. And I had an Honours in English. I said to Eprile when I joined that the pay was low for my qualifications. He said that it wasn't my academic qualifications that were important here but experience in journalism, and as I was just starting I had to be on the same scale as the other reporters. I had no choice so I took it on.

When I finished at *Drum* I was still getting £43 a month, it hadn't gone up at all. If anybody got a raise it was for something spectacular. When Can Themba was assistant editor he wasn't getting anything for that position.

Arthur Maimane: The basic thing is that Jim Bailey and his editors practised apartheid by not paying blacks and whites equally. The salaries were bad for the blacks. When I ended up as news editor of the Sunday paper I was one of the best paid among professional black people, excluding doctors in Johannesburg. I was better paid than schoolteachers or university lecturers but my salary was the same as the editor's secretary's salary: £62. 10s. I started at £3.10s.

The last time I complained was when I was news editor on *Golden City Post*. Because we were black we couldn't get passes to go to police press conferences. As you can imagine, there were a lot of things we couldn't do in the public domain. The editor said he thought we needed a white reporter to cover these issues. I agreed, but I immediately asked how much he would be paid. I was told £120, which was double what I was being paid as news editor. I complained. The editor got angry and said *Drum* would never pay me £100 a month, that I must be mad if I thought it would.

We were told that we didn't need the same money as whites, that our standards of living were lower so we didn't require as much. Jim Bailey was one of the meanest employers anyone could ever have had. When it came to money he tried to screw everybody. Even the whites he paid as little as possible. But it was still double the black wages. We were, however, still very well paid as black people in Johannesburg but as journalists working for *Drum* we were badly paid when compared with the *Rand Daily Mail* staff or anyone else. And we were in a position where we couldn't resign because there was nowhere else we could get the same money. We were trapped.

Obed Musi: Of course we didn't get paid a good wage. It was all nonsense, peanuts, £13 a month with a first-class matric. You couldn't make ends meet on that. We did ask for more money: in 1957, Nat Nakasa, myself and Lewis Nkosi and others submitted a memo to Bailey. I remember the preamble read: '*Drum* publications purports to be a non-racial, democratic little island, but the way we are treated is no better than those who work on the nationalist press.' So we asked for an increase in our salaries. But Jim Bailey being Jim Bailey had a selective process whereby some guys got increases and others not.

Before we went in to Bailey we wrote to our colleagues at the coastal offices, Cape Town, Durban – where G. R. Naidoo was in charge – and they said that they were quite satisfied with what they were getting. But it came out years later that they were paid on a different scale because they were either coloured or Indians – and this from a non-racial organisation. The whites on the staff were all right but we were not paid on their salary scale.

Jurgen Schadeberg: As far as I can remember I used to get more or less the same as the black writers, maybe slightly more. Certainly in the early years I got the same as Henry. I think people like Can and Henry, who were considered seniors like myself – that status had nothing to do with age, but our responsibilities – I think we more or less got the same to my knowledge. Probably people like Lewis, who was regarded as a junior, may have got less, but that's the way it is everywhere. To my knowledge Jim never made any money out of *Drum*. It was all private money and it never came back.

And Bailey's response: We suffered from a dislocation in salary scales between blacks and whites. You paid them a competitive rate for a black journalist. This was related to the annual advertising result, which was remarkably little because advertisers in South Africa all advertised to the white public and wouldn't advertise to the black public. So when you brought in a white journalist you had to pay him in relation to the white newspaper rates, which created a dislocation in salaries between black and white journalists which was unavoidable. I don't feel they [the black writers] were underpaid because we scraped along as best as we could on what income we could get, which was remarkably little. I made no money out of *Drum*, so they all got paid better than I did. I got paid a large negative sum. Some years we broke even; otherwise it was a capital loss. I only continued with the magazine because I thought it was a unique moment when one could contribute to half a continent on a substantial scale and I was able to afford it.

From Drum 2

69

TERROR IN THE TRAINS by Can Themba

Friday night, and the end of the month to boot. That's why, joining the hordes that flowed into Park Station, Johannesburg, Isaac Moeketsi of Dube – and thousands like him – was scared. He had, to a more intense degree, that sinking, uneasy feeling he always got when he had to board any of these location trains. More intense because he knew that robbers would be making that extra effort on this most special of nights.

Isaac had his pay packet in his inside coat pocket. Once on the train he would press his right arm against the pocket every now and then to make sure the money was still there. But he would do it in such a way that nobody would notice anything, he hoped.

Then he plunged into that throng. For him there was no safety in numbers. He knew that in this crowd were pickpockets, gangsters, robbers, hard-boiled thugs, beat-up men and even downright killers. Of course most of the people were just potential victims, but Lord, who's who?

Maybe he'll make it home safely, or maybe he will be another bruised, battered, embittered hard-working man who tells his stunned wife: 'It's not even much good going to the police.' But there are thousands of others who know and understand his fear. For pay-day is panic-day for all of them. Mothers, wives, workers, even chance visitors.

Congestion on the trains has become virtually

unbearable during peak hours. The few third-class coaches, the all too, too few trains, jam-packed with gasping, frightened humanity – oh what a chance for their criminal stepbrothers.

There is little method in the operations of these criminals. Many pickpockets just put their hands into your pocket and take what they want. More likely as not you will not feel anything as you struggle for breath in the crowd. If you do, what matter? They out-brave you and threaten you with violence. The younger pickpockets go down on their knees, cut a hole into your trousers with a razor blade, and then let slide into their hands whatever comes forth.

But the true terror for train users comes from the rough-house thugs who hold people up at the point of a knife or gun or simply rob and beat up passengers. The fear among passengers is so deep that some people don't even want to admit that they have been robbed. And pay-days – Fridays, month-ends, from half-past four in the afternoon – are the Devil's birthdays.

The other day we went to see for ourselves. We got to Park Station about three o'clock in the afternoon. People were already beginning to stream in. Almost everyone was in a hurry, and had an anxious expression. It was Friday again. Then we went through the barriers, down the steps, and into the swarms on the platform.

Flush on our arrival, plain-clothes policemen were arresting a man for robbing somebody on the platform. They twisted him round, and pushed him off through some cursing people. The drama had begun. We let a few trains pass, for we wanted to see how the people in this thick mass boarded them.

Whee! In rushed an electric train. A man in brown overalls yelled the destination and the stops on the way, but his voice, already hoarse, couldn't rise above the din. People were jabbing at each other frantically, asking, 'Where is it going? Where does it stop?' Before everyone could get in, the train pulled out. Men and women were hanging precariously outside open doors, squeezing for all they were worth to get in. And the train slid out of sight. The same thing happened with train after train.

We chanced a Dube train. It was packed, jammed like putty. On all sides humans were pressing against us. In the passage, between seats, on seat-backs – humans. Four on three-men seats, three on two-men seats. Crammed. One woman screamed for help because somebody pressed against her hard and her purse seemed to be sliding out of her pocket. At intermediate stations more and more people forced their way in.

At Phefeni Station many people got off, and we had some relief. As the train moved off, in a sparkling flash, I saw a man poised on the platform like a baseball pitcher. Then he flung a missile. Crash! It struck a window. We all ducked. It looked like somebody doing it just out of hatred. Maybe he'd tried to rob people in an earlier train and failed.

Nothing much happened for the rest of the trip – that is, 'nothing' except periodic pickpocketing and stealing of parcels which we learned about later. On our way back we met a man who was so drunk that he didn't know that he was being robbed. He got pushed out of the train and landed on his back.

In the coach next to ours three thugs assaulted a man who resisted their attempts to go through his pockets. After this the other passengers were afraid to interfere with the thugs, who robbed a few more people before getting off the train.

We met a man whose suitcase was thrown out of a window as the train passed a station. He had to get off at the next station and come back to look for it. Wonder of wonders! He found a woman who had taken charge of the suitcase and he got it back intact. It happened in Johannesburg.

There are various gangs operating on trains or near railway stations on the Reef. In the Moroka-Jabavu-Mofolo area and in Pimville it is mainly the 'Torch' gang. They specialise in 'dark patch' operations – robberies in unlit areas just outside the stations. Suddenly a man finds a torch flashed into his face, blinding him for a moment. Then a stunning blow on the head. Next thing he is lying in the grass, beaten up and robbed.

In the Orlando area there is the 'Mlamlankunzi' gang, a bunch of youngsters who work in the trains. One will come from behind and give you an elbow-lock round the neck. Another will point a knife or a screwdriver to your belly, and then they rob you. If you resist, they throw you out of the running train.

There has been some violent reaction to these train robbers, and *tsotsis* in general, in the Dube area. Propped-eared Zulus* first ganged together to beat them up. This was a natural reaction of harried people at the end of their tether.

But it then went all haywire. Some Zulus went about hitting people indiscriminately. They have a saying, 'Hit a cap and a *tsotsi* will jump out'. So anybody who wore a cap was in danger of being clubbed. Recently they went even further, beating up old women in their homes after saying, 'Your son is a *tsotsi*.' They smashed houses without having done the most elementary research.

Then a few weeks ago, the situation became electric, and the two main opposing tribes in the area poised themselves for violence. The Zulus, chiefly from Dube Hostel, and the Basotho, with reinforcements from as far as Evaton and Vereeniging, clashed during a bloody

---

* Some Zulus insert large, round, colourful earrings into, rather than through, the lobes of their ears. *Prop* in Afrikaans means plug.

weekend of violence. They went at each other with murderous weapons, including battleaxes. During three days about forty people were killed and one hundred injured. The police were kept busy day and night keeping the blood-mad warriors from each other, and sometimes the police were forced to shoot.

What caused this sudden violent explosion? In a certain sense, it has not been a surprise to those of us who live in these townships. We have lived with terrorism so long that we have always feared that one day there would be an eruption. You can't live with assault, robbery and murder without something big happening eventually.

The situation has been aggravated, according to many people, by the policy of ethnic grouping, which has led the more tribal among us to think of other tribes as 'foreigners, enemies'. We are not allowed to learn to live together in peace, say the train-using, bus-boarding philosophers to whom the Dube wave of terror has become a matter of life and death.

The two sides are threatening to go on fighting until Christmas, which will become the Devil's dance in this bloody affair. They must be stopped!

(October 1957)

70

THE LIFE AND DEATH OF KING KONG by Nat Nakasa

Ezekiel 'King Kong' Dhlamini – that rugged, ever unkempt giant with the iron muscles of a Durban rickshaw puller – is back in the limelight. Within two years a legend has emerged round the man who threw himself into a dam rather than face the grey sameness of prison life.

That is as he would have wished. That the whole land should remember his death. That the whole land should remember the strange, fabulous incidents that crowded the thirty-two-year life of 'Lightning Marshal'.

Right this moment, here in Johannesburg, King Kong's gorilla face is on red posters pasted on to walls, his name splashed in the papers and pasted on car windows. A musical, an elephant-size job with over fifty men and women on the stage, is being made on King's life. The estimated cost of the opera's production is £6,000.

The 'Spice Smasher', the 'King Marshal' – Mandlenkosi Dhlamini if you want to be official – met his first boyhood days in the district of Vryheid, Natal, around the year 1925. After showing up, fairly regularly, in a Roman Catholic school for two years, King Marshal turned his back for the last time on a classroom.

Only about fourteen then, according to his brother Elliot, King Kong went to work in Vryheid, herding a white family's milk cow and keeping their little garden in lookable condition. There wasn't much in the way of pay. But what a pleasure to be away from his father's whip in the family fields!

Only a few months hurried by and King Kong was gone. Nobody had any idea where he was. The next to be heard of him was when he wrote – at least supervised the writing of a letter to his mother – reporting that he was in Durban. But Durban was too quiet for this tall Tarzan-youth.

So without much waste of time, King Kong took his exit from Durban. Off to the wild, stabbing, over-populated Johannesburg. Much, much further away from his parents, and his three brothers and two sisters, all his juniors.

Not bothered for one moment about getting himself a job and a boss, King Kong tried his big hands at gambling with cards and casting dice – just to knock together some kind of a living. It was a gambling argument that landed the King in gaol, after a man had been battered to death. King was acquitted, and swaggered straight back into his old life.

In those days he used to visit places like training gyms and singing or dancing hang-outs, since he had tons of time on his hands – which 'won't work' hasn't? He found his way to the sparring rooms at the Bantu Men's Social Centre – a den with hard-hitting boys under the famous hand of William 'Baby Batter' Mbatha.

Those who tell the story of King's first day in the gym have now turned it into a joke for entertaining guests at the township parties. He is said to have laughed himself sick at the sight of people fighting with 'cushions' round their fists.

'Why don't they use bare fists, these chaps?' King is said to have asked.

To King Kong the whole thing looked silly. He told the boys he could lick them all in a row, gloves or no gloves on. What's more, when he was shown the trainer, he repeated his words: 'I can lick your boys any time all in a row, including you, their boss.'

The trainer laughed it off and went his way. But when King insisted, getting more insulting and aggressive, trainer Mbatha got into a pair of gloves and flung two to King Kong. In two or three rounds Mbatha sent this Goliath to the ground, proving his point.

But this didn't stop the King from being stubborn. In fact, the defeat made him angry as a wild beast. Yet some sense had been knocked into his head. The defeat made him want to take lessons from Mbatha. After some time, results began to pop out. In many a tournament King was awarded a walk-over win since there were no opponents in his division, the heavyweights. Promoters told the black giant: 'Your trouble is that you are too heavy. Try to reduce.'

King listened to the advice, and the trick seemed to work. In 1946 King was matched against Joe Maseko, then a seasoned amateur boxer in the middleweight shelf. King lost on points to Joe, just like everybody had expected. This, of course, meant a serious grudge against Joe Maseko. For King Kong always had a grudge against anyone who got one up on him.

Then came a big moment for the King, when he was matched against Gilbert 'Kwembu' Moloi, a respected and thoroughly feared boxer from Jo'burg's Sophiatown. King Kong was fresh throughout the night, and put Kwembu down every round, to win the fight on points.

King Kong showed plenty of his unorthodoxy that night. Every time he dropped the humiliated Moloi, he would refuse to go to his neutral corner. He stood over Moloi with his fists clenched, ready to pummel him to the ground should he get up.

In a South African Amateur Championship tournament down in Durban that same year came King's next tussle in the ring. The opponent was Durban's sleepy-eyed heavyweight, Nat Mngoma. When the King lost this fight, it only meant one more creature's name in the long list of those he was going to 'fix up one day'. Mngoma should have counted himself among the lucky guys because King Kong did not run after him in the streets, challenging him to a return fight. And King could have done this without any persuasion.

The story has been told time and again how King Kong once cornered one of his challengers at the Durban railway yards. Here's how it goes: a light-heavyweight in Durban, Sam Langford, said something which sounded like he was keen to face King Kong. The King heard of this, so he took a single ticket to Durban – four hundred miles from Johannesburg – just to see this boxer who dared challenge him. The poor fellow was busy sweating away a day's work when King Kong confronted him at the railway.

'Are you the chap who wants to fight me?' King enquired impatiently. 'Let's get going now.'

'But how can we fight here in the yard at work?' Sam protested. 'These things are done through promoters and managers and trainers. And it must be in a ring.'

'Listen, boy,' King cut in. 'You said you can beat me anytime, any day of the week and twice on a weekend. Now what are you scared of?'

King Kong was already weaving and bobbing in the yard when a third party – a fellow worker of Sam's – intervened. Some sense was spoken into the King's head, and he walked off, satisfied that Sam was a damn yellow guy.

Round about September 1951, King got a fight for the Transvaal heavyweight title against John Sullivan – roundly hailed as a tough in the boxing game. The BMSC hall in Jo'burg was packed to the roof that night.

Famous for his unfailing stamina, King chased poor Sullivan round the ring from corner to canvas, piling face-tearing punches with the speed of a flyweight. King would stand hands up or rubbing his tummy while Sullivan landed feeble punches all over the giant's front. After a few rounds King got to work again, giving Sullivan the powder that brought the fight to a sudden end.

The next step in the King's programme was to become the South African champion – to beat every heavyweight in the game here. And he got what he wanted. That's when he beat Joe Mtambo in Cape Town.

But then again King Kong found himself without opponents. It got so bad, this lack of opposition, that the King landed up doing bare-fist fighting on Sunday afternoons. The boxing bug was in him. He had to exchange blows with some willing victim.

For weeks on end he would travel long distances to Pretoria and the mine dumps on the Reef. Pedi tribesmen would pay his fare and offer him stakes if he came to their open-air bare-fist fights. The lonely champ would line them all up and knock them out one by one. Even at these fights the South African champion wore his maroon and blue 'King Marshal, Spice Smasher' gown.

Not satisfied with these bare-fist goes, King Marshal would occasionally show up in Johannesburg's busiest streets – all gowned up for exercises. Stunned shopping crowds on hot summer days would watch this oversized six-footer shadow-boxing on the pavements and on street corners.

It was during these eccentric times that King Kong's last fight – against Simon Greb Mthimkhulu – was clinched. Greb was a real good and tough boxing man. But nobody really expected to see him beat the King.

There was big confusion when the King failed to show up on time. But still the crowds waited on him. In the mean time the King was trotting the two-mile

distance from Jeppe Hostel, the usual big crowds running behind and around him. When he ultimately made
the ring and flew over the ropes in his characteristic
boastful style, he was soaked in his own sweat.

With a fourteen-point weight advantage over Simon
Greb, King Kong toyed around with his opponent. Two
friendly jabs and a slap on the face sent Greb breathless
on to the canvas for a short count. It became a foregone
thing the King was going to crush Greb anytime. But
then King Kong started dancing about, swinging his
arms like a policeman during a drill session. What's
more, he left himself open for attack.

It happened in the third round. Greb rushed in with
a stinging right to the tummy and pressed home a
butchering left on the King's jaw, sending the champion
to an immediate, peaceful sleep. The King lay flat on
his back, his fans shocked.

This was to be a turning point in King Kong's life.
From then the great King Kong lost some of his glamour. He wouldn't have anyone look or laugh at him.
'What are you looking at me for?' he would ask. 'What's
so funny about me?'

Yes, his reputation had been injured. But his strength
and skill remained with him. He could have easily
beaten Greb had he not done those ballet gimmicks in
the ring. But his end in boxing was near. It came in a
secret sparring session in Johannesburg with the white
man-mountain, Ewart Potgieter.

Potgieter sent the black giant twice over the ropes.
The King got so hurt that doctors urged him not to fight
again for some time. King Kong himself felt he was
getting weaker and weaker each day, but still he had
one more fight.

'He used to grumble a lot to me,' says Elliot, his
brother, who is in Johannesburg. 'He used to tell me
that some doctor had given him an injection that

reduced his strength. He always said wildly that he would kill that doctor if he found out who he was.'

That was the end of the King's ring career. But even a king must live, so the man with the strength of ten began operating as a bouncer in gangster-infested dance halls. With his change of occupation came new kinds of trouble – with the law. While bouncing one night he stabbed a troublesome knifeman to death. He pleaded self-defence, and was let off.

But the big conflict – with the law and with himself – was still ahead. It was a night in 1956 at the Polly Centre Hall. The King was out with his only known girl, Maria Miya. The King suspected that the girl had been unfaithful to him for some time. So when a misunderstanding came up between them, the King stabbed her to death. While a shocked crowd muttered around, the King himself ordered them to call the police.

The police came, to find the giant standing in the hall, a knife in his hand. 'Drop that knife,' the police ordered. The King refused. They warned that they would take action if he did not drop the knife. The King still said No.

With the hall all tensed up, the police opened fire on King Marshal. Three bullets went through his body and hit two policemen behind him. Everybody thought his end had come – but the King lived on. He was taken to hospital, where he stayed only a short while. Before he had recovered, he was taken to the Fort gaol at his own request. A rather strange choice. But he was granted his wish.

The peak of the drama in his life was now near. After a few months he was in the Supreme Court, tried and sentenced to twelve years in gaol. Even the trial of King Kong was not to be without its touch of the fantastic: he begged the judge to give him a death sentence instead of gaol.

A reporter who spoke to him before he was locked

up says King Kong had this to say: 'I have nothing to say. I'm not bothered at all about my girl's death. My only worry is that by the time I come out of gaol I will be too old to fight.'

If there's one thing King Kong never feared, it was gaol. Those with him tell that he had a royal time in the cells. Neither the guards nor the fellow convicts wished to be involved in a brawl with him.

It was the dull, disciplined life of gaol he must have hated. In the outside world he was constantly surrounded by crowds of people. People who talked about his fame and his might. This admiration was a part of his life. Not the grim-faced crowds, like a bunch of hard-labour convicts, who saw him hurl his life away, saw him drown himself in a dam at the Leeuwkop Farm Gaol on 3 April 1957.

The King had himself granted his death plea to the judge.

(February 1959)

71

NUDE PASS PARADE by Can Themba

Naked. Humiliated. Hoping to God time's going to go quickly. Trying to pass off awkwardness with a shrug and wry jokes, big-shot businessmen, professional men, ordinary guys just come for a pass stand around stripped in the waiting room of the Non-European Affairs Department in Johannesburg each workday of the week. Hundreds of them, each day.

You want a pass. Right. You go into a structure that looks like a public convenience. It is on the corner of Albert and Polly Streets in Johannesburg. You find a 'blackjack' – one of those black-uniformed municipal policemen – sitting on a high stool. He barks at you that you should not be an idiot: can't you join the queue! You join the queue of hundreds of other Africans, and you get counted off.

If you are in the batch that is to see the doctor for a medical certificate you get a little ticket that permits you to enter the eastern gate to the great building of the city's Non-European Affairs Department. You join another queue that goes in and out of iron railings and right into the building.

Inside you meet white-coated clerks and medical aides who yell you into removing your top clothing, yell you into joining a queue that leads to a green-curtained room, and yell others off from this sacrosanct queue.

In due course you get your turn to step up to the X-ray machine, hug it according to instructions, and your chest gets X-rayed. Then you pass into an inner room where you are curtly told to drop your trousers, all of you in a row.

You may be a dignified businessman, a top-class lawyer, a jeweller, a wood merchant, or anybody. You will find yourself naked. Well, you wanted a permit to work in Johannesburg, didn't you? The official world is not finicky about your embarrassed modesty.

Recently the Non-European Affairs Department issued a new instruction that all Africans who work for a European must also be registered. This edict includes some of the elite members of African society: business-men, doctors, musicians, lawyers, and also those who are still looking for work.

There seems to be an obvious connection with the panic over the Reef's crime wave, for many people have blamed the workless Africans for the crimes, and some of the businessmen are blamed for encouraging thefts and robberies by receiving stolen goods.

Mr John Raditsebe of 71 Victoria Road, Sophiatown, Johannesburg, is a watch maker. He has a little shop near the corner of Ray Street. Behind his shop are living quarters. Sometimes he has to work deep into the night to cope with the demand for his services.

Like so many others he had to go fix his passes. He, too, had to walk the gauntlet of humiliation. 'This pass, however,' he says, 'is so precious that one shuts one's eyes and goes through with the miserable experience.'

And there's Mr W. Lubengu, of Sophiatown, a wood merchant; Mr Rufus Khoza of the famous Manhattan Brothers, a world-famous singer now. And more and more.

One of the most startling things that have come from this strange business is the verdict of the people affected themselves. Terse, tired. 'Official contempt!', that is all they say.

The authorities claim that the humiliation of the mass

naked parade is unavoidable. If they tried to give everyone individual attention they wouldn't have time to get through their work, they say.

Pressed further, one official said, 'What's so wrong with this, after all. Why, during the war, old men, young men had to strip all together. They thought nothing of it.'

But, Mr Official, Mr Non-European Affairs Department, Mr Everybody who thinks things like this are OK: we aren't at war. There's no emergency. We're a civilised country, we keep telling the rest of the world.

(December 1957)

72

WITCHCRAFT by Nat Nakasa

There's a hunt for witches around the little Transvaal town of Bronkhorstspruit. People are scared.

First three little kids vanished from their parents' huts. No signs of them although the parents looked and looked, and whole villages helped. Gone.

Then an old white man who lived in the village disappeared. Later someone stumbled across a blood-stained shirt in the veld. Soon afterwards someone else found the old man's tobacco pipe, and a few strands of messy hair on some rocks. It didn't seem like an ordinary murder. It looked like a medicine killing. Had the same thing happened to the kids?

People began to talk. They looked at each other suspiciously. Even the whites caught the fever. One white woman who lives alone on her farm told her friends that she heard noises every night, and found bones and '*muti*' on her verandah each morning. She thought someone was trying to cast a spell over her.

One night she caught up her courage and looked out of her window. She saw four Africans climbing on the roof of her farmhouse. Then they ran off, she said, looking like monkeys.

'You see those four trees over there? They climbed up those four trees, and they disappeared. Each man had his own tree that he climbed.'

I looked at the trees. They looked ordinary trees to me. How could a man climb up a tree and disappear? Did he climb into heaven?

But the dirty happenings looked as if they had to do more with hell. 'Black magic,' people whispered.

The children disappeared more than a year ago. No sign of them yet, in spite of the long search. They were toddlers, just walking. They couldn't have gone far by themselves.

One of the children was eighteen-month-old Elizabeth, granddaughter of Diamond Matiye. The old man still grieves for her.

'She's dead now, for sure,' he told me, shaking his head. 'She just went off the way children go, to play with the next-doors. She didn't come back.'

When the old white man Kosie van den Berg disappeared, local farmers and the people who lived on the farms combed the hills. Two hundred policemen from Pretoria came into the area to help look.

Then the shirt, the pipe, the hair were found – but no sign of the old man himself.

Meantime the police had been making their enquiries, and before long they swooped, dragging six medicine men into court. They were charged with murder.

A court case followed, in which forty witnesses or more were called. But in the end the six men were let loose: Not guilty, the Supreme Court said.

Then there were new events, nothing to do with the murder.

A white woman, forty-two years old, with a small face on a big body, was arrested and charged with witchcraft. Detective I. J. Breytenbach of Bronkhorstspruit was the man who searched her home to find her secrets. In court, he told the magistrate: 'I found a bag made of rabbit skin, and inside the bag there were bones. In one room I also found a monkey-skin, a porcupine quill, horns, roots and mixtures. I also found a doll in the yard.' Then the other witnesses trooped into the witness box.

Africans told the court how, for a fee of 5s., the white

woman, Mrs Christina Magdalena Rademeyer, produced her bones and threw them on the floor to find out what the patients were suffering from.

Ageing Amos Ratlou, who lives in Tweefontein, brought his evidence too.

'My child was ill and I took it to her,' Ratlou said. 'She asked me into her house and took some powder that looked like flour.

'She threw it on some paper, lit it with a match, and it went "Pheew!" exploding. She put a horn to her ear and nodded her head. At the same time she wrote in her book.

'She said the child was sick – but not really the child, but the mother. She gave me a bottle of medicine which was for the mother and the child. I paid 5s., which she said was for the use of the bones. She said I must pay £1. 19s. for the medicine. I didn't have the cash, so I paid her with a goat.

'I signed the receipt so that she could not be accused of having stolen the goat.'

Mrs Rademeyer got into the box to speak in her own defence. She told the magistrate that she had had a licence for selling medicines, explaining that it had lapsed on 31 December.

'I came to Tweefontein four months ago and brought some medicines with me to test the market,' she said. 'I saw that it would not pay.'

Then the magistrate asked, 'Was the competition too keen?'

'The natives here have no money. They want to exchange,' said Mrs Rademeyer.

Mrs Rademeyer denied that she burned powder or listened to a horn. Instead, she said, 'I burned a taper because of the bad smell. That talk about paying 5s. to throw the bones is also untrue.'

At the end the magistrate coughed for silence. 'I find you guilty of practising witchcraft,' he summed up. The sentence was a £75 fine, or six months in gaol, suspended for three years . . .

It was within twenty-four hours of this sentence that I went to see Mrs Rademeyer and her family in their farmhouse – an old white-walled bungalow surrounded by bushy plains and clusters of tall trees. The whole family – Mr and Mrs Rademeyer, a teenage daughter and a barefooted son, plus a crawling baby – were relaxing on the verandah.

'Kaffirs are liars, *jong*! I won't have anything to do with them. Now you get out of here . . .' Those angry words came from Mr Rademeyer.

But he blurted on: 'That monkey-skin they showed in court. It was from a dead pet we kept here. We used to call it Anna. I shot it myself after it attacked some children.'

And the horns had come from a pedlar. 'I paid 2s. 6d. for them,' said Mr Rademeyer.

I left the Rademeyer farm for the other parts of Bronkhorstspruit, where Africans have been squatters on white farmers' lands for more than fifty years. Here there are clean Ndebele kraals, surrounded with thick and well-levelled mud fencing, and decorated with red, white and black figures – famous primitive art.

This is where the three children disappeared – victims of an unknown African witch-doctor – and simple folk now say, 'We don't know each other any more. We fear each other in the night and in the day.' I met these folk. Any mention of the missing children still causes them to nod their heads, grieved and agreeing that 'there is something wrong with this place'.

(July 1959)

Witchcraft is always a good story and it occurs fairly regularly in *Drum*. Like this case reported in April 1952 from Swaziland: '. . . [A] chief, thirty-year-old Mahlabindaba Dlamini, was weak and inexperienced when he became the head of his tribe, the Mkweli, and his uncles decided to increase his power by obtaining medicine from human flesh. They chose as their victim the twelve-year-old herd-boy, brother of the chief. The boy was caught, given powder to weaken him, and taken to a riverbed where he was tied to a tree and then kept for months, fed every day on roots.

'One witness described how the boy's eyes were white and the whole of his body was white as white paper. He was running on his knees and the backs of his hands like an animal. Eventually he was struck on the back of the neck with an axe, his throat was cut with a pocket-knife and various parts of his body were removed, including the nose, lower lip, tongue, a thumb and an eye. These were brought back to the kraal, and cooked in a clay pot; the chief and his elders then put their fingers in the pot, licked them, and spat towards the east. This done, the ceremony was complete.'

73

RUSSIAN FAMO SESH! by Can Themba

A dark figure swathed in a coloured blanket swerved from the muddy pavement into a dark yard of a house. Soon similar figures appeared, men and women, the men looking ferocious and carrying sticks, the women lascivious with blue, artificial pimples or 'beauty' lines painted on their faces. Now and then a giggle would come from the dark, and straining eyes would discern two dark forms clinging to each other. From the house came the music of an organ, harmonicas, the shrieking of voices, the stomping of feet. That is *famo*, the famous sex dance of the Russians, Basotho gangsters of the Reef. The place was Germiston Location.

We slid out of the car and went in. It was a stunning scene, so cramped with swarming life and sweating bodies. There were long, wooden benches along the walls, and Russian men and women had filled them in the order of man and woman, man and woman, man and woman, right round the room. In the centre were sweating dancers yelling their heads and the roof off.

The men just swayed. The women were the stars. They danced a primitive thing that looked strangely like jive. Now and again, at little climaxes in the song and the dance, the women kicked up their legs to show panties, and with some of them, no panties. The men ogled and goggled.

But in their ogling and goggling they were secretly choosing the women who seemed to promise them most. There was liquor, too, mostly KB. Then in bustled mine hostess. She was a short Mosotho woman, nicely stacked, beaming hospitality now, bristling hostility a moment after. As she approached us I saw she carried a gourd with beer. She did a prancing dance in front of us and yelled, 'Eu! Eu! Eu! Eu! Eu!' She thrust the gourd at me, and to show my manliness I took a big long swig.

Suddenly commotion broke loose in one corner. Men with raised sticks rushed at a young man with a girl on his lap. It looked like murder. I went closer to find out what it was all about. Everybody was jabbering. I waited for a forest of sticks to rain down on the young man, and they were poised in the air like the spears of a barbarian horde.

Manyeu, mine hostess, shouted above the din: '*Khele, le sele!*' (Hell, but you people are naughty!) Everybody laughed and sticks came down slowly. It was all a rough joke. I wiped the sweat off my brow.

The organ went groaning again, harmonicas wailed, human voices took up the lament, and the crowd started dancing. I watched a young woman near me. She was dancing a dance all her own. She stood in one spot, but her body was darting back and forth like a cobra preparing for an attack. Suddenly she kicked up her leg. A flash of petticoat, a dash of panties. Not content with that attack on my modesty, she whirled round, stopped before me, and yanked her dress up over her head in a swift movement so that I saw knees, thighs, black panties, belly and a navel. She threw out a leg clean over my head. I bought more hooch.

As the night wore on I noticed that the crowd was thinning. I went out of the stuffiness into the night air. I noticed that some of the girls who had been dancing were walking off, arm in arm with blanket-robed Russian men. I went to the yard. I hurried back: I had seen enough. In the open, couples were making love.

(March 1958)

The Whole Thing was Shattered

74

The last two years of the decade: there is a feeling that it's all winding down. *Drum* is running the same stories with different characters and just doesn't look as vibrant as in the middle years. But then Henry Nxumalo's dead, Es'kia Mphahlele's gone, Bloke Modisane's packing, as is Arthur Maimane. Todd Matshikiza will soon be off to England. Can Themba will soon be fired. Of course, Casey Motsisi's there, and Lewis Nkosi and Nat Nakasa, but it's not the same.

It's not the same outside the *Drum* doors either. Sophiatown has almost been flattened. There are whites in two of the grand houses that were not bulldozed, and here and there homeless people sleep on verandahs or in the boarded-up shells. In the Pretoria Supreme Court sits Nat Nakasa, covering the mammoth Treason Trial that began in early 1957 and continues and continues . . . Until:

> 13 October 1958: the mild, cloudy Pretoria morning on which the most sensational of things happened for the ninety-one men and women of all races facing a charge of high treason.
>
> Mr Pirow, leader of the Crown team at the trial, rose to his feet, touched a colleague who was still addressing the court, and brought the microphone to his mouth. 'Your Lordships, I withdraw the indictment against the accused,' he said in his hoarse voice.
>
> The height of the trial's drama had come. Up in the packed non-white gallery, black faces lit up and swung round to take swift looks at the judges, still wondering if they had heard aright. Pirow settled in his chair while

Justice Rumpff collected his books and made the dramatic announcement adjourning the court. Without any waste of time the large crowd of accused loomed to the outside, many almost dancing with excitement, while others strolled out with cynical, non-smiling faces.

Out in the street, where spectators and photographers were pressing on the accused, shouts of 'Afrika' rang high and firm, victory handshakes spelled the day's relief.

Only a few seconds before, tough, tensioned argument had filled the court, deciding the defendants' fate.

Mr Pirow had begun the day by asking the court to let him make further alterations in the indictment. The alterations would help speed up the case, Pirow said. Almost at the same time, he told the court, 'If my application to further amend the indictment is not granted, I will withdraw the indictment against the accused.'

Even before the defence lawyers could reply to this, drama, anxiety and sheer excitement were piling up, Justice Rumpff throwing in his remarks in between points. 'Then I do not know what is conspiracy,' said Justice Rumpff, commenting on some of the statements by the Crown.

Replying to Mr Pirow's application for alterations again, Justice Rumpff brought fireworks into the case. 'You are aware, Mr Pirow, that you are removing nine-tenths of the Crown case?' he asked.

From all this moving drama, one of the accused, Phineas Nene, was absent. He was hauled in later in the day allegedly charged with murder. But even Phineas Nene was in time to witness the next, exciting moments of the trial.

Moments when loud joyful talking flared up while some people worriedly asked, 'Does it mean the whole case is finished?'

Was it finished indeed? Or were the harrowing

delays, the family separations, the anxiety and expense endured by the accused to be protracted even further – while the Crown thought out some new, legally more effective method of attack?

That was a question only time could answer.

(November 1958)

The answer was that in 1960 charges of treason were again laid against thirty of the original defendants. The new hearing continued through to March 1961, when the judges found that the state had failed to prove their case. The defendants were discharged.

Walter Sisulu: We weren't expecting anything like the scale of the Treason Trial arrests. [Initially 156 people were arrested, but charges were soon dropped against sixty-five of them, excluding Sisulu.] They came as a complete surprise. Obviously we constantly expected arrests for minor violations, but never had we dreamed of anything like the Treason Trial.

I think the government totally overestimated what was going on. It didn't need to respond with that kind of hysteria, which only served to give us greater prestige than we would otherwise have enjoyed.

But because they were misreading the situation, they saw plots and conspiracies and they became desperate, they were scared. In 1956, when we were arrested, the whole structure of apartheid had not yet completely solidified. The government was worried, and the security police were very worried. In fact I think they misled the government.

For us, the Treason Trial gave us time to consolidate, we were able to discuss things, able now to create a united leadership and co-ordinated efforts throughout the country . . . Of course by then we had already had the Congress of the People, which gave rise to greater consolidation between the various parties, so the trial became a training ground in co-operation.

*

It was the Cape ANC leader, Z. K. Matthews, who first called for a Congress of the People as a united front that could more forcefully articulate demands for change. Sisulu recalls that the idea came at a time when the leadership was in a vacuum after de-escalating the Defiance Campaign. 'Matthews had introduced the concept at the Cape Conference in 1953 and then it was adopted by the Executive at the end of the year. It became a centre-point. Something which we could plan towards, which would activate people throughout the country. We immediately started approaching other organisations with this concept and that's how the Congress of the People began.

'But it wasn't easy to consolidate our activities. The government was placing more and more people under banning restrictions. At the time I was banned so I couldn't work officially as secretary-general, but I continued to operate underground. In addition, our records were in shatters yet we succeeded in organising our biggest campaign of the '50s. By the time the Congress of the People came into being there was a thorough organisation throughout the length and breadth of the country.'

The Congress held its first meeting on 26 June 1955. It was a highly significant meeting, as it adopted a Freedom Charter which called, among other things, for equal rights for all ethnic groups and put forward the tenet that South Africa belonged to all its inhabitants. Although there were some socialist principles regarding commerce, the ideal was for a democratic state, not black majority rule.

However, to many black nationalists the Freedom Charter was anathema, largely because they felt white interests were too dominant. To Africanists this weakened the ANC, indeed deprived them of their most effective ideological call to the masses: nationalism. In addition, these initiatives smacked of white self-interest and served to perpetuate black dependency on them. In short, the Freedom Charter was a betrayal of African nationalism which caused an ideological rift within the ANC. These grievances simmered until an ANC conference at the end of 1958 when finally the AFRICANISTS CUT LOOSE, as *Drum*'s headline proclaimed. The story read:

> It was one of the stormiest conferences for many a day. Tempers flared, sticks were brandished. But it was not violence which made the drama. The high moment, the real tension, came with the decision of the Africanists to split from the Transvaal Congress.
>
> Saturday 1 November 1958. The threat of rain in the air, of political uproar in the area. We wait impatiently outside the Sekgapa-madi (Blood-spilling) Hall in Orlando, Jo'burg, where many a bloody Congress fight has broken out in the past. Scheduled to open at 2 p.m., the conference does not being until well after 3.30 p.m. Meanwhile, feverish and furtive movements to and from a house near the hall – and another house that purveys beer – show that last-minute plans are being polished up.
>
> Dramatic things are expected at this conference of the Transvaal branch of the African National Congress. For long months the Africanists, the nationalist wing of Congress, have been organising a *putsch* to oust the Freedom Charterist leaders of the ANC in the province. This is to be the first step towards grabbing control of the National Executive.
>
> But, the test of their strength is still to come.
>
> It is about three-thirty and we go into the hall. In row upon row sit the Congressites. On the stage are Oliver Tambo, suave Johannesburg lawyer, acting as chairman; portly Chief Luthuli, national president-general; Y. Puthini, national president of the Youth League; A. Nzo, ex-bus boycott leader. Then clerks and interpreters.
>
> Chief Luthuli gives the presidential address. He makes calculated jabs at apartheid, how it has deteriorated race relations. But he says that we Africans should

not emulate that line of thinking, and follow a narrow nationalism. We should co-operate with the whites. I fancy I can see Africanist ears twitching.

During his speech a horde of Africanists enter the hall at the back, to the booming sounds of heavy boots. They are a surly crowd, with a dash of Basuto blankets here and there. And with their coming, the atmosphere is galvanised into high tension.

Then the debate on the presidential address, and the sparks fly. Mr Z. Mothopeng is the first speaker. Flushed and simmering with internal wrath, he says that he doesn't care about the multiracial society. In this country the people are divided into two groups only: the oppressors and the oppressed. There can be no co-operation with the oppressors.

Then speaker after speaker makes the points: This presidential address asks us to co-operate with apartheidists; We don't accept the whites at this stage; Let us not forget our origins; We shall consider co-operation when we have come into our own first.

Sunday 2 November: for many people milling around the hall, this Sunday does not start with very holy thoughts. Tension is still in the air, but a vital change has been wrought overnight. Scores of young men are milling about, openly wielding sticks, clubs and sjamboks. And they look as if they are ever so willing to use them. Yet there across the road still stand members of the Special Branch and the police, arms folded, in passive amusement.

Things are different from yesterday, however. The Charterists have rallied their own strong-arm men 'to resist Africanist force with force', and these men are guarding the conference, which is in closed session.

Not an Africanist in spitting distance. But a little further away, a group of Africanists stand ruefully. Now and then a knobkerrie charge, and some Africanist flies for his life.

Then I hear that most of the Africanists have been refused entrance into the conference hall, and they are deliberating in that house nearby on what to do.

Later, Mr Rosette Ndziba comes to the hall in a blue suit. Stopped there, he explains that he is an accredited delegate from Mofolo North, and that he has a letter to read to the conference from the Africanist group.

This letter contains the fateful decision of the Africanists to secede from Congress and go it alone as 'the custodians of the principles of African nationalism formulated originally and pursued up to the time of the Congress alliances' with the Indians and the white Congress of Democrats.

Mr Ndziba is refused entry. The fateful letter is forcibly removed from him, and a few young men chase him down the steps, hitting at him. He turns and menaces them with his hand in his pocket. But all he produces is a little garden fork. His supporters come in a group and walk him off.

What remains of the conference elects a new Transvaal Executive Committee. New? From the names it is clear they are mostly the same old members. This means that this conference, at least, has considered that there are no more any grievances against the Transvaal executive.

Eventually the curtain goes down on the stormy conference and rises again on a new scene in African politics.

But nothing is clear in the new picture etched out of the split, and the questions follow hot-foot on one another.

Will there be two African organisations: one a sharp left, the other a dark black?

Will all South African politics now be extremist? Will there be an extreme Afrikaner nationalism? Extreme African nationalism? Extreme Congress policies? Will . . .?

(December 1958)

A few months later, in April 1959, the Pan Africanist Congress was formed under the leadership of Robert Sobukwe. At the start of the '50s Sobukwe had been an ANC man, but became gradually disenchanted with their policies. He wanted Africa for the Africans, as he told a *Drum* reporter. The magazine's response, despite their strong ANC bias, was to do a glowing profile of the new leader.

'A few weeks ago the name Robert "Mangaliso" (it means Wonderful) Sobukwe meant little to people outside the inner circle of African politics here. Today the tall, suave, thirty-five-year-old Witwatersrand University lecturer has become a man with a hand on the strings of political destiny.'

At the time the ANC predicted that the PAC was of little importance, and perhaps that would have been the case had it not been for an unexpected tragedy.

Walter Sisulu: Sobukwe was with us in the Youth League, but he was not a top man. The people who went to make up the PAC were insignificant in our movement. There is not one member of the Executive who went out. No. Mostly the PAC consisted of young people inspired by an idea of nationalism. But apart from that they had nothing tangible. At no time did they have support except in 1960, and even then, in the lead-up to Sharpeville, you will see that the support was for the ANC.

The role of the PAC in the lead-up to Sharpeville came about by accident. It was certainly not because of any planning. History has given credit to the PAC for creating a situation in the country which panicked the government into shooting. But that has nothing to do with the status of the organisation or its ability to plan a nation-wide strike. It was the ANC that called the strike on 31 March. The PAC was not in a position to have done so. It had support in two places: Cape Town and Vereeniging. That's all. If there had been no shooting at Sharpeville the PAC would have died. That massacre raised the image of the PAC in the eyes of the world and particularly in Africa.

*

In most of this Sisulu is supported by political historians, but as for whether the PAC would have dropped away – that is speculation. Certainly the PAC didn't have the organisational ability of the ANC and was relying on the naïve belief that if their leaders defied the pass laws and were arrested, the nation would be stirred to insurrection.

Decisions to stage resistance campaigns had been taken in December 1959 by both the ANC and the PAC. According to a carefully worked-out schedule, the ANC's passive protests were to start on 31 March, the anniversary of the 1919 pass burnings. The PAC had set no date.

The hated pass – known colloquially as the '*dompas*' or 'stinker' – focused the campaign. Some months earlier, this story from Nat Nakasa had appeared in *Drum*. It was headlined CRIMINALS WITHOUT CRIME:

A desperate father-to-be dashed from his house in Orlando Township, Johannesburg, to call a midwife. It was midnight, and he snatched a piece of iron to protect himself in case he met any thugs.

But there were no thugs to worry him. Instead he met the police. '*Ja, jong*! What do you want in the street at this time? Where's your pass? You're a thug. Where are you off to with this piece of iron?'

'I'm only going to call a nurse for my wife, she's going to have a baby,' the man rattled off, explaining. 'If you must arrest me, gentlemen,' he pleaded despairingly, 'let's at least pass a clinic and call a nurse.'

But the police weren't in any mood to listen to any 'nonsense' about babies.

They took the man – call him Henry Musi – to a cell and locked him up until the next day. Mrs Musi, back in Orlando, struggled and groaned throughout the night, giving birth without any help.

The white press published this story for all South Africans to read. But of course, like other similar incidents, it was soon forgotten. The police continued their normal routine, arresting thousands of people for petty offences regardless of pleas. A night or more in gaol for no night pass, for a glass of wine, for no house permit, for being in arrears with rent, for trespassing.

It's happening every day in the Union's bigger centres. And it's been that way for years. But lately the newspapers and leading citizens have started to say things about it.

'About 1,250,000 natives brought to court for petty offences in a year. Gaols are busting. Too many people are being arrested for minor offences.'

In 1956, 79,975 people were arrested under the curfew laws alone. Thousands more were arrested under the laws dealing with the registration and production of documents.

Among these latter thousands was a simple working man from Nyasaland, John Nangale. John did not have his pass with him when the police stopped him in a Johannesburg street. He was immediately arrested and packed off to a farm prison. Frustration over the loss of his job and at being parted from his family combined to spell his plight. He ended up a madman. The police had carried out their duties.

Again, the police were only carrying out their duty when they arrested more than twenty-two thousand people in 1956 – most of them Africans – for being in possession of liquor.

And it is not only the large numbers which shock those people still capable of human feelings. It is the way many of the arrests are made. The police swoop down on any of our townships, any day, any time. In a matter of minutes they are seen herding through the streets dozens of handcuffed 'criminals' – guilty perhaps of having left a pass hanging up in a pocket.

In a cool, matter-of-fact way, these messengers of justice pick their way through the townships, scolding their victims, threatening to bash noses in, causing general unrest.

In the municipal townships, municipal police raid tenants who are in arrears with their rent at any hour of the night. Mrs Julia Moloi, of Phiri Location, Johannesburg, is one recent victim: 'They knocked at my door at 2 a.m.,' she tells. 'I explained that my husband had long passed away, and that I have three little children to look after.'

The police chose 'to carry out their duty'. They hauled the widow out of the house there and then. Her children were left alone in the house, while she joined the dozens of men and women who were being marched to the superintendent's office. It meant a long wait – till after ten in the morning.

Look in at 'E' court in Johannesburg, where many of the city's petty offenders come up. The trials last less than five minutes. Most of the folks these days simply plead guilty. They'd rather pay a fine of £2. 10s or £1 and hurry off to their jobs. If you plead not guilty, you could be remanded in custody and get involved in delays which might lead to your losing your job or keeping your family on edge for days.

What's more, life is real tough in the cells. How many men get their first taste of crime through being locked up for a couple of days with thugs and gangsters? How many men acquire a contempt for the law and a familiarity with law-breaking through being imprisoned for a trifle? How many hot-blooded ones swear to themselves, 'It'll be for something real next time'?

These are questions people have been asking for years. Now at last, the minister of justice, Mr Swart, has begun to give a hopeful answer – through paragraph 23 in his Criminal Law Amendment Bill. When this becomes law, thousands of us will get a long-wanted break to breathe. For under it, a policeman will be expected to serve an offender with an order to appear in court, instead of arresting him on the spot, provided the offence is not likely to involve a fine of over £15.

The minister is obviously up to good work here. A thorough handshake for him. And this is a valuable first step. If others follow, a gigantic load of misery and harassment will be lifted from the shoulders of our people. A huge waste of time and money would be stopped. The biggest barrier to goodwill between black and white would be lifted.

But is it not time now to reconsider these 'offences'? To consider whether they are in fact offences at all? As things stand, the raids on people will go on. Mr Swart has himself declared that these raids are valuable to our society.

Insults will continue to be flung at people, strengthening the old, cynical truth: 'In this country a white man runs to the police for safety. The black man must flee from the police in order to survive.'

(April 1959)

As the days of March 1960 passed, the PAC began to feel a need to pre-empt the ANC's first mass demonstration at the end of the month, if they were to be given any credit for leading the campaign against the pass laws. So Sobukwe decided to launch the campaign on Monday 21 March. The ANC didn't take him seriously. Nor did the police, and in the main they were right. Except at Sharpeville, and at Langa, outside Cape Town.

75

My mother came to wake me on that morning. She was very much worried. There were no buses and no telephones, she said. She said it was better that I didn't go to work. 'I must go to work, Mother,' I said. 'This is not my business.' 'Aw,' she clicked her tongue angrily. 'There is trouble out there.'

The township was quiet and nobody stopped me until I was on the road to the factory. Then this young man came up to me.

'Haven't you heard what Mangaliso has told us?' he asked.

I nodded.

'Go back,' he said. 'We must be as one today. We must alter this pass law which is hard on us.'

So I went back and sat in the yard until my friend came to fetch me. Everyone was at the police station, he said. Mangaliso was going to make a speech. Also there was to be an announcement about the pass laws. The pass laws were over, he said. I didn't believe him but we could hear the people singing. There was much excitement.

Outside the police station there were crowds and crowds. More people than I have ever seen gathered before. Although everyone was happy and singing and giving the thumbs-up Afrika sign, I could feel there was going to be trouble. You could see the police didn't know what to do. They were afraid. They tried to get us to go home. When they spoke to us they carried rifles and pistols but no one would go home.

'There is going to be trouble here,' I told my friend. 'We should go.'

But he wouldn't leave. 'We must stay,' he said. 'We are part of the people.'

So we stayed all morning under the sun on the dust and gravel.

We shouted, '*Izwe Lethu*' (Our land).

'Afrika,' we shouted.

Then the jets came. Nobody heard them they were so low, just over the roofs. Their sudden noise filled the whole sky. People screamed. We ran. We fell on the ground. Again they came at us, so close you could see the pilots. They were going to bomb us, I thought. But I couldn't run away because there were too many people. I started struggling and pushing, even hitting people to get out of my way because there was so much noise in my head. But people just laughed at me and said they wouldn't bomb us because they might hit the police. So we stayed there and the jets came once more and then flew off.

'You see,' said my friend, 'we are stronger than them.'

'Where is Mangaliso?' I asked.

'He is coming,' people replied.

But all that came were more police. They came from behind us, a grey car and three Saracens. Some children waved at the policemen on the Saracens and they waved back. Then the men climbed inside and closed the hatches. They drove slowly towards the police station.

'Aw, that is Major Spengler in the car,' someone said.

I could see where the Saracens were, in front of us. Nobody minded them. People walked about, laughing. Children played round the police.

You must not ask me how it happened. One moment it was all right. The next moment it was trouble. People say a policeman was pushed over and was frightened, so he pulled the trigger. People say there was an order to shoot. Myself, I didn't hear or see any of this. The first I knew there was trouble was when the cry came. The cry came from the women. '*Izwe Lethu*.' You could hear it start over near the Saracens and then it came towards us and passed on over the crowd. *'Izwe Lethu.'* Hands went up. People gave the Afrika salute.

Toc-toc-toc-toc, I heard the guns.

People started running. They were running towards me but I couldn't run. Women, children, men. Running, leaping, laughing. But I couldn't run and they knocked me down. I could see the people falling everywhere.

Toc-toc-toc, I heard the guns.

There were men on the Saracens. One man I could see with his Sten gun, with the gun at his hip, swaying gently as he shot the people. He moved so slowly, like a man in a dream.

I saw the woman fall. She fell there in front of me where there was some grass. Her friend, a young man, he turned back to her with a wide grin. He tried to help her up but her chest was shot away and his hand was full of blood. For a long time he stood bent over her with his hand outstretched. I heard him say, 'My God! She's gone.'

When the guns stopped there was silence. I have never heard that silence again. It is the silence when nothing lives. Only slowly does the living come back into that silence. But for a long time it was very quiet.

All over there were bodies. A man walked past me, fell down and didn't move again. I got up and walked through the bodies. People groaned and tried to get up on their elbows. A woman sat with her head cupped in her hands. There were so many shoes all over the place. So many people dead without their shoes. Then the police came and stood among the killed with their guns. And the people came back to help the wounded and find their dead.

76

At Sharpeville sixty-nine people died and 180 were wounded. At Langa two people were killed when the police opened fire. Following a suggestion by Nat Nakasa, the ANC president Albert Luthuli called a national day of mourning on 28 March.

Although *Drum* had the only pressman, Humphrey Tyler, and the only photographer, Ian Berry, in Sharpeville during the massacre, it was six months before they could use their story or the photographs. On 30 March a state of emergency was declared and made retroactive for four days. Its terms banned coverage of the massacre, so the *Drum* report and photographs were published in the London *Observer* and the *New York Times*.

77

Drum continued through the early years of the '60s, but its vigour had clearly gone. Tom Hopkinson returned to England. Nat Nakasa went into exile on a one-way permit and died in New York. A year later Lewis Nkosi followed him into exile, also on a one-way permit. The only old hand left at *Drum* was Casey Motsisi.

On the news-stands sales were declining and Jim Bailey tightened budgets. *Drum* searched vainly for sensational stories but couldn't come up with enough to keep its readership. Then, for reasons which are not entirely clear, it was banned between 1965 and 1968 and inserted as a fortnightly colour supplement into *Golden City Post*.

Today *Drum* still appears each month although it is nothing like the magazine that recorded the '50s. Ironically, it is now owned by the Afrikaans publishing giant Nasionale Pers.

Select Bibliography

Barnett, Ursula A., *A Vision of Order*, Cape Town: Maskew Miller Longman, 1985

Caccia, Angela (ed.), *The Beat of Drum*, Johannesburg: Ravan Press, 1983.

Chapman, Michael (ed.), *The Drum Decade*, Pietermaritzburg: University of Natal Press, 1989

Hopkinson, Tom, *Under the Tropic*, London: Hutchinson, 1984

Huddleston, Trevor, *Naught For Your Comfort*, London: Collins, 1965

Lapping, Brian, *Apartheid: A History*, London: Paladin, 1987

Lodge, Tom, *Black Politics in South Africa Since 1945*, Johannesburg: Ravan Press, 1985

Matshikiza, Todd, *Chocolates For My Wife*, Cape Town: David Philip, 1985

Mattera, Don, *Memory is the Weapon*, Johannesburg: Ravan Press, 1987

Modisane, Bloke, *Blame Me On History*, Johannesburg: Ad Donker, 1986

Motsisi, Casey, *Casey & Co.* ed. Mothobi Mutloatse, Johannesburg: Ravan Press, 1983

Mphahlele, Es'kia, *The Wanderers*, Cape Town: David Philip, 1984

Mphahlele, Ezekiel, *Down Second Avenue*, London: Faber & Faber, 1989

Nakasa, Nat, *The World of Nat Nakasa* ed. Essop Patel, Johannesburg: Ravan Press, 1975

Nkosi, Lewis, *Home and Exile*, London: Longman, 1965

Sampson, Anthony, *Drum: An African Adventure – and Afterwards*, London: Hodder & Stoughton, 1983

Schadeberg, Jurgen (ed.), *The Fifties People of South Africa*, Johannesburg: Bailey's African Photo Archives, 1987
The Finest Photos from the old Drum, Johannesburg: Bailey's African Photo Archives, 1987

Stein, Pippa, and Jacobson, Ruth (eds.), *Sophiatown Speaks*, Johannesburg: Junction Avenue Press, 1986

Themba, Can, *The Will to Die*, Cape Town: David Philip, 1982
The World of Can Themba ed. Essop Patel, Johannesburg: Ravan Press, 1985

Index